THE GLOBAL RESUME AND CV GUIDE

Mary Anne Thompson

John Wiley & Sons, Inc.
New York • Chichester • Weinheim • Brisbane • Singapore • Toronto

Library of Congress Cataloging in Publication Data:
Thompson, Mary Anne, 1955–
    The global resume and CV guide/by Mary Anne Thompson
      p.   cm.
    Includes index.
    ISBN 0-471-38076-8 (pbk: alk. paper)
    1. Resumes (Employment)   2. Employment in foreign countries.   I. Title: Global resume and CV guide. II. Title
HF5383 .T53   2000
650.14—dc21

                                        00-039234

To my parents, Paul and Mary Jeannette
For your love, support, and encouragement
and to
Harrison
Never stop reaching for the sky

ADVANCE PRAISE FOR *The Global Resume and CV Guide*

Karen Hinchliffe, Global HR Solutions partner with PricewaterhouseCoopers
"The Global Resume and CV Guide creates a "win-win" situation for everyone. With the great increase in cross-border recruiting, this book will provide HR managers with a one-of-a-kind resource for evaluating resumes/CV's from other countries. In addition, by reading *The Global Resume and CV Guide,* job candidates will know in advance how to best describe their backgrounds relative to the particular market. The similarities between the country requirements are many, but not understanding the differences can have deadly consequences for even the most qualified candidates."

Hans Rosengren, Senior Consultant for the global recruitment firm, Mercuri Urval "International candidates who read *The Global Resume and CV Guide* will have a greater likelihood of a successful job search by presenting their credentials in the various formats recommended by the experts in this book. Our ability to find the best candidate is greatly enhanced when the applicant understands how to relate his/her background and experience in terms that we (the local recruiting company) can readily understand and use a basis for comparison."

Paul McMahon, COO of AMROP International, one of the world's largest executive recruitment and search organizations, explains: "Any person aspiring to a position of responsibility should live and work in at least one other culture. Mary Anne Thompson's book delivers more than its title suggests. It will serve as your guide to choosing a country and then provide you with the tools to make a positive first impression. *The Global Resume and CV Guide* contains critical information on how to 'culturally sensitize' all aspects of the international job search—from detailed advice on how to write a resume/CV to practical tips on how to handle yourself in the interview."

Contents

viii   Contents

Acknowledgments _____

For my family, first and foremost, Paul, Mary Jeannette, Edith, Jim, and Harrison. For supporting me in this (ad)venture and many others. Above all, for always believing.

For my support staff, Frank, Paula Satterfield, Barbara S. Nolan, Kasie Fanning, Joan Orleans, Aimee Thompson, and Allison Aarons-Stridth. For working day and night to make this project a reality.

For my friends in the human resources field who encouraged me from the very beginning, Lee Perrett of The Coca-Cola Company and Karen Soderberg Hinchliffe of PricewaterhouseCoopers. The world, as they say, continues to grow smaller, while the opportunities abound.

For the executive search professionals who believed in and supported this project by sharing their expertise with the CEOs of tomorrow. Hans Rosengren and Roger Hagafors of Mercuri Urval; Sue Speight of Signium International; Paul McMahon and Hanneke Visser of Amrop International; Alannah Hunt, Andrea Tubbs, and Pamela Leri of PricewaterhouseCoopers; and the dozens of recruiters around the world who contributed the material for this book.

For Michael Hamilton and Kimberly Vaughn of John Wiley & Sons, Inc. A special thanks for believing in this innovative project despite the hundreds of other resume books on the market. Thanks to you, young professionals around the world now have another tool for helping them turn their dreams into reality. A special thanks also to Alan Kaufman, my lawyer and adviser, for his patience and assistance in guiding a novice through the publication process.

For the hundreds of students and young professionals who kept asking the question—"How do I write a resume/CV and look for a job in another country?" Here is your answer.

Introduction:
Give the World a Twirl _____

Interest among college graduates and young professionals in pursuing international careers has skyrocketed in recent years. Such interest has been enhanced by chronic personnel shortages in home markets that are causing companies to actively search beyond their borders for talent.

This new generation of employees is not waiting to be hired at whim by just any employer. Young professionals around the world are targeting specific destinations *first* and then choosing career partners who can take them there. A recent survey of the chief executive officers of many of the world's largest companies lists working abroad as the most important employment experience for young professionals who are interested in becoming the CEOs of tomorrow.

Each chapter of *The Global Resume and CV Guide* is written by a local expert in that market. Well-respected headhunters associated with many of the leading executive search firms in the world have shared detailed advice on creating a culturally correct resume/curriculum vitae, including up-to-date information on job information sources, the Internet, work permits and visas, and interview advice. The similarities are many, but the differences could essentially put an end to the employment process before it even starts.

Resume/CV guidelines are in a constant state of change. There are no hard-and-fast rules that are 100 percent appropriate in every case. Best advice: Do your homework—find out what is appropriate vis-à-vis the corporate culture, the country culture, and the culture of the person making the hiring decision. The challenge will be to incorporate several different cultures into one document.

Some general advice:

► The terms "resume" and "CV" (curriculum vitae) *generally* mean the same thing the world over—that is, a document describing one's educational and professional experience that is prepared for job-hunting purposes. When there is a difference, a CV is typically a lengthier version of a resume, complete with numerous attachments. The *average* length for a resume or CV is two pages—no matter the country, no matter the position. There are some country variations to this general rule, and you are advised to check that chapter for specific guidance. Never ever try to "get around the rules" by shrinking your font size to an unreadable level or by printing your resume on the front and back sides of one piece of paper. Neither is an acceptable technique under any circumstance. If you have limited work experience, one page is adequate. Never stretch your resume to two pages but also never sell yourself short by limiting yourself to one page.

▶ Different countries use different terms to describe the specific aspects of what a resume/CV should contain. For example, cover letters are called "letters of interest" in some countries and "motivation letters" in others. When you see the word "Note" in bold in a chapter, that is intended to highlight a unique aspect of writing a resume/CV in that country. It is meant to alert you, the reader, to pay particular attention to conforming your resume/CV to that country's unique requirement. For example, it is not appropriate to attach photographs to resumes in the United States; and, if one is enclosed, the employer is required to dispose of it. In my lectures, I am constantly confronted by job seekers who are insistent about attaching their photos to U.S. applications, no matter the rule. Why would you want to highlight to an employer that, although you would like to work in that culture, you have not taken the time to find out what is appropriate or, for some reason, wish to ignore the rules?

▶ Education requirements differ country to country. In almost every case of cross-border job hunting, merely stating the title of your degree would not necessarily be an adequate description. The reader still might not have a clear understanding of what topics you studied or for how many years (i.e., in some countries, a university degree can be obtained in three years and in other countries it takes five years to receive a degree). Especially if you are a recent graduate and depending heavily on your educational background to get a job, provide the reader with details about your studies and any related projects and experience. The general rule is that educational background becomes strictly a line item on your resume (i.e., no further details needed) once you have five or more years of professional experience.

▶ If you have specific training, education, or expertise, use industry-accepted terminology in your description. Use language and terms that any professional in your field would understand, no matter where in the world he or she lives.

▶ Pay particular attention in each chapter to advice about whether to write your resume in chronological or reverse chronological order. Chronological order means to start by listing your first or oldest work experience. Reverse chronological order means to start by listing your current or most recent experience first. Most countries have definite preferences about which format is more acceptable. If there are no specific guidelines given, the *general* preference is that a resume/CV be written in a reverse chronological format.

▶ The level of computer technology and accessibility to the Internet varies widely from country to country. Even if a company or individual lists an e-mail address, there is no guarantee that your e-mail was actually received. Always make sure to e-mail your resume as an attachment and in a widely accepted format, such as Word. I would always recommend sending a hard copy of your resume/CV via "snail mail" just to make sure that it is received.

▶ Computer skills and language skills are always important, no matter the job, no matter the country. Take care to describe your skill levels in detail in both categories.

▶ If you are submitting your resume in English, find out if the recipient uses British English or American English. There are numerous variations between the two versions. A reader who is unfamiliar with the variations just presumes that the resume contains typos. Most European companies use British English, though most United States companies—*no matter where they are based in the world*—use American English. Almost every computer today provides you with both options.

▶ Spell check, spell check, spell check, then get a human being to spell check your resume/CV. Incorrectly spelled words or typos are frowned upon by human resources professionals the world over. The presumption is that if you submit a sloppy, careless resume, you will be a sloppy, careless worker. A human spell checker is especially valuable for catching words that are spelled properly but are *used* incorrectly. The same is true for taking the time to double-check the correct title, gender, and spelling of the name of the recipient of your resume. In the United States, "Jan" is usually a woman's name whereas it is a man's name in Europe.

▶ If you can, get someone who is a native speaker of the language in which your resume/CV is written to review your document. Resumes/CVs written by non–native-language speakers tend to include terms which, though correct in the exact translation, are never used on an everyday basis. For example, sometimes foreign resumes/CVs submitted to U.S. employers describe university/college education as "tertiary" education. Although "tertiary" is literally correct, it is a term that is almost never used in the United States. One goal of your resume/CV is to show your familiarity with the culture by using culturally appropriate language. Anything else just highlights that you may not be a candidate who can hit the ground running.

▶ Be aware that business stationery or paper has different dimensions in different countries. The United States standard is 8.5 by 11 inches (215.9 × 279.4 millimeters) whereas the European A4 standard is 210 by 297 millimeters (8.4 × 11.9 inches). When you are transmitting your resume/CV via e-mail, go to "page setup" on your computer and reformat your document to the recipient's standard. Otherwise, when it is printed out on the other end, some of your material might be missing! The same is true for sending a fax. If you transmit material typed on irregular-size paper, some of it can be missing on the other end. If at all possible, purchase stationery that has the same dimensions as the recipient's and e-mail/fax your resume on that stationery.

▶ Most multinational companies will expect you to speak both the language of the country where you will be working and English, which is widely accepted today as being the universal language of business. Have your resume/CV drafted in both languages and be prepared for your interview to be conducted in both languages. Most companies want to see and hear actual proof of your language skills early in the hiring process.

▶ This book contains a few examples of resumes/CVs from various countries. The safest way to ensure that your document is culturally correct is to review as many examples as possible. Ask the employer or recruiter for examples of resumes that they thought were particularly good.

▶ Work permit and visa regulations appear to be very similar from country to country. In very general terms, most employers who want to hire "foreigners," "aliens," or "expatriates" must be able to certify to the government that they were unable to find locals with the required skill sets. The fastest way to be hired abroad is either to actively seek a country where there is a shortage of people with your skills—information technology (IT) backgrounds are pretty hot everywhere—or to be an intracompany transfer from another country. Be aware that obtaining a work permit can take many, many months.

▶ Lastly, to be successful and enjoy your experience abroad, you must be flexible and open-minded, both eager and willing to learn new ways of doing things. You must be willing to "when in Rome, do as the Romans do." To hold fast to your own cultural traditions even when they offend another or render you ineffective is a waste of everyone's time. People everywhere appreciate individuals who are at least interested in getting to know them and learn about their ways of doing things. Enormous cultural faux pas are forgiven of pleasant individuals who are making honest attempts to fit in. On the other hand, arrogant know-it-alls can sink million-dollar deals just by their boisterous attitudes. Be patient and observant. Ask questions; show your interest in learning and broadening your horizons. Be aware that you represent your country to everyone you meet. You may be the first Aussie that a German has ever met. Both of you will walk away from the initial encounter assuming that all Australians or all Germans are just like you. Representing an entire country is a major responsibility and one that you should be aware of with everything you say and do.

So, go out and give the world a twirl. Here are the tools. The rest is up to you!

Employment Advice by Country

Argentina

Dr. José M. Llaberia, PricewaterhouseCoopers

COUNTRY OVERVIEW

The continental area of Argentina is approximately 2,800,000 square kilometers. It is the second largest country (in population and area) in South America, after Brazil. It is divided into 23 provinces and the federal district, Gobierno Autónomo de la Ciudad de Buenos Aires. Argentina comprises six major regions: northwestern, northeastern, western (Cuyo), central (Pampeana), southern (Patagonia), and the metropolitan area (city of Buenos Aires and environs). The climate ranges from tropical in the north to subantarctic in the south.

Almost 40 percent of the country's population live in Buenos Aires and the city's massive, sprawling suburbs. About 85 percent of the population are of European descent, primarily Spanish or Italian. Mestizos (people of mixed American Indian and Spanish ancestry) and blacks together make up a small percent of Argentina's 36 million people. Probably the best-known manifestation of the Argentine popular culture is the tango—a dance and music that have captured the imagination of romantics worldwide.

Despite its turbulent political history, Argentina has been a democracy since 1983 and has remained one of Latin America's most prosperous nations. The economy has been stabilized, and inflation is currently not a problem; gross domestic product (GDP) is US$283 billion. Government-owned companies have become privatized and the economy is now open to foreign investment. Nevertheless, the unemployment rate is around 18 percent.

It is hard to determine a social class among Argentineans. There is an upper class, a middle class, and a lower class. The middle class has grown weaker, resulting in a smaller upper-middle class. Today, there is a noticeable difference in income distribution between the higher and lower social classes.

RESUME SPECIFICS

Education

In presenting your academic qualifications, start with a description of your college/university education. State the name of the educational institution, graduation year, major, title of the degree, and grade point average (in Argentina, 10 points is the maximum). Briefly describe any student internship or diploma work (thesis), including length of time and subject. Continue with a description of any postgraduate or master's degree. State the name of the institution, your graduation year, grade point average, and if you have studied abroad.

Note: After high school (secondary school) in Argentina, one may go on to earn a college degree at the university or an intermediate-level degree (*terciario*), which may be obtained either at the university or at a special institute.

After describing your college/university studies, briefly review your high school education. List the name of the school, your graduation year, grade point average, and whether you studied abroad.

Note: In Argentina, high schools allow different specialization areas for study. These may be industrial (*industrial*), commercial (*comercial*), or humanities (*bachiller*).

Extracurricular Activities

You may describe the extracurricular activities in which you participated, such as arranging different types of student activities, working within the student administration, and so on.

Awards/Honors

List any awards or honors received for scholastic achievement.

Additional Education/Specialized Training

Any additional college or university courses should be mentioned in this context. Also, include courses or training in specialized areas. Specify the institution where you attended the course, and the title. State the period of time in which you performed each activity and/or the number of hours that the activity demanded (for example, "from June 1999 to August 1999: 60 hours").

Work Experience

Start by listing the name of your current (or most recent) employer. Describe some characteristics of the company, such as: principal activities or products, sales, turnover, headquarters, and country of origin. Specify the employment dates and your job title. If you have held different positions within the same company, it is important that you list them all, mentioning the period of time corresponding to each one, starting with the most recent.

Give the details of your work and your field of responsibility, number of people under supervision and their positions, type of tasks you perform(ed), as well as principal achievements. Emphasize information that is relevant to the position for which you are applying. You may add information about the contractual relationship with the company and whether it was a full-time or part-time job.

Shorter periods of employment performed prior to your professional career should not be mentioned if they are not relevant. If there are any gaps in your employment history, or if you have held different positions in several companies for brief periods of time, it is important that you explain the reasons for the situation.

Achievements/Accomplishments

Any awards or special recognition received during employment should be highlighted.

Special Skills

Proficiency in foreign languages and knowledge of specific computer skills should be noted. Depending on the position, it may be important to mention if you have participated in the implementation of an ERP (Enterprise Resource Planning).

Professional Affiliations

List any professional affiliations relevant to your focus area. Include information about your involvement with special activities within the organization or any leadership roles.

Military Experience

It is not necessary to include information in your resume/CV about your military service (which is no longer mandatory in Argentina).

Volunteer Experience

You are not expected to include this kind of information, although it could be mentioned during a personal interview. Nevertheless, you may include a brief list of activities with associations, clubs, or areas of personal interest (connected to sports, charities, etc.).

Personal Information

You must include your date and place of birth, marital status (in Argentina, "civil" status refers to marital status), and personal identification number. You may include the number of children you have and their ages, although it is not necessary. You are not expected to describe your personal interests.

Note: Never mention religious or political beliefs, views, or interests.

References

Provide a list of references connected to your professional experience, such as previous employers. Those people should be well acquainted with your work performance and be rather recent in time.

RESUME PRESENTATION

Format and Layout

Your resume/CV should present a clear picture of what you are able to do and what type of job you are interested in. You may include information about your personal interests or hobbies; however, it is better to mention this information in a personal interview.

Note: In Argentina, if you are not applying for a specific position, it is very common to include, after the name and address data, a section entitled "Objectives." In that part you explain the types of activities you are interested in pursuing.

Begin your resume/CV by describing either your educational background or your professional experience. It is better to begin with your most recent experience (reverse chronological order). Use a business letter format.

Length

Your resume/CV should be no longer than three pages.

Attachments

Copies of your grades, certificates, and letters of reference will be requested when necessary. Do not include them with your CV. You may include a small photo to personalize your application.

E-mail Applications

It is highly appreciated by Argentinean employers to receive information and have the ability to contact applicants through e-mail.

COVER LETTERS

An application should always include a personalized cover letter, and preferably two copies of a complete resume (one in Spanish and the other in English). The cover letter should be brief and specific.

Note: A typed application in letter format is preferred, but you may be requested to send a handwritten letter as well. In Argentina, some companies perform graphological studies of handwritten documents.

If you are responding to an employment ad, your response should be sent as soon as possible. An instantaneous response shows the future employer your strong interest in the position and the company.

Content/Detail

Your cover letter should start with a phrase stating the position for which you are applying. The content of the letter should present a clear picture of your personality. It also provides a good opportunity to show your special interest in the position and the particular company. Your letter should be concise and clear.

Begin by describing your education, job title, years of experience in comparable positions, and the companies where you have been performing similar activities. Also include a description of key achievements. Continue by explaining why you are interested in this particular position. Describe what experiences, characteristics, or skills you have that may be valuable to the company. Although it is important to appear to be self-confident and to catch the reader's attention, do not overstate the facts. You should not use colors or features that will distract the reader.

If it is required, include details concerning your ability to relocate and your availability for travel, and so on. Please note: Often the applicant's salary preference is requested in the employment advertisement. If so, you are expected to mention that information in the cover letter. End your letter by stating you are very interested in scheduling an interview so that you can describe your experiences and interests in more detail.

JOB INFORMATION SOURCES

Newspapers

The main daily papers that contain employment ads are *Clarín* and *La Nación*. Both of them cover the entire country and have complete recruitment supplements that are published on Sunday. At times, it is possible to find ads published in different languages (e.g., English, German, Portuguese, etc.). Recruitment ads are also published in the economical supplements. You may also find some employment ads published on the papers' web sites.

Clarín
Phone: (05411) 4348-7746
Web site: www.clasificados.clarin.com.ar

La Nacíon
Phone: (05411) 4318-8888
Web site: www.lanacion.com.ar

Chambers of Commerce

Argentino Británica (British Chamber of Commerce in Argentina)
Fax: (54-11) 4312-9001
E-mail: info@ccab.com.ar

Argentino Brasilera (Brazilian Chamber of Commerce in Argentina)
Fax: (54-11) 4812-9466
E-mail: cambras@interlink.com.ar

Argentino Austríaca (Austrian Chamber of Commerce in Argentina)
Fax: (54-11) 4394-2168
E-mail: ccargaust@impsat1.com.ar

AmCham (American Chamber of Commerce in Argentina)
Fax: (54-11) 4371-8400
E-mail: amcham@amchamar.com.ar

Franco Argentina (French Chamber of Commerce in Argentina)
Fax: (54-11) 4331-2494
E-mail: ccifa@ccifa.com.ar

Italiana (Italian Chamber of Commerce in Argentina)
Fax: (54-11) 4816-5902
E-mail: camcomit@impsat1.com.ar

Suizo Argentina (Swiss Chamber of Commerce in Argentina)
Fax: (54-11) 4312-8573
E-mail: camsuiz@camsuiz.com.ar

Internet Sites

It is not common for companies to advertise open positions on their web sites. However, if you are interested in a particular company, you could send your resume by e-mail. There are several new employment web sites in Spanish:

www.bancodetrabajo.com.ar
www.laborum.com
www.hotjobs.com
www.weblaboral.com.ar
www.empleo.com.ar
www.bolsadetrabajo.com
www.bumeran.com
www.computrabajo.com
www.monster.com

Telephone Directory/Industry Directories

In the telephone directory Yellow Pages, you will find companies listed under the relevant trade headings. There is also a compact disc (CD) version. This can be a fruitful way to start looking for companies in your field of interest. There are also different directories for various industries where you can find data related to the companies in a particular industry.

WORK PERMITS/VISAS

Visas

Expatriate employees with long-term assignments in Argentina, and any accompanying family, require at least a temporary visa, which represents a work permit valid for one to three years. The temporary visa may be renewed for one-year periods. In addition, after the first visa has expired, the expatriate may also apply for a permanent visa. Temporary and permanent visas are obtained by filing identity papers, good conduct certificates, and health certificates issued by the Argentine consulate in the country of origin and a written petition to the Argentine Immigration Authority. For further information, see the web site: www.migraciones.gov.ar.

Residence and Work Permits

Residence and work permits are required for all foreign citizens who want to work in Argentina. The company that wants to hire you is in charge of applying for the work permit after you have signed an employment contract. A written offer of employment must accompany the work permit application. Work permits are processed and approved by Dirección Nacional de Migraciones (National Directorate of Migration). The telephone number is (54-11) 4317-0200, and the e-mail address is info@migraciones.gov.ar.

Note: All persons employed in Argentina are required to pay income tax. Depending on your country of origin, there might be a special arrangement to avoid double imposition of the social security tax. If you are a director of a firm, you have to pay into the pension fund as an "autonomous" (independent) worker.

INTERVIEW ADVICE

▶ Many important international companies from all over the world have been established in Argentina. You should be aware that their management styles, values, and cultural characteristics are quite different from one another.

▶ Other international companies, in order to set up branches in Argentina, have acquired local companies in recent years. Those acquired companies, which used to have vertical structures, are now initiating change programs to modernize their processes and structures to remain competitive. Therefore, you should be prepared to face a changing business environment.

▶ It is rare that an employment advertisement mentions a specific person to contact. The person in charge of recruiting (an internal or external recruiter or headhunter) will get in touch with you if you fulfill the position requirements. Nevertheless, if the name of a person is listed in the advertisement, you may contact him or her after sending your resume, to introduce yourself or ask for additional information. However, do not persistently telephone to check the status of the recruitment process.

▶ Once the personal interview is set up, it is important to be punctual. Informal attitudes, incorrect vocabulary, and casual clothing are not appropriate.

▶ Express your ideas in a clear and concise way. Explain in detail what you consider relevant. Always respond directly, but not aggressively, to the questions. If you do not understand a question, it is better to ask the interviewer to rephrase the question than to change the subject or not answer what you are asked. You are expected to appear self-confident, but not dominant. In competitive environments, aggressive and ambitious characteristics are appreciated. Nevertheless, one should not exceed what is considered to be appropriate behavior.

▶ It is common that interviewers ask for personal information during the meeting. Some people from other countries may consider the requested information to be too confidential or private. In this case, you should explain that you feel uncomfortable with that type of question, but never do so in a manner that faults or blames the interviewer.

CULTURAL ADVICE

▶ Bank, government, and other business offices are open from Monday through Friday, usually during the morning and to some extent in the early afternoon.

▶ Business offices sometimes close for lunch for one to two hours, between 1:00 and 3:00 P.M.

▶ Dinner often begins at 9:00 or 10:00 P.M. Argentines are accustomed to working overtime (although they may not receive extra payment). It is not unusual to leave the office at 7:00 or 8:00 P.M.

▶ Annual vacation (two to five weeks) is taken between December and March. This period is a difficult time for conducting new business.

▶ While Argentines dress casually for most recreational activities, informal dress is normally inappropriate for conducting business, dining at some restaurants, and formal events. Earrings or long hair on men could be considered informal and not appropriate for a business setting.

▶ Women were not expected to assume high positions in business several years ago. Today, they are performing key managerial functions in many important companies. Their contributions to the development of business have risen dramatically. However, in some traditional industrial companies the old concept remains.

Australia

Watermark Search/Signium International

COUNTRY OVERVIEW

Australia is not only a continent; it is also the largest island in the world. Australia is part of the Asia-Pacific region, and has the largest landmass in the South Pacific; its area is just short of that of the United States of America. Australia is an enormous country, with most of its vast, barren land uninhabited. It has a population of nearly 19 million, most of whom live in the major cities, especially along the southeast coast. Australia's premier and oldest city is Sydney, the capital of New South Wales. Other major cities include Melbourne, Brisbane, Adelaide, Perth, Hobart, Darwin, and Canberra, the nation's capital.

While the official language spoken in Australia is English, it is renowned for its cultural diversity. Australia's Anglo-Irish heritage has been revitalized by the large influx of immigrants from Italy, Lebanon, Greece, Turkey, and all over Asia. Australia's original inhabitants, the Aborigines, have had the longest continuous cultural history in the world, although today they represent only a small percentage of the population.

Australia is a democratic country led by an elected parliament and prime minister, although it is still part of the British Commonwealth. It has a market economy, with a very extensive social welfare system providing benefits for unemployment, child care, education, and health, to name only a few. Social welfare is supported by a progressive personal income tax system, which is soon to be overhauled with the introduction of a goods and services tax, similar to the value-added tax (VAT) system in Europe. Australia's major trading partners are in the Pacific Rim countries, including Japan and New Zealand.

Australia is basically a middle-class society. Equality between men and women is considered one of the most important social issues, and Australia is a world leader in environmentally friendly practices.

RESUME SPECIFICS

Education

In Australia, it is not necessary to provide any in-depth details about your secondary or high school achievements, beyond stating the name of the school, the level attained, and, if you wish, the year of graduation. (Legally, employers cannot specifically ask for graduation years. These must be provided voluntarily.)

Note: In Australia, the highest secondary education level attained is the higher school certificate. This is a relatively generic, broad-based study.

It is considered more important in Australia to include details about your university or college education. You should state the place of your study, the course name (and major if applicable), and level attained. Again, it is a good idea to state your graduation year. You should list your most recent educational qualifications first (reverse chronological order).

Extracurricular Activities

It is not necessary to list any extracurricular activities, especially those related to secondary education. It is important, however, to list any professional affiliations you may have, such as being a member of the Society of Chartered Practicing Accountants. These are normally listed directly after your educational qualifications.

Awards/Honors

Any outstanding awards or honors received for scholastic achievement should be listed, along with the specific educational qualification that each applies to. For example, if you graduated with first class honors in your bachelor degree, this may be mentioned.

Additional Education/Specialized Training

Any additional management courses and technical/specific skill training should be mentioned here.

Employment

List your employment history in reverse chronological order (beginning with your most recent experience), clearly specifying the name of your employer, your exact title, and the period of employment (identifying the month and year). If you had various positions with one employer, categorize these separately (with dates). For each employer and specific position, list your responsibilities and the scope of your position, such as reporting relationships and team size. Also include a brief description of the organization (including annual revenue and staff numbers), and list any of your achievements. In addition, if you have had any temporary or part-time work experience, list this information in a separate category first (especially if you are a new job seeker or recent graduate). Highlight any skills you attained and your responsibilities.

Volunteer Experience

Volunteer experience is not normally included, unless, of course, you have participated in volunteer work that was directly related to your area of work for an extended period of time.

Personal Information

Only your basic personal details should be listed.

Note: It is common to include your date of birth, although legally this information can be withheld. You should also list any languages spoken other than English, and your visa or resident status. Describing some of your personal interests such as hobbies and sports activities is not mandatory, but is common. List your personal interests in one or two lines only; do not provide in-depth details. It is up to you whether you state your marital status; this is not a requirement, but it is common to do so.

References

You should select references who are relevant to your professional employment experience. These people should know your responsibilities, skill level, and job performance. The references you choose should be able to provide rather detailed responses to these areas; therefore, they should be people with whom you have worked quite closely, and who held a senior position to you. For each reference, include name, current job title and organization, and contact details such as telephone and address. Alternatively, if you want this information to remain confidential until a later stage, you can state, "References will be supplied on request" in your resume.

RESUME PRESENTATION

Format and Layout

The most important areas of your resume should be your college/university education and professional employment experience. Details on these areas should be clear and concise and, most importantly, should highlight your strengths. All education and employment details should be arranged in reverse chronological order.

Note: Your resume should always begin with basic personal details, such as your name, date of birth, and contact details. These should be followed by education details and professional affiliations, and any additional education and specialized training you have had. Your professional employment details should then be listed, followed by any personal interests and finally your references.

Length

Generally, your resume should be no longer than five pages, with plenty of space and wide margins.

Attachments

When initially applying for a job, it is not usually necessary to include any attachments, such as certificates or grades. It is more appropriate to bring them to the interview, neatly presented in a presentation folder. Some people do, however, attach their letters of reference.

E-mail Applications

It is now very common for organizations to place their e-mail addresses in job ads, and others will provide them if requested. Attach your resume to the e-mail with a brief note stating your intentions and the job applied for.

COVER LETTERS

When applying for a job, it is vital that you include a personalized cover letter loosely attached to the front of your resume. This cover letter should generally not be more than one page.

Content/Detail

Your cover letter should start by stating the position you are applying for, including any job ad reference numbers. You should show that you have understood the key criteria described in the ad by briefly relating them to your professional experience. This should be followed by a short description of why you are applying for the position. Identify your key skills and strengths and also discuss briefly your desired career path. You should also include one paragraph about your educational and employment history, with additional details about your current employment status (if you are unemployed, this should be stated).

JOB INFORMATION SOURCES

Newspapers

Daily newspapers and some trade journals and magazines include employment ads. Most newspapers are state-based. These are some of the most popular newspapers for advertising jobs (most of these also place their job ads on the Internet):

The Sydney Morning Herald
Distribution days: weekdays and Saturdays
Distribution area: New South Wales
Web site: www.smh.com.au

Note: Jobs are advertised every day, although the Saturday edition of *The Sydney Morning Herald* provides a very extensive separate employment section. The Tuesday edition focuses on information technology (IT) jobs.

The Australian Financial Review
Distribution days: weekdays and Saturdays
Distribution area: Australia-wide
Web site: www.afr.com.au

Note: Most of the jobs advertised through *The Australian Financial Review* are in the finance and banking industries. Many higher-level executive positions are also advertised.

The Age
Distribution days: weekdays and Saturdays
Distribution area: Victoria
Web site: www.theage.com.au

Note: *The Age* also has a separate, extensive employment section on Saturdays.

The Australian Newspaper
Distribution days: weekdays and Saturdays
Distribution area: Australia-wide
Web site: www.news.com.au

Note: *The Australian Newspaper* also has a separate, extensive employment section on Saturdays.

Internet Sites

There are a number of popular employment web sites, as well as web sites for career advice and assistance. Most of the major recruitment companies also have web sites where you can register your details. Some of these web sites include:

Job Network	www.jobnetwork.com.au
Employment Opportunities in Australia	www.employment.com.au
Mycareer.com.au	www.mycareer.com.au
FutureStep	www.futurestep.com.au
Seek	www.seek.com.au
Morgan & Banks International	www.morganbanks.com.au

Telephone Directory

In Australia, the Yellow Pages for each geographical area (for example Sydney) are an excellent way to find companies listed by their business activities. The yellow pages can be accessed on the Internet by visiting www.yellowpages.com.au.

Country Employment Office

The Australian employment bureau is Employment National; it has a job-seeker hot line number and over 200 branches across Australia. Local addresses and telephone numbers can be found in the White Pages at www.whitepages.com.au.

WORK PERMITS/VISAS

Visas

Australia has strict immigration laws. There are a number of different visas depending on the type of visit you are planning. For example, the conditions and entitlements of a working-holiday visa are very different from business entry visas. The Australian Department of Immigration and Multicultural Affairs has a very detailed web site listing all the types of visas and conditions. Their web site address is www.immi.gov.au.

INTERVIEW ADVICE

▶ Many people call the contact person listed in the job ad before sending their resumes. Many also make follow-up calls to ensure that their resumes have been received. However, it is not a requirement in Australia that you do either one.

▶ Doing your homework before the interview is important; you should know a little about the activities of your prospective employer.

▶ For higher-level positions, it is not unusual to have two or three rounds of interviews (or more), so be prepared.

CULTURAL ADVICE

▶ Australians enjoy their summer (December to February), and most people take at least some of their four-week annual holiday during this period, especially around Christmas.

▶ The Australian way of life is relaxed, and the pace is slower than in other countries. However, don't be fooled—Australians have quite a competitive nature in all aspects of life, from work to sport!

Austria

Bernadeet Hasslinger and Doris Furthmayr,
Jenewein Management Consulting/Amrop International

COUNTRY OVERVIEW

Austria is located in southern Central Europe. Geographically, its territory encompasses both the eastern Alps (which cover some two-thirds of its surface area) and the Danube region. Austria has a land surface of 83,858 square kilometers (32,369 square miles). Given its location, it has always been a crossroads of trade routes between the major European economic and cultural regions. Austria has common borders with eight other countries: Germany, the Czech Republic, Slovakia, Hungary, Slovenia, Italy, Switzerland, and Liechtenstein.

Austria is a federally organized country consisting of nine federal states: Burgenland, Carinthia, Lower Austria, Salzburg, Styria, Tyrol, Upper Austria, Vorarlberg, and last, but not least, Vienna, the capital of Austria. The Austrian population totals slightly more than eight million inhabitants. The official spoken language of the country is German. English is, by far, the leading second language and is understood and spoken by a large percentage of the population.

Austria's business activities are primarily focused toward the European Union and Central Eastern Europe. Many international companies locate their headquarters for Central and Eastern Europe in Austria. The currency unit is the Austrian shilling (ATS). One U.S. dollar currently equals approximately ATS12.80. On January 1, 1999, the euro was introduced and in 2001, the euro will officially replace the Austrian currency.

RESUME SPECIFICS

Always start your CV by indicating your full name, title, address, telephone numbers, and date of birth. If you wish, you may mention religion and information concerning your parents.

Note: It is very important in Austrian CVs to list your date of birth, nationality, marital status, and number of children.

Education

The Austrian school system differs from the Anglo-American system. Give details about junior and secondary schools attended in a chronological listing, with the years spent at each. Provide similar details about your college and university education, including major courses studied. Of special interest are periods of study at foreign universities.

Note: In Austria, students have four years of junior school (*Volkschule*) followed by at least four years of secondary school (*Gymnasium*). After four years of secondary school, a teenager can decide to either stay for another four years of high school, go to a technical high school (*Berufsbildende Schule*) for five years, or do an apprenticeship (*Lehre*). For further education, one goes on either to university or to college (*Fachhochschule*).

Extracurricular Activities

State your extracurricular activities, such as participation in organizations, special events, or specific activities. Such information gives your prospective employer some interesting insights about your personality.

Awards/Honors

Prizes or special recognition of scholastic achievements should be highlighted.

Additional Education/Specialized Training

List any additional college/university courses or job-related training.

Work Experience

There should be a clear distinction in the CV between part-time work or internships (before or during college) and full-time employment periods. In both cases, the name of the employer should be given, with perhaps a brief description of the nature of the business. Dates of employment should be clearly stated, as well as the positions held and descriptions of your key areas of responsibility. Quantifiable parameters such as turnover, personnel, and project or team responsibility should be stated to give the reader a clear indication of the scope and nature of your role.

Achievements/Accomplishments

Any awards, special recognition, or promotions received during employment may be mentioned.

Special Skills

It is crucial to give an exact overview of your language skills. Always state your level of knowledge (fluent, good, or basic). Furthermore, computer skills are of major interest. List all applications you are familiar with; information technology (IT) specialists should give specific details about all the technologies with which they are proficient.

Professional Affiliations

List any professional affiliations relevant to your focus area. Include information about your involvement with activities within the organization or any leadership roles.

Military Experience

Mandatory military service, or alternative civil service periods, should appear in the resume. State beginning and ending dates and if there is continuing involvement.

Volunteer Experience

Briefly list your charitable, social, or other voluntary roles.

Personal Information

Mention your hobbies and interests outside of studies or work.

References

References have to be provided only on request.

Other

It has become standard to add a recent passport-type photograph to the CV. If you wish to make a good first impression, send it with your CV and cover letter. Be sure to write your name on the back if the photo is loosely attached.

RESUME PRESENTATION

Format and Layout

All data given should be presented in chronological order. Your resume should be clearly structured and presented in five succeeding sections:

1. *Personal details.* Your full name, title, address, phone numbers, date of birth, nationality, marital status, and number of children.
2. *Education.* Primary, secondary, and high school education as well as college and university courses.
3. *Work experience.* Full-time business experience as well as part-time work.
4. *Other skills.* Language skills, computer skills.
5. *Interests and hobbies.*

Length

Your CV should be a maximum of two pages—leave the reader wanting to know more about you!

Attachments

Note: In addition to the cover letter and your resume, it is standard practice in Austria to include a passport-type photograph and the testimonials of former employers in your application. These testimonials give details of the employment dates, the role and responsibility encompassed in the position, as well as a commentary on personal and professional performance. Copies of university and school diplomas should be included as well. Enclosing diplomas of every single course is not necessary.

E-mail Applications

The number of e-mail applications is increasing steadily. Sending your cover letter and CV via e-mail is regarded as sufficient for the first contact. Do not send lavish digital presentations; the addressee might not have the equipment to read them.

COVER LETTERS

Content/Detail

Your cover letter should follow the same form and layout as a business letter. For example, many modern business letters now use the so-called full block style, which places addresses and the date at the left margin.

Always write your letter to a specific person. If no name is given in the job advertisement, phone the company and find out to whom the letter should be addressed.

A good way to structure the letter is to divide it into three sections:

▶ First, explain why you are applying for the specific job. If you are replying to a job advertisement, address the major criteria listed in the ad.

▶ Second, highlight what is special about your application and why you have chosen that particular company.

▶ Third, at the end request an interview.

Note: Never send a handwritten cover letter; this is regarded as extremely old-fashioned.

Length

The cover letter should be no longer than one page.

JOB INFORMATION SOURCES

Newspapers

Note: The major daily papers in Austria contain employment ads in their Saturday editions.

The most important newspaper source is *Kurier*, which covers all employment openings throughout the entire country. For top and middle management, *Der Standard* and *Die Presse* are the most important sources.

Kurier (daily newspaper; all areas in Austria; all employment levels except top-management)
Phone: +43-1-52 100-0
E-mail: leser@kurier.at *or* online@kurier.at

Der Standard (daily newspaper; main emphasis on Vienna, surrounding areas, and other major cities; primarily top and middle management; increasingly focused on high-tech specialists)
Phone: +43-1-531 70-0
E-mail: documentation@derstandard.at

Die Presse (daily newspaper; main emphasis on Vienna, surrounding areas, and other major cities; primarily top and middle management)
Phone: +43-1-514 14-0
E-mail: internet@presse-wien.at

Wirtschaftsblatt (daily paper for important Austrian business news; less important for job ads)
Phone: +43-1-919 19-0
E-mail: info@wirtschaftsblatt.at

Important Regional Papers

Salzburger Nachrichten (Salzburg region; all employment levels)
Phone: +43-662-83 73-0
E-mail: anzeigen@salzburg.com

Tiroler Tageszeitung (Tyrol region; all employment levels)
Phone: +43-512-53 54-0
E-mail: anzeigen@tirol.com

Kleine Zeitung (Styria and Carinthia; all employment levels)
Phone: +43-316-875-0
E-mail: anzeigen@styria.com

Oberösterreichische Nachrichten (Upper Austria; all employment levels)
Phone: +43-732-78 05-0
E-mail: anzeigen@oon.at

Internet Sites

Usually companies advertise their open positions on their own web sites in Austria. The web site of the Austrian Employment Office (www.ams.or.at) carries ads and gives a number of useful links to other employment web sites.

You will also find job ads on special employment web sites, such as:

www.jobnews.at
www.jobpilot.at
www.zbp-mc.at
www.jenewein.at
www.job-consult.com
www.dv-job.at

The important newspaper web sites are:

Kurier	www.kurier.at
Der Standard	www.derstandard.co.at
Die Presse	www.diepresse.at
Wirtschaftsblatt	www.wirtschaftsblatt.at
Salzburger Nachrichten	www.salzburg.com/sn
Tiroler Tageszeitung	www.tirol.com/tt
Kleine Zeitung	www.kleine.co.at
Oberösterreichische Nachrichten	www.oon.at/ooen

Chambers of Commerce/Trade Councils

Austrian Chamber of Commerce
Wirtschaftskammer Österreich
Wiedner Hauptstrabe 63
A-1040 Wien
Phone: +43-1-501 05-0

Industriellen Vereinigung
Schwarzenbergplatz 4
A-1031 Wien
Phone: +43-1-711 35-0

Country Employment Office

The Austrian Employment Office (Arbeitsamt), with offices in each city of major importance, can be contacted through the Internet at www.ams.or.at. For professionals, however, the Austrian Employment Office is not the right source for job search.

WORK PERMITS/VISAS

Technically, non–EU citizens entering Austria for the purpose of accepting employment need a visa; such visas are issued free of charge by the Austrian embassies and some of the consulates. This applies only when working for an Austrian company. Visa requirements are in effect when remaining in Austria in any employment for more than three months or for citizens of countries that have no mutual agreement with Austria. EU citizens need neither visas nor work permits to work in Austria.

For detailed information concerning visa requirements, please see: www.botros.at/travel/visa.

INTERVIEW ADVICE

▶ It is of absolute importance to be dressed formally for job interviews. In daily business, the dress code varies according to company and position.

▶ Austrians are usually punctual in business life. If you risk arriving late, call ahead to announce your delay. Plan on the possibility of traffic jams, train delays, and so on when scheduling interviews.

▶ Austrians tend to stress their personal, political, and social networks. Do not focus on name-dropping, but on what value these contacts could have for your potential employer.

CULTURAL ADVICE

▶ In Austria, the cultural and social life plays a major role in business. Good communication skills and keeping up-to-date on important cultural events (such as the Viennese Opera Ball) are regarded as vital qualifications for senior management positions.

▶ It is unusual to discuss private issues, like family or holiday trips, during business meetings.

▶ Most socializing takes place in the course of evening events, always together with a buffet and cocktails. Austrians appreciate good food and drink.

The Baltic States:
Lithuania, Latvia, and Estonia _____

Audrone Tamullonyte and Dr. Woody Sears, Aon Consulting

COUNTRY OVERVIEW

The three Baltic States—Lithuania, Latvia, and Estonia (south to north)—lie on the eastern shore of the Baltic Sea, flanked by Poland to the south, Belarus and Russia to the east, and Finland to the north. They are relatively small countries with a population of about nine million among them. Lithuania is the largest and most homogeneous—Lithuanians comprise 80 percent of the population. The climate is mild, with average temperatures of 20°C in July and –7°C in February. As the Baltic countries lie quite far north, they are blessed with long hours of daylight during the summer and cursed with long hours of darkness during the winter.

After enjoying a brief period of independence between the World Wars, all three countries were forcibly annexed into the Soviet Union in 1940. A half-century later, on the leading edge of the processes that led to the collapse of the Soviet Union, Lithuania, Latvia, and Estonia reemerged as independent countries in 1991, after the failed Moscow putsch. However, they had suffered 50 years of Sovietization, which left a legacy of economic and political problems, inefficiency, and corruption that the countries are still struggling to overcome.

Lithuania, Latvia, and Estonia are often grouped together and have many features in common. Their recent history has made them very conscious of their independence—an independence made possible by their stubbornness and strong nationalist feelings. They have similar dress and eating habits, consider themselves to be hardworking, and tend to be cautious and suspicious, especially of officialdom. All three countries have a varying, but real, desire to integrate into the European Community, though they fiercely guard their individuality.

Each country is a distinct nation with a character of its own. All three have difficult-to-learn languages. Lithuanian (considered the oldest living Indo-European language) and Latvian are Baltic languages, while Estonian belongs to the Finno-Ugric language family, together with Finnish and Hungarian. Lithuania is primarily a Roman Catholic country; Latvia and Estonia are mostly Protestant. Latvia and Estonia are also more multiethnic than Lithuania. While all the Balts tend to be reserved, it is perceived that the Estonians are the most serious and restrained, while Lithuanians are the liveliest of the three and are sometimes even referred to as the "Italians of the North."

RESUME SPECIFICS

Education

Describe your higher education by indicating the universities/colleges you attended, with dates, your areas of study, degrees, and honors.

If you have no, or limited, higher education, indicate the year you graduated from secondary school. If you were involved in special programs that support your capabilities to perform tasks within the job to be filled, highlight them.

Extracurricular Activities

Use the presentation of this information to emphasize work-related skills you had an opportunity to develop. Singing in a choral group probably required some discipline, but if you arranged transportation or performed other administrative support that is the point to emphasize. (Example: "Travel coordinator for high school chorus; also sang tenor.")

Awards/Honors

These add important dimensions to the self-portrait you create with your resume. Include them, even if they do not seem relevant to the job. They say something about discipline, diligence, and acceptance by peers or teachers.

Additional Education/Specialized Training

Indicate any specific training you received that directly relates to the job for which you are applying.

Work Experience

Begin by listing dates, employers, and job titles. Highlight the experience that directly relates to the job objective you have. Shorter periods of employment can be summarized (especially if you have extensive work experience). It is best not to leave any gaps in employment history; but if necessary be prepared to explain the gaps in the interview.

Note: It is important to describe each position, your scope of responsibility, the skills you have used and developed, and the results you have achieved. This is especially true in the Baltic countries where CV writing is relatively new and the same job title often can indicate very different kinds of responsibilities.

Achievements/Accomplishments

Any special recognition received during employment should be indicated.

Special Skills

There are two skills in particular that will help you—languages and computer literacy. Indicate your knowledge of languages as well as the proficiency level of each. Also, as most businesses are computer-dependent, indicate your ability to work with computer programs such as Word, PowerPoint, and Excel. A valid driver's license is also worth mentioning.

Note: Competency in spoken and written Lithuanian, Latvian, and/or Estonian, as well as English and/or Russian is a *big* plus for your application.

Professional Affiliations

Memberships in professional or honorary societies relevant to your goal are a plus and should be indicated. Stress any leadership or organizational role you played.

Military Experience

Detailing military experience is not necessary unless your experience adds significantly to your CV—for instance, you received special training related to your job objective or had organizational or managerial experience.

Volunteer Experience

In a region where volunteerism is still rare, and in which service organizations still have not yet fully evolved, the fact that you gave your time and effort to contribute to your community in some way will be a positive element on your resume.

Personal Information

Include some of your personal interests and hobbies in your CV. Make sure you are truthful about your interests, as you might be asked about them in the interview. If you list jazz as your personal interest, be sure you really do like and know about jazz, because the interviewer just may share your interest.

It is typical in this region to include personal information such as date of birth and marital status. Age and birth date are optional, especially if a picture is included, unless there is an age limit in the job posting. In that case, you might want to establish that, despite your experience, you are within the upper limit.

Note: Lithuania is the only country in Central and Eastern Europe with Equal Employment Opportunity legislation and an official ombudsman to whom issues of discrimination can be referred for resolution.

References

Have a list of people who know you, have taught you, or have worked with or supervised you. If a potential employer asks for references, what he or she wants to find out is whether you can learn new things quickly and have shown yourself to be dependable. It is unnecessary to put on your resume, "References available upon request." Potential employers know that, and will not ask for references until you are among the final applicants for the position. It is best to inform those whom you intend to use as references. Then, when the resume reviewer or potential employer calls a person you have listed as a reference source, the person will not respond, "Jane Doe? I don't know a Jane Doe."

RESUME PRESENTATION

Format and Layout

Your resume is your personal representative—the first thing about you seen by someone who may become important in your life. First impressions *do* count! Make sure your resume makes a favorable first impression by using high-quality white paper (A4) and crisp, black type that is easy to read (no script or fancy typefaces).

It is important that your CV shows your education and work experience, highlights your skills and accomplishments, and includes some information about you as a person. List in the following order: your name, education and training, work experience, and special skills. The type of resume most often used, and easiest for the recruiter or employer to follow, is a reverse chronological format, which shows your current or last position first. Do not include anything that will not strengthen your application for the job. Do not lose sight of the purpose and function of your resume. As long as the format and sequence of information prescribed here is followed, neatness and readability are the important criteria. Check resume handbooks and the resume examples at the back of this book for the format that best fits your information.

Remember, your resume is a self-portrait! Invest the time necessary to make it sparkle—research time, data collecting time, and time for multiple drafts.

Length

One page is preferable; two pages is the maximum length (and this is only for persons with extensive experience and accomplishments).

Attachments

In this region, it is standard procedure to attach a passport-type photograph (a head-and-shoulders photo) in the upper right-hand corner of your resume. Never submit a vacation pose, one that includes your dog, cat, baby, or motorcycle. Do not attach anything not specifically requested. In rare instances, employers will want photocopies of diplomas, special licenses, certificates, or permits. Never send original documents. You may never get them back, even if you provide a stamped, self-addressed envelope. If employers want more information from you, they will ask for it.

E-mail Applications

If an e-mail address is provided in the job advertisement, it probably means applications can be received via that medium.

Note: If you send your resume as an attachment, make sure it goes as a Word 97 as well as Word 95 document, as not all Baltic offices have the newer version of Word. Also, use a universal font such as Times New Roman to ensure that the receiver can read your document. Make sure as well that the recipient can open your document, because if not you are unlikely to be asked to resend it.

COVER LETTERS

A cover letter should be included with a CV, especially when applying for a specific position. It should be brief—no more than three or four paragraphs—and focused. A typed cover letter on white paper (A4) is preferable, but a neatly and legibly handwritten one is also acceptable.

Begin the letter by explaining what you are applying for (i.e., whether you are responding to a specific advertisement or are interested in a particular type of job). Continue by writing several sentences about why you are interested in a particular position and what you can offer. Include information about your background that is relevant to the sought position. It is important that the letter reflects your personality and is not a canned version from a resume guide or computer program.

JOB INFORMATION SOURCES

In addition to the sources listed next, there are consulting firms and placement agencies that match candidates and employers for a fee (usually paid by the employer). Frequently, you can find listings in professional journals, in local newspapers, and on the Internet. Personal references by local people are recommended. Also, temporary agencies from the West are opening offices in the Baltics, and one of these may be a place to begin your search.

The "In Your Pocket" books, issued bimonthly, are the single best sources of information about Vilnius, Riga, and Tallinn (and many other European cities). With maps, as well as hotel, restaurant, transportation, and basic city information (including some key words and phrases), plus listings of scheduled events, they are an indispensable resource, even for natives and longtime residents. (As you look at services offered, you may spot a potential employer.) A bargain at about US $1 per copy, they would be cheap at three or four times the price. For *Vilnius in Your Pocket*, call (+370) 2 22 29 76; web site: www.inyourpocket.com. For *Riga in Your Pocket*, call (+371) 722 05 80; e-mail: riyp@mailbox.riga.lv. For *Tallinn in Your Pocket*, call (+372) 631 33 50; e-mail: tiyp@infonet.ee.

Internet Sites

The only employment web site in the Baltic States is: www.cv.takas.lt.

Note: This web site only accepts CVs written in Lithuanian.

Newspapers

Most communities have job postings in the local languages. Some advertisements appear in English. To see what's happening across the Baltics (in English), check out the *Baltic Times*, issued weekly (e-mail: btimes@auste.elnet.lt).

▶ Lithuania: The best source of jobs is the Saturday issue of *Lietuvos Rytas*, the main daily published in Vilnius (www.lrytas.lt). For a business perspective, check out *Verslo Zinios* (vzinios@vzinios.lt).

▶ Latvia: Try *Diena* (www.diena.org.lv) or the business daily *Dienas Bizness* (bizness@db.lv).

▶ Estonia: Try *Postimees* (www.postimees.ee), *Eesti Paevelehe* (www.zzz.ee/epl/epl.html), or the business daily *Aripaev* (www.mbp.ee).

Chambers of Commerce

Lithuania
American Chamber of Commerce
Lukiskiu 5-204, Vilnius
Phone: (370 2) 61 11 81
Fax: (370 2) 22 61 28
E-mail: acc@post.omnitel.net

Latvia
American Chamber of Commerce
Jaunuiela 24, Riga
Phone: (371) 721 22 04
Fax: (371) 782 00 90
E-mail: amcham@mailbox.riga.lv
Web site: www.amcham.mt.lv

Estonia
American Chamber of Commerce
Harju 6, Tallin
Phone: (372) 631 05 22
Fax: (372) 631 05 21
E-mail: acce@datanet.ee

WORK PERMITS/VISAS

Visas

Citizens of many countries do not need visas to visit the Baltic States. But if you are planning to stay for more than 90 days, it is wise to obtain the necessary visas and permits before you arrive. A permanent resident or work visa is required for all foreign visitors staying for more than 90 days. To obtain more information, it is best to call the consulates of Lithuania, Latvia, and/or Estonia in your home country.

Residence and Work Permits

If you are already "in country," to obtain a residence and work visa contact:

Lithuania
Immigration Department
Saltoniskiu 19, Vilnius
Phone: (370 2) 72 58 64

or

Immigration Service
Verkiu 3, Vilnius
Phone: (370 2) 75 64 53

Latvia
Citizenship and Migration Board
Visa Section
Raina 5, Riga
Phone: (371) 721 94 24
Fax: (371) 782 03 06

Estonia
Foreign Ministry
Ravala 9, Tallin
Phone: (372) 631 74 40

INTERVIEW ADVICE

► Do your research before you go to the interview. Find out about the company, where its European headquarters are, what the main lines of activities are, and if possible what types of activities the company performs in the Baltic countries. Be prepared to talk specifically about what you can offer. Remember that the job market is tight and unemployment is currently rising, so you will be in competition with qualified local professionals.

▶ Make sure your choice of clothes is appropriate for work, especially during interviews—shirt, tie, and jacket for men, blouse and jacket for women. For both, make sure slacks or suit pants are pressed.

▶ It is natural to be nervous. The better prepared you are for the interview, the less this will be a problem. Do some relaxation exercises before the interview. During the interview *listen* to what the interviewer is asking and answer questions concretely and concisely.

▶ Expect interviews to be more formal than informal. Be familiar with the information on your resume, and be prepared to answer the predictable questions about your last job, reasons for leaving, feelings about your former manager, what is appealing about the job for which you are applying, and so on.

▶ Be prepared to state your salary expectations during the first interview.

CULTURAL ADVICE

▶ Do not remind Balts of their Soviet legacy or talk about Soviet mentality too much. Remember that national honor and identity are important for them; treat them with respect as Europeans or as independent Balts.

▶ Never compare their languages to Russian or any other Slavic language. While Russian is common to all three Baltic countries and is widely known, there is a hesitancy to use Russian, especially in Estonia. The Balts appreciate any attempt to learn the local language and are tolerant of mistakes.

▶ Many people still are struggling to learn new ways, and have not prospered as members of free-market economies. Try to be tolerant even if you find behaviors strange or offensive. Their actions might be caused by lack of knowledge and awareness.

▶ If you are invited to someone's home, bring flowers. Champagne or wine is also appropriate. Be punctual, but do not come early.

Note: Always bring an odd number of blooms, as even numbers are for mournful occasions.

▶ In most homes, shoes are left near the door and exchanged for slippers (because of the snow, sand, and salt stains that are unavoidable in lands with such long and wet winters). Not surprisingly, shoe shines are important, too.

▶ Most people will observe good manners, but truth is somewhat elastic and evasiveness about personal issues is to be expected (though you may get probed about your own personal affairs).

▶ The high level of poverty contributes to the high level of theft. Pickpockets are active, and "smash and grab" thefts from cars and homes are common, though personal assaults are infrequent (except for people who flash money or jewelry in bars and get robbed on the way home).

▶ Always drive defensively and walk especially carefully. Drivers tend to drive aggressively, often too fast for conditions, and may not yield to pedestrians or cyclists.

Belgium

Fanny Bodart, Nicholson International

COUNTRY OVERVIEW

The population of Belgium is approximately 10 million, of which 55 percent are Flemish (Dutch-speaking, in the northern part), 33 percent Walloon (French-speaking, in the southern part), a minority is German-speaking, and 10 percent are foreigners. The capital is Brussels, which is one of the world's few officially bilingual capitals. Brussels is the economic and political heart of the country and home to nearly one million people. Other major Belgian cities include Antwerp, Ghent, Charleroi, Liège, and Bruges. Belgium is a constitutional parliamentary monarchy.

Brussels is an economic center, thanks to its favorable location and extensive transportation network. Housing several European Union organizations, Brussels is also called "the capital of Europe." A multitude of international companies have their European headquarters there. The export-oriented Belgian economy focuses on services, agriculture, and chemicals. The GDP (gross domestic product) per capita is US$21,000.

Bordered by the Netherlands, Germany, Luxembourg, and France, Belgium is mainly flat. The southern part of the country is dominated by the Ardennes, a wooded plateau which forms, along with the North Sea coastline and the historical cities, the country's primary tourist attractions.

Belgian people are entrepreneurial, friendly, and rarely boastful. Most Belgians speak English in addition to French and Dutch. Belgian food is highly regarded throughout Europe. National specialties are french fries, brussels sprouts, endives, beer, and chocolate.

RESUME SPECIFICS

Education

State the beginning, as well as the graduation date, of your studies and the name of the university or college you attended. Include the title of your major and additional specialization areas. Mentioning the topic of your thesis can be useful for new graduates. Include a list of other studies, even if you did not complete the entire program or receive a degree.

Note: The American term "high school" corresponds to what is known as "secondary school" in Belgium. The Dutch term "hogeschool" in Belgium means college, that is higher education on a non-university level. In Belgium, one can go to university and obtain an academic degree or attend a college and get a more practice-oriented education. A college degree usually takes three years to obtain. You then receive a degree on the *A1 level* (that's the official name). A college degree is not considered to be an academic degree. Holders of university degrees usually fall under a higher salary scale.

Extracurricular Activities

Extracurricular activities reveal something about your personality, so feel free to refer to them in your resume. These may include participation in student or youth movements, weekend work during studies, travels, language summer school, and so on.

Awards/Honors

Awards and honors achieved are useful and should be mentioned.

Additional Education/Specialized Training

Include additional courses, seminars, and training you attended during your studies or during your professional career. List the dates, the teaching institution, and the time attended (e.g., one-year evening course, five-day training program).

Work Experience

Give a reverse chronological description of your employment beginning with your most recent experience. Start with the employment dates, the company name and address, and the title of your position. Describe the overall function of your position and then list your responsibilities in complete sentences. Give the title of the person you reported to. If possible, support your descriptions with numbers/percentages, especially for sales and management positions. Give specific numbers on how you increased the sales budget, the number of new clients you brought in, specifics of the budget system you created, and so forth. Link your experience to the requirements of the position you are seeking. Young professionals can list their apprenticeships in this category.

Note: If you had different positions within the same firm, state these separately and add the beginning and end dates for each position. In addition, it is useful to give some information about the company, especially if it is not globally known.

Achievements/Accomplishments

Describe any special accomplishments that are of interest/relevance.

Special Skills

Give a summary of your knowledge of any computer languages, applications, and/or programs, as well as a description of your language skills.

Note: Belgium is a multilingual society; therefore, language skills are an important asset to your resume. Note your proficiency in speaking, writing, and reading each language that you list.

Professional Affiliations

Mention these if applicable.

Military Experience

Give the date and the duration of your military service, where you were based, and what duties you performed. In Belgium, fulfilling a military service is no longer obligatory.

Volunteer Experience

If applicable, include any activity performed on a voluntary basis (e.g., leadership in a youth movement, membership in a parents' committee, etc.). Together with the extracurricular activities, this tells something about your personality.

Personal Information

State your address, telephone number(s), and e-mail address. Also, include your nationality, civil (marital) status, and date of birth. Briefly provide information about your personal life: sports, cultural activities, other hobbies, and so on.

References

A resume does not necessarily include references. These will be checked at a later stage of the application process. Your future employer will usually seek your approval prior to contacting your references.

RESUME PRESENTATION

Format

Begin by listing your personal details (name, address, etc.) and continue with a brief description of your education. The largest part of your resume should be dedicated to describing your professional experience in reverse chronological order, beginning with the most recent. End by detailing your language skills, computer skills, and other information (extracurricular activities, etc.).

Note: Writing a CV in English is acceptable, since this is often the official business language of the larger corporations. It is also politically correct, because the person to whom you address your application can be from any number of countries.

Layout

Depending on your profile, the company's image, and the position you are applying for, the correct CV can be any style from somber to splashily original! A CV that is appropriate for a position as an art director would not be suitable for an accountant.

Length

Although there is no definitive rule, the perfect CV is usually no longer than three pages. If responding to an advertisement and your background speaks for itself, you can keep it shorter and send a "one-pager."

An unsolicited application sent to a recruitment agency should be more elaborate. Consultants like to have a clear and detailed view of your professional background. If you send a spontaneous application to search and selection offices, they will probably put your CV in their databases and not invite you for a visit until there is a matching position. Stating a preferred salary level is unusual, but it can be done.

Attachments

You may attach a photograph to your CV, but it is not necessary to include any other documents with your application. You can provide them later on request.

E-mail Applications

Make sure you refer to the position in the subject line. Also, send both the motivation letter (cover letter) and the CV in an attachment using a common format (e.g., Word).

COVER LETTERS

Content/Detail

Your cover letter should be tailor-made for each application. Using the same letter for every application gives an impersonal impression.

Refer to the position of interest and how you learned about the opening (newspaper, Internet, etc.). Mention something about why this particular company interests you. Explain why you are the perfect solution and what you can do for the company. Do not just repeat what is in your CV. Most importantly, beware of spelling errors.

Length

Your motivation letter should be one page in length.

JOB INFORMATION SOURCES

Publications/Newspapers

In Dutch

The major weekly job publications are:

Vacature (Inserted in different media)
Phone: +32 2 452 03 50
Fax: +32 2 469 08 31
Web site: www.vacature.be

JOB@ (Inserted in the weekend issue of *De Standaard, Het Nieuwsblad,* and *De Gentenaar*)
Phone: +32 2 467 27 27
Fax: +32 2 467 97 97
Web site: www.jobat.be

Employment ads are listed in the weekend issue of the following newspapers:

De Morgen and *Het Laatste Nieuws*
Contact: *De Persgroep*
Phone: +32 2 556 68 11
Fax: +32 2 520 41 92

Gazet van Antwerpen
Contact: *De Vlijt*
Phone: +32 3 210 02 10
Fax: +32 3 233 74 80

De Financieel-Economische TIJD
Contact: *Uitgeversbedrijf TIJD*
Phone: +32 3 286 02 11
Fax: +32 3 286 02 10
E-mail: Abo@tijd.be

Het Volk
Phone: +32 9 265 61 00
Fax: +32 9 265 61 11

Employment ads are listed in the following weekly magazines:

Knacks and *Trends*
Contact: Roularta Media Group
Phone: +32 2 737 51 00
Fax: +32 2 737 51 39

De Standaard Het Nieuwsblad and *De Gentenaar*
Contact: V.U.M.
Phone: +32 2 467 27 27
Fax: +32 2 467 97 97
E-mail: Info@jobat.be

In French

Le Soir Employ (Inserted in the newspaper *Le Soir* on weekends)
Contact: Rossel & Cie
Phone: +32 2 225 55 55/225 52 08
Fax: +32 2 225 59 04
Web site: ww.emploi.lesoir.be

Vacature Employ (Inserted in the weekly magazine *Le Vif and Trends Tendances*)
Contact: Roularta Media Group
Phone: +32 2 225 55 55/225 52 08
Fax: +32 2 225 59 04
Web site: ww.emploi.lesoir.be

General Interest

The Bulletin
Phone: +32 2 373 99 09

Trade Publication

MoveUp (Annual career guide for young professionals/graduates)
Phone: +32 2 734 90 00
E-mail: Moveup@moveup.be
Web site: www.moveup.be

Business Organizations

Chambre de Commerce et d'Industrie
  de Bruxelles
Louizalaan 500
1050 Elsene
Phone: +32 2 648 50 02
Fax: +32 2 640 93 28

American Chamber of Commerce in
  Belgium
Kunstlaan 50/5
1000 Brussels
Phone: +32 2 513 68 92
Fax: +32 2 513 35 90

Internet Sites

Address	Language
www.jobs-career.be	French, Dutch, English
www.amasis.be	Dutch, French, English
www.adecco.be	Dutch, French
www.creyfs.be	Dutch, French, English, German
www.interlabor.be = www.randstad.be	Dutch, French, English
www.interimpartnership.be	French, Dutch, English
www.konvert.be	English, French, Dutch
www.jobscape.be	English, French, Dutch
www.jobstoday.be	French, Dutch, English

www.belgium.hotjobs.net	Dutch, French
www.work4u.com	English
www.jobworld.be	English
www.orbem.be	French
www.vdab.be	Dutch
www.fws.be	French, Dutch, English
www.expat.org	French
www.moveup.be	Dutch
www.forem.be	French

WORK PERMITS/VISAS

European Union citizens can enter Belgium on an official identity card. Citizens from Australia, Canada, New Zealand, Japan, the United States, and other countries need a passport that is valid for at least three months after arrival. Citizens from other countries need to apply for visas. Your employer in Belgium must obtain a work permit for you. This will be handled by the Belgian regional employment office. There are two possibilities for obtaining a residence permit:

1. Your employer sends the work permit to you, and then your local embassy/consulate provides you with a residence authorization.
2. Upon arrival in Belgium, you can obtain a residence permit from the town hall where you will live by submitting your work permit. This permit is valid for one year and can be extended. For executives, this permit has no time limit.

European Union Citizens

With written proof of employment provided by the employer, EU citizens can obtain a temporary identity card, valid for six months, which can be extended to a five-year identity card. EU and non-EU citizens who do not have work upon arrival can stay for up to three months to seek employment.

CULTURAL ADVICE

▶ Belgian law prohibits mentioning age and gender requirements in advertisements.
▶ Belgians are very easygoing people. Belgium is known as the country of compromise, so be gentle and polite.
▶ Although Belgians are easygoing, you should behave rather formally when visiting someone's home for the first time.
▶ Do not come empty-handed to a social event at someone's home.
▶ Do not ask someone about his or her salary. Most Belgians are rather discreet about their incomes.
▶ Do not use someone's first name before you are invited to do so.

Brazil

Maria Paula Sampaio, Maria Paula Sampaio Consultores/
Marlar International

COUNTRY OVERVIEW

The Brazilian territory covers an area of 8,547,403 square kilometers in the eastern part of South America. Only two countries in South America—Chile and Ecuador—do not border Brazil. The eastern, southeastern, and northeastern regions of the country are bathed by the Atlantic Ocean.

Although 90 percent of the country is in the tropical zone, more than 60 percent of the population live in regions where the altitude, sea breezes, or polar cold fronts make the temperature pleasant. The cities that are located on plateaus, such as São Paulo, Brasilia, and Belo Horizonte, offer amiable climates, with average temperatures of 19°C. Cities like Rio de Janeiro, Recife, and Salvador, located on the coast, have hot climates soothed by the constant presence of the *alísios* winds. The southern cities of Porto Alegre and Curitiba have subtropical climates similar to some regions of the United States and Europe. In these regions, below-zero (Centigrade) temperatures occur frequently during winter.

Brazil is a federative republic comprised of 26 states. Brasilia, the country's capital, was founded in 1960 and is located in the central-eastern part of the country. The economic center of Brazil is concentrated in the highly industrialized cities around São Paulo, Rio de Janeiro, and Belo Horizonte (southeastern region). Most of the country's population is concentrated in these two regions. The area is rich in minerals and agriculture, and hosts numerous global companies from various segments (e.g., electronic/appliances, automobiles, telecommunications, food, chemicals, pharmaceuticals, etc.). The headquarters of the largest national and multinational banks are also located here.

The southern region represents a high level of development, balancing the rural and industrial sectors. Toward the south, the plateau transforms into vast plains called pampas, where traditional cattle ranching gave birth to the gaucho, the Brazilian equivalent of the cowboy. Toward the west, on the border between Brazil and Argentina, is the Cataratas do Iguaçú, one of the world's most splendid waterfalls. The largest city in this region is Porto Alegre, the capital of the state of Rio Grande do Sul, Brazil's southernmost state.

RESUME SPECIFICS

Education

Give a description of your college/university education. State your graduation year, major, and education title and whether you have studied abroad.

Extracurricular Activities and Awards/Honors

These do not need to be mentioned in Brazil.

Additional Education/Specialized Training

Any additional college/university courses should be mentioned in the education section. Also include information about courses or training in specialized areas, such as language or computer training.

Work Experience

Start by listing your job title and the name of the employer. Specify the employment dates. Give the details of your work and your field of responsibility. Emphasize information that is relevant to the position for which you are applying. Describe how your skills have developed through your tasks and achievements. Summer jobs and shorter periods of employment performed prior to your professional career should be summarized. If there are any gaps in employment history, it is important that you explain the reason for each gap in reasonable detail.

Achievements/Accomplishments

Any awards, special recognition, or promotions received during employment should be highlighted.

Special Skills

Proficiency in foreign languages and knowledge of specific computer programs should be noted.

Professional Affiliations

List any professional affiliations relevant to your focus area. Include information about your involvement with activities within the organization or any leadership roles.

Military Experience/Volunteer Experience

These do not need to be listed in Brazil.

Personal Information

List your home address, telephone numbers, age, civil (i.e., marital) status, and e-mail information.

References

The references you select should be connected to your professional experience, such as previous managers. These people should be well acquainted with your work performance, and be rather recent in time.

RESUME PRESENTATION

Format and Layout

Your resume/CV should present a clear picture of your education, internships, and employment, as well as other important experiences that might interest an employer, such as professional association memberships. A reverse chronologically arranged list with the aforementioned headings is best.

Note: Always begin your resume/CV by describing your educational background, followed by the details of your professional experience.

Length

Your resume/CV should be no longer than two pages.

Attachments

Grades, certificates, and letters of reference do not have to be included with your application.

E-mail Applications

It is increasingly common that employers in Brazil accept applications via e-mail. In this case, always attach your resume to the letter/e-mail.

COVER LETTERS

An application should always include a personalized cover letter along with a complete resume. A cover letter of one page typed in A4 format is preferable. A handwritten letter is acceptable provided that the writing is legible.

Content/Detail

Your cover letter should start with a phrase stating the position for which you are applying. Remember that the letter aims at raising the reader's interest, so try to let your personality influence the content. Everything you say in the letter should also be found in your resume/CV. Start by describing your education, your proficiency in foreign languages, and your field of professional experience.

Explain why you are applying for this job. Analyze your experiences and emphasize those which are connected to the position for which you are applying. Continue with a concentrated description of your previous professional experiences. Include information about relevant longer periods of foreign travel and your future professional goals. If you are unemployed at present, you should state that in the letter. Also, include details concerning your personal situation: ability to relocate, availability to travel on business trips, and so forth.

JOB INFORMATION SOURCES

Newspapers

Daily papers contain employment ads. The most popular daily papers in Brazil are *O Estado de São Paulo* (São Paulo) and *O Globo* (Rio de Janeiro). Every state has its own newspaper containing employment ads in that region. Sometimes ads are published in English, especially if the employer is a multinational company.

O Estado de São Paulo
Phone: (55 11) 856-2122
E-mail: anuncios@estado.com.br

O Globo
Phone: (55 21) 534-5500,
        (55 11) 811-3232
E-mail: Globoncomercial@
        oglobo.com.br

Internet Sites

Through the Internet, companies usually advertise open positions on their web sites. The most popular employment web sites in Brazil are www.catho.com.br and www.vagas.com.br.

Telephone Directory/Trade Publications

In the Brazilian telephone directory Yellow Pages, you will find companies listed under the relevant trade headings. This can be a fruitful way to start looking for companies that interest you. There is also another publication called *Exame* magazine (www.exame.com.br), which annually lists the largest organizations in Brazil (published by Abril Cultural; www.abril.com.br).

Country Employment Office

In Brazil, this office is suitable only for locating nonexecutive positions.

WORK PERMITS/VISAS

Visas

A business or permanent residence visa is required for most foreign visitors. For further information, contact the Brazilian embassy/consulate in your country.

Residence and Work Permits

Residence and work permits are required for all foreign citizens who want to work in Brazil.

INTERVIEW ADVICE

- ▶ Be on time, even if you know that your interviewer might be late.
- ▶ It is customary to begin the interview with a quick chat about the weather, traffic, or soccer.
- ▶ It is customary to find more horizontal structures, and positions with more responsibilities/independence in the multinational Brazilian companies. Small and medium-sized national companies tend to utilize a more centralized management style.
- ▶ It is not customary to contact the person who is offering the job to obtain more detailed information. It is advisable to send the application and wait to be contacted.
- ▶ It is wise to avoid discussing salary and other parts of the compensation package early in the process.
- ▶ Brazil has only a few, but strong, trade unions. Regulated vacation is four weeks per year.

CULTURAL ADVICE

- ▶ Brazilians are generally warm people. However, there are substantial regional differences in behavior, style, and even accent, derived from different types of colonization, economic activity, and climate.
- ▶ It is wise to show a humble spirit and style. To brag or to appear aggressive or overly ambitious is considered in poor taste.
- ▶ Workers receive a one-month holiday per year. This time is usually concentrated during the summer, or during the Carnival season (February or March). There is also a two-month school break in the summer, when many professionals take their vacations.
- ▶ The current legislation regarding traffic violations (alcohol, speeding, parking, etc.) is very severe.
- ▶ It is forbidden to smoke in public places, in commercial establishments, and in restaurants.

Canada

Charles M. Lennox, PricewaterhouseCoopers

COUNTRY OVERVIEW

Situated north of the United States and between the Atlantic and Pacific oceans, Canada is the world's second largest country. It extends 7,700 kilometers (4,775 miles) east to west and 4,600 kilometers (2,850 miles) north to south. Nearly 90 percent of Canada's 30 million people live along the 6,379-kilometer (3,955-mile) southern border with the United States. Ottawa, located in eastern Canada, is the capital, with 314,000 inhabitants. Other major cities include Halifax, Montreal, Toronto, Winnipeg, Calgary, and Vancouver. Canada has over 129 national historic parks and 12 areas of such natural significance that they are listed on the United Nations' World Heritage list.

Canada has four distinct seasons, which vary slightly in their arrival across the country. A significant factor in the country's climate is latitude—it becomes increasingly colder the further north one travels. The warmest areas in the south are the most populated. There are six time zones ranging from Newfoundland standard time in the east to Pacific standard time in the west.

Canada is a constitutional monarchy with Queen Elizabeth II as head of state and a democratically elected prime minister as head of government chosen every five years. Canada has a market-driven economy, with an extensive social welfare system. Government benefits are funded by high personal taxes and include health care, unemployment insurance, and a pension plan. The United Nations has rated Canada the most livable country in the world six consecutive times.

Canada has a complex three-dimensional character resulting from traditions derived from indigenous native peoples and the country's two founding peoples— the French and the English. Culturally, the country is influenced heavily by its close proximity to the United States. Canada is a thriving multicultural society with a variety of languages and racial origins; the 1996 census lists over 200 separate countries and territories of birth for Canada's immigrants. In fact, Canada absorbs more immigrants per capita than any other country. Although English and French are the country's two official languages, the influence of other nations can be felt across the country. The country's cultural diversity enhances the Canadian identity.

RESUME SPECIFICS

Education

It is not necessary to include details of your high school education. If you have studied beyond high school, known as "post-secondary" in Canada, it is understood that you graduated from high school or possess an equivalent designation. Details of post-secondary studies should include the university or college attended, the course of study, the diploma or degree received, and the year graduated.

Note: Canada makes a clear distinction between college and university. "Colleges" are viewed as institutions granting diplomas in job-specific areas of study. "Universities," on the other hand, are more academic in nature and are degree-granting.

Extracurricular Activities

Describe any extracurricular activity in which you participated, such as arranging different types of student activities, working within the student administration, participating in clubs or sports teams, and so on.

Awards/Honors

List any awards, honors, bursaries, or scholarships received for scholastic achievement or outstanding performance in other areas.

Additional Education/Specialized Training

Any additional college or university courses should be mentioned in this context. Include courses or training in specialized areas such as languages, information technology, or sales.

Work Experience

Start by listing your most recent job title and employer. Specify the employment dates (years only) and if it was a part-time job (it is assumed to be full-time if not otherwise specified). List the details of your work and your areas of responsibility, utilizing a well-structured bullet-point format. Emphasize information that is relevant to the job for which you are applying. Describe your accomplishments in each position, emphasizing those that are quantifiable achievements. Summer jobs and shorter periods of employment performed prior to your professional career should be summarized.

If there are gaps in your employment history, it is important that you be prepared to explain the reason for each gap should you be granted an interview. Also, for part-time employment, be prepared to explain the reason why you chose not to work full-time.

Achievements/Accomplishments

Any awards, special recognition, or promotions received during employment should be highlighted.

Special Skills

Proficiency in foreign languages and knowledge of specific computer programs should be noted.

Professional Affiliations

List any professional affiliations and memberships relevant to your professional career. Include information about your involvement in activities within the organization or any leadership roles you hold or may have held. Include this information only if you have been an active member.

Military Experience

Military service is not mandatory in Canada. If you have military service experience, include the information in your resume as you would any other professional experience—rank (job title), military organization (employer), areas of responsibility, and accomplishments. Include the dates and location of your service.

Volunteer Experience

Details of any previous or current volunteer activities should be given. These may include activities with associations, clubs, or areas of personal interest (connected to your children's school, sports, charity, etc.).

Personal Information

Describe your personal interests such as hobbies and sports activities. These activities reflect, in part, what type of person you are. Be mindful of listing only solitary pursuits if the position to which you are applying is one that requires interactivity with others. Be careful not to exaggerate, as it is important to appear believable.

Note: In Canada, it is illegal for a prospective employer to ask your marital status/sexual orientation, ethnicity, or age.

References

The references you select should be connected to your professional experience, preferably previous managers, college instructors, or university professors. These people should be well acquainted with your recent work performance and capabilities. Providing the names of three references (along with title, organization, and contact information for each) is sufficient.

RESUME PRESENTATION

Format and Layout

Your resume should represent a clear picture of your professional experience, education, and community and volunteer activities, as well as other important experiences that might interest an employer, such as professional association memberships. A reverse chronology (most recent experience appearing first) with the aforementioned headings is recommended. A short profile of your skills and abilities, in well-structured bullet-point sentences, should appear first.

Note: Your resume should begin with a short profile followed by either your educational background or details of your professional experience—all in reverse chronological order.

Length

Your resume should be no longer than three pages.

Attachments

Transcripts of grades, certificates, and letters of reference should not be included with your application, as you can present them at the interview should you be asked.

Note: Personalizing an application with a small photo is considered inappropriate in Canada and is not encouraged.

E-mail Applications

It is increasingly common that employers in Canada accept and appreciate receiving applications via e-mail. In this case always include your cover letter in the same electronic file as your resume. Video recordings are not recommended.

COVER LETTERS

An application should include a typed personalized cover letter of one page and a complete resume of no more than three pages.

Content/Detail

Your cover letter should start with a phrase stating the position for which you are applying. Remember that the letter aims to raise the reader's interest, so try to let your personality influence the content. In other words—be yourself. Everything you say in the letter should also be found in your resume. The cover letter should be more than a simple restatement of facts in the form of sentences; it should seek to tie all your experiences together and convey a sense of reason and harmony to the many steps taken along your career path.

Explain why you are applying for this job. Analyze your experiences and emphasize those that are connected to the position for which you are applying to show your suitability for the position. If you are unemployed at present, you should state that in the letter.

JOB INFORMATION SOURCES

Newspapers

Newspapers and trade journals contain employment advertisements. Canada has a number of daily newspapers—with one or more in each large urban area. The country has two English-language national newspapers—*The Globe and Mail* and *The National Post*. *The Toronto Star* is another large-circulation English-language daily newspaper, but it is concentrated in Canada's densely populated southern Ontario region.

The Globe and Mail (national newspaper)
Phone: 416-585-5000
Web site: www.theglobeandmail.com

The National Post (national newspaper)
Phone: 416-350-6100
Web site: www.nationalpost.com

The Toronto Star (southern Ontario only)
Phone: 416-367-2000
Web site: www.thestar.com

Southam Inc. (publishes several newspapers across Canada)
Phone: 416-445-6641
Web site: www.southam.com

Employment Publications

Canada Employment Weekly is the largest career newspaper in the country and typically includes leads on over 1,000 new jobs across Canada. The paper is distributed in every province and territory in Canada as well as in 16 other countries. More information is available by visiting www.mediacorp2.com.

Chambers of Commerce

Canadian Chamber of Commerce—Ottawa
350 Sparks Street
Suite 501
Ottawa, Ontario
K1R 7S8
Phone: (613) 238-4000
Fax: (613) 238-7643

Canadian Chamber of Commerce—Toronto
BCE Place
Heritage Building
181 Bay Street
Toronto, Ontario
M5J 2T3
Phone: (416) 868-6415
Fax: (416) 868-0189

Internet Sites

Through the Internet, companies usually advertise open positions on their web sites. It may be worthwhile to look for companies in your field of interest. The most popular employment web sites in Canada are: www.careermosaic.com, www.globecareers.com, www.jobshark.com, and www.monster.ca. The newest and largest web site for jobs is a joint venture of Canada's two largest newspapers, *The Globe and Mail* and *The Toronto Star*: www.workopolis.com.

Telephone Directory

Each Canadian city or large geographic area publishes its own telephone and Yellow Pages directory specific to its local area. In the Yellow Pages directory you will find companies listed under the relevant trade/business heading. This can be a seemingly easy way to start looking for companies that interest you. In the White Pages telephone directory, all companies are listed in alphabetical order. A national telephone directory is available online at www.Canada411.sympatico.ca. A national Yellow Pages directory is available at www.canadayellowpages.com.

Canada Employment Offices

The Canadian federal government operates Canada Employment Offices across the country. Local addresses and telephone numbers can be found at the web site for the Canada Employment Office at www.canada.gc.ca/programs/jobs.

WORK PERMITS/VISAS

Applying as an Independent Immigrant

Most independent immigrants are skilled workers who are expected to have the education, skills, work experience, language ability, and other qualities needed to participate in the Canadian labor market. The selection criteria, known as the point system, focus on occupation, education and training, experience, age, and knowledge of English and/or French. Bonus points are given if the applicant has relatives in Canada who are Canadian citizens or permanent residents. The visa officer also gives points for personal suitability. Skilled workers must obtain a minimum of 70 points. Immigrants to Quebec must meet selection criteria set by that province. The self-assessment guide, which comes with the application kit for independent immigrants, will help you evaluate your chances of success. For more information, please see the web site www.mrci.gouv.qc.ca. The processing fee is not refundable, so if you appear unlikely to qualify, you may decide not to apply. The Canadian federal government is responsible for medical examinations and background checks.

To see if your skills are needed in Canada, check the General Occupations List. If your occupation is not on the list, you will not qualify, unless you have arranged employment. If an occupation is not on the list, it usually means that there are enough Canadians qualified in that occupation to meet the demands of the labor market. It is important to remember that even if your occupation is on the list, that is no guarantee of employment in Canada. Labor market needs can change. You may not meet Canadian standards for your occupation and may need upgrading.

More information is available at the Citizenship and Immigration Canada web site www.cicnet.ci.gc.ca.

INTERVIEW AND CULTURAL ADVICE

- ▶ It is wise to show a humble spirit and style. Bragging or appearing aggressive or overly ambitious is considered in poor taste.
- ▶ Canadians are almost always punctual, both professionally and socially, and expect the same from others.
- ▶ Canadians are polite, deferential to authority, consensus-oriented, and inclined to avoid confrontation.
- ▶ Telephoning the contact person listed in the employment advertisement before sending in your application for further details or just to introduce yourself is not encouraged. However, sending a brief note of thanks by e-mail or regular mail after an interview is considered polite.
- ▶ It is wise to avoid discussing salary and other parts of the compensation package early in the interview process. However, if requested, you should state your salary preference.
- ▶ Since most Canadians take their annual vacation during the warm summer months of June, July, and August, the period immediately prior to and during the summer is a difficult time for conducting new business.
- ▶ In social circumstances, it is common for men to shake hands and for men and women to briefly embrace. In professional circumstances, it is common for people to shake hands when beginning their discussions.

Chile

Veronica Morgan, MV Amrop International

COUNTRY OVERVIEW

Chile is best understood as a land of ethnic diversity. The father of Chile, Bernardo O'Higgins, was the son of an Irish immigrant; the founder of Santiago, Pedro de Valdivia, was a Spaniard; but the spirit of Chile is derived from Lautaro, the Mapuche chief who defeated the Spaniards. Chileans are descendants of Mapuches, Spaniards, French, Germans, British, Italians, Scandinavians, and Asians. A land of magnificent scenery, aesthetic pleasure, and cultural delights greets guests from all over the world. The population of Chile is almost 15 million. Santiago accounts for 40 percent of the total population, and only 15 percent of the population actually live in rural areas.

Chileans believe in hard work, responsibility, and efficiency. Additionally, they have the ability to overcome adversity and view the future with confidence. The official language is Spanish, but English is spoken in the larger business environments.

Chile's president is elected by popular vote for a six-year term. The bicameral National Congress (Congreso Nacional) consists of two houses. The Senate (Senado) has 48 seats, 38 elected by popular vote and 10 military appointees. Members serve eight-year terms, with one-half elected every four years. The Chamber of Deputies (Cámara de Diputados) has 120 seats. Members are elected by popular vote to serve four-year terms. The Congress is located in Valparaíso, a port city located less than 100 kilometers west of Santiago.

Chile has a broad layer of small, medium, and large private firms capable of organizing and carrying out ambitious investment and marketing programs. Chilean entrepreneurs have also shown an ability to see beyond its borders—recent export expansion has been impressive.

Business opportunities in Chile include: electricity generation and related products, pollution control equipment, telecommunications equipment, computers and peripherals, mining and construction industry equipment, building materials, medical equipment, port equipment, food processing equipment, air-conditioning and refrigeration equipment, and security equipment. There are also excellent opportunities in consumer products and service industries such as tourism, high technology, and infrastructural-type products. Chile is well known for its transparent regulatory systems and friendly disposition toward foreign businesspersons. The Chilean economy is expected to grow more than that of any other Latin American country.

JOB INFORMATION SOURCES

Newspapers

El Mercurio is the most important and extensive newspaper in Chile. Section E, "Artes y Letras," is published every Sunday. It is in this section that private companies and consultant companies advertise their personnel requirements.

El Mercurio
Avenida Santa María 5542, Vitacura
Santiago, Chile
Contact: Eugenio Olivares
Phone: 562-3301523
Fax: 562-2289289, 562-2282813

Chambers of Commerce

Many countries have independent chambers of commerce where useful assistance can be obtained (such as company directories, special seminars, etc.):

American Chamber of Commerce
Avenida Américo Vespucio Sur 80
9th floor, Las Condes
Santiago, Chile
Contact: Felipe Reyes
Phone: 562-2909700
Fax: 562-2060911
E-mail: felipe.reyes@amchamchile.cl

French Chamber of Commerce
Marchant Pereira 201 of 701, casilla 5-d
Santiago, Chile
Phone: 562-2255547
Fax: 562-2255545
E-mail: cfcc@netline.cl

Spanish Chamber of Commerce
Carmen Sylva 2306
Santiago, Chile
Phone: 562-2335280

British Chamber of Commerce
Avenida Suecia 155-C
Santiago, Chile
Phone: 562-2314366
Fax: 562-2318211

Internet Sites

The Internet has several special web sites where people can find jobs, apply to job offers, and register themselves in employment databases. The most popular are:

www.laborum.com
www.Vitae.cl
www.Trabajando.cl

Telephone Directory

In the Yellow Pages, you will find the companies listed in alphabetical order under the relevant trade headings.

Executive Search Firms

Formal searching for executives by search firms or headhunter companies is relatively new in Chile.

WORK PERMITS/VISAS

A work permit is required to work legally in Chile. The employer or company that is hiring the employee submits the required paperwork to the Ministerio de Relaciones Exteriores along with the work contract. Once the Ministerio approves the application, the employee brings the documents, along with a personal certificate, to the local Chilean consulate, which issues the work permit.

INTERVIEW AND CULTURAL ADVICE

- ▶ Do your research before you go to the interview. Find out about the company and also about the competence required for the position. Be clear about what you can offer and contribute to the company.
- ▶ Interviews are formal and you should dress accordingly. Be prepared to answer questions about your most recent job, reasons for leaving, what you expect from the job you are applying for, and so forth.
- ▶ It is wise to avoid discussing salary and other parts of the compensation package early in the process.
- ▶ Do not persistently telephone for the status of the search process.
- ▶ Job references are very important.
- ▶ Chilean people like to work as a team.
- ▶ Most Chileans take their three-week annual vacation between December (Christmas holidays) and February.
- ▶ Chilean people are very traditional and formal, and foreigners should behave in the same manner.
- ▶ Chileans are not punctual, especially in social situations.
- ▶ In social circumstances, it is nice to arrive with a small present for the hostess.

China

Fiona Yung, PricewaterhouseCoopers

COUNTRY OVERVIEW

Situated on the western seaboard of the Pacific Ocean north of the equator, the Asian landmass of the People's Republic of China (PRC) is as large as the whole continent of Europe. It can be divided into five regions: Western China, Northeast China, North China, South China, and Southwest China.

China is governed by the State Council, which is the executive committee of the National People's Congress (NPC). Under the State Council are various ministries, commissions, and other government bureaus responsible for specialized fields. The State Council has the power to formulate administrative measures, issue directives and orders, and verify their execution in accordance with the Constitution, laws, and decrees.

Note should be made of the role of the Communist Party of China (CPC), which is the key policy-making body in China. The policies adopted by the CPC are implemented by government agencies. In the past, the CPC and the government have been virtually impossible to separate. Recently, efforts have been initiated to separate the CPC from the government in terms of policy implementation, with the CPC responsible for policy making and strategy.

Putonghua, or Mandarin, based on the Beijing dialect, is the national language, spoken by 70 percent of the population. It is taught in all schools and is the spoken language of the government. There are numerous other dialects such as Cantonese, Shanghainese, Fukienese, and Hakka. The written language, which is ideographic and not phonetic, is uniform.

The education system has undergone dramatic changes since 1977. In 1986, a compulsory education program was introduced, mandating the implementation of a nine-year education system for school-age children. The education system will be reformed gradually. Under the new system, schools are run primarily by the government and various social organizations. Entrance to universities and middle schools is still very competitive.

Living standards are highest in the coastal areas because of the more advanced industrial development and the establishment of a larger number of foreign investment enterprises, particularly in the Special Economic Zones. There is a growing disparity between urban and rural incomes. When combined with regional income growth differentials, these income disparities contribute to increased migration pressures.

China has a great cultural heritage, which includes opera, historical monuments, and museums. Recently, developments have been seen in such areas as the fine arts, theaters, films, publishing, libraries, and radio and television broadcasting. The major cities, such as Beijing and Shanghai, offer numerous leisure activities. Competitive sports are also played on an international level.

The Chinese economy is principally a state and collective economy, with a limited, but increasing, amount of private and individual ownership. State-owned enterprises have been responsible for the highest proportion of total industrial output in the past. However, the cooperative and private-sector industrial output is increasing and is now beginning to account for a larger proportion of total output.

SPECIAL LABOR CONSIDERATIONS

This special section on labor considerations is included for your reference because the PRC is still very much a developing labor market. This has an impact on the type of employers seeking overseas executives as well as on job sources available for interested parties.

The economic reforms begun in the early 1980s, which encouraged joint ventures with foreign businesses, highlighted the gulf between locally available skills and those required to compete a market economy. The role of the Chinese manager in the centrally planned economy was primarily to fulfill production quotas defined by the state. In this environment, there was little need for skills such as marketing, since prices were determined by the state.

Now, some 20 years into sweeping economic reforms, many foreign enterprises operating in China still find it hard to recruit local managers with an understanding of international business strategy. Although the labor supply is plentiful, the recruitment of skilled and managerial staff is often difficult. This inevitably has a direct impact on the cost of establishing a business in China. Many companies will require an expatriate presence for some time to come. The situation has improved in recent years, particularly in the large cities. However, it will take a few more years for young Chinese midlevel managers to become seasoned.

As a result of this shortage, employers tend to recruit Western and Asian professionals with the required technical and language skills or Chinese nationals who have been out of China for some time, either working or studying. Many Chinese M.B.A. graduates are returning to China and are highly sought after for their newly acquired management skills and fluency in English. This type of employee usually commands a higher salary than local Chinese nationals, though not generally as high as typical expatriate salary levels. One problem in recruiting the overseas-educated Chinese is that they tend to incur the jealousy and envy of their local Chinese colleagues who resent what is considered to be the special treatment they receive.

RESUME SPECIFICS

As described earlier, the impact of the economic reforms has attracted many foreign investment enterprises (FIEs) to operate in the PRC. Typically, these entities (U.S., European, or Asian) will transfer in-house qualified executives to start and subsequently run their businesses. This group typically has the technical understanding of the particular business sector as well as the corporate understanding. Due to the shortage of middle management, however, these FIEs often look externally to recruit executives with the language skills and understanding of doing business in the PRC to support the management team. At present, many qualified financial, sales, marketing, and engineering executives (primarily Asian) are working for FIEs in the PRC.

In addition, with the establishment of local PRC private and exchange-listed companies, there is a need for experienced executives with an understanding of Western management techniques. Again, Asian executives have been attracted to help develop these companies.

Thus, there is no set recommendation for the preparation/presentation of a resume or application letter, as the employer reviewing the application could be one of many nationalities and could be headquartered outside the PRC. Therefore, the applicant will need to assess the nationality/domicile of the employing entity and tailor his or her resume accordingly.

In addition, the applicant will need to clearly demonstrate language skills, prior PRC work experience (if applicable), and a genuine desire and commitment to be based in the PRC. If the applicant intends to take his or her family, this should also be stated, as the employer will need to assess the suitability of the assignment location for a family.

JOB INFORMATION SOURCES

Newspapers/Trade Publications

Foreign investment enterprises, joint ventures, and private companies are able to place advertisements in national and regional newspapers. Approval needs to be obtained from the Labor Bureau and a copy of the business license submitted with the application. Most papers are printed in Chinese. There is one English-language national newspaper, the *China Daily*. Advertisements appearing in the Chinese media are primarily aimed at local PRC nationals. Some more senior positions aimed at expatriates are advertised in the *China Daily*. In addition, advertisements for PRC-based expatriate positions are placed in Hong Kong, Singapore, and Taiwan.

There are also specific industry journals that advertise for more technical positions (e.g., telecommunications, engineering, pharmaceutical, and medical); again, these are aimed primarily at local PRC nationals.

Business Organizations

It is not common for recruitment to be handled by business organizations.

Internet Sites

This will become a more effective medium but, at present, few businesses have access to the Internet. There is an increasing number of new entrants in the Asian market offering online job search/recruiting portals. They offer subscribing member companies throughout Asia (including the PRC) the opportunity to post available positions and to search and view selected resumes. Two major companies offering this service are Jobs Dbase (www.jobsdb.com) and Jobs Asia (www.jobasia.com.) New Internet recruitment web sites include www.futurestep.com, www.futurego.com, and www.pacificbank.com.

Campus Recruitment

Many sizable multinational companies in China sponsor the top universities and business schools through the provision of scholarships. These universities in turn provide a pool of graduates for management training programs with major multinational companies. Although overseas students often opt for Mandarin-intensive language courses at these universities, preference by multinational companies conducting on-campus recruitment will usually be for PRC nationals.

WORK PERMITS/VISAS

Foreigners who wish to enter, pass through, or reside in the PRC must obtain permission from PRC diplomatic missions, consular posts, or other agencies authorized by the Ministry of Foreign Affairs of the PRC to issue visas. Under special circumstances, foreigners may apply at visa offices situated at the ports designated by the PRC government: Beijing, Shanghai, Tianjin, Dalian, Fuzhou, Xiamen, Xi'an Guilin, Hangzhou, Kunming, Guangzhou (Baiyun Airport), Shenzhen (Luohu, Shekou), and Zhuhai (Gongbei).

Nonimmigrant Visas

Tourist Visa

Foreigners who wish to travel to the PRC should apply for the "L" visa, which is obtainable upon application to a PRC visa post abroad. The visa is usually valid for three months. Foreigners who wish to stay in the PRC for longer periods may apply for visa renewals. Tourists may seek a three-month renewal and, under special circumstances, a further three-month renewal from the Public Security Department in the PRC.

Transit Visa

Foreigners are not required to produce visas if they are only in transit and continuing on international flights within 24 hours. For temporary departures from the airport, permission must be obtained from the appropriate authority. Please note that since November 1995, British passport holders have not been eligible for this visa-free treatment. They must obtain a visa even if they are only in transit.

Business Visa

Foreigners who travel to the PRC for business visits, for speaking engagements, or to exchange knowledge on scientific and cultural topics in the PRC should apply for an "F" visa.

Employment Visas and Permanent Residence

Foreigners who wish to work in the PRC must be sponsored for a "Z" visa by their PRC employer. This process is done in four stages. First, the employer must sponsor the foreigner (the employee) for an Employment Permit; second, the Employment Permit will then be forwarded to the appropriate location (i.e., where the employee is located) for processing; third, the employee will need to enter the PRC and obtain an employment certificate; and fourth, the employee will then need to obtain a Permanent Resident Card or Foreign Resident Permit (the name depends on which part of the PRC the employee will work in).

Residents of Taiwan, Hong Kong, and Macau (THM) are required to apply for an Employment Approval instead of an Employment Permit. If, however, the

THM resident will serve as either the general manager or deputy general manager of a foreign investment enterprise (i.e., Sino-foreign equity or cooperative joint venture, wholly foreign-owned enterprise, or a holding company), the THM resident is not required to secure the Employment Approval.

INTERVIEW ADVICE

▶ As noted earlier, it is difficult to be specific regarding job interview advice, as the employer could be any nationality—a U.S., European, Taiwanese, Hong Kong, or Singaporean company, each with its own diverse culture. In addition, there are tri-venture entities operating in the PRC—thus the ultimate management team could be comprised of three different cultures.

▶ Ensure that you have a good understanding of who the employing entity is.

▶ If it is a joint or tri-venture, try to identify which entity has management control.

▶ Ensure that the reporting lines and job requirements are fully understood.

▶ If the employment is on an assignment basis, ensure there is a clear understanding about the assignment objectives and the proposed assignment length. Usually expatriates are employed to:

Transfer skills to the local entity; the skills may be technical, managerial, or a special knowledge of the organization (i.e., how it works internationally, and its values and corporate culture).

Provide strong leadership skills, help to build up organizations, act as the instrument of change, or design the strategic plan.

Communicate with the home office.

Ensure the Chinese office is performing its fiduciary duties, and safeguard the company's interests.

Train the local Chinese staff to operate according to international standards.

▶ For an expatriate going to work in the PRC for the first time, it is recommended the following also be considered:

A preassignment visit should be arranged.

Sufficient background information about the city/town (i.e., hospital/ medical care, school facilities, availability of housing, etc.) should be supplied.

There should be an opportunity to meet with other expatriates working for the same employer.

The employee should have a good understanding of the Chinese culture and the way of doing business in China.

The employee's spouse should also buy into the assignment.

China

Sheldon Zhou, Amrop International

COUNTRY OVERVIEW

China is the world's most populous country. Geographically, China refers to mainland China, Taiwan, Hong Kong, and Macao. In political and economic terms, China generally refers to mainland China with a central government based in Beijing. Situated in the eastern part of Asia, mainland China occupies a huge territory of almost 9.6 million square kilometers. With a population of 1.2 billion, the whole country covers one-fifteenth of the land surface of the globe, and makes China one of the largest countries in the world. The country has a long coastline that extends from Northeast China to South China. Several economic centers are located along that coastline (i.e., Beijing-Tianjin area, Yangtze River delta area, Pearl River delta area). In addition to the capital city—Beijing—other major cities include Harbin, Changchun, Shenyang, Dalian, Tianjin, Nanjing, Shanghai, Fuzhou, Xiamen, Guangzhou, Xi'an, Wuhan, Chongqing, and Chengdu. Over 60 percent of the inhabitants live in rural areas.

China is still a Communist-ruled country, although market mechanisms have been gradually introduced through economic reforms that started 20 years ago. The government, parliament, and legal systems are all controlled by the Communist Party of China (CPC). Economically, reform has brought about huge changes over the past 20 years in people's day-to-day life.

At the current stage, private business and overseas-funded business sectors account for more than 60 percent of the country's GDP. However, the state-owned enterprises (SOEs) still receive most of the political and financial support from the Communist-led government. These SOEs have performed poorly in recent years; more than half of them are in the red. The government once promised to turn SOEs around, but there is a long way to go. Due to the increasing integration into the global economy, the government is likely to relax its control over many areas in which private and foreign businesses are currently not allowed.

The official language of the country is Mandarin Chinese. However, given the country's huge size and multicultural historic background, many dialects are spoken in different geographical areas. In general, Mandarin is used for business communications in most of the country. With more and more multinational companies establishing their operations in China, English has become increasingly more important in the business community, especially for people working for foreign companies or engaging in business with foreign companies.

RESUME SPECIFICS

Personal Information

List your name, sex, marital status, date of birth, nationality, permanent address, and telephone numbers (both home and mobile if available).

Career Objective

Briefly describe what you want to achieve and the type of position you are seeking.

Education

Provide information about your secondary school/high school studies, with reference to specific courses and programs.

Continue with a description of your college/university education. State your graduation year, major, and education title. Briefly describe any student internship or diploma work: length of time, number of credits, and references.

Note: This information is required only if you are still a college student who has yet to graduate.

Extracurricular Activities

Describe relevant extracurricular activities in which you participated, such as arranging different types of student activities, working within the student union, and so forth.

Awards/Honors

List any awards or honors received for scholastic achievement or outstanding performance in other areas.

Additional Education/Specialized Training

Any additional college or university courses should be listed in this context. Also, include courses or training in specialized areas, such as languages, computers, sales, and so on.

Work Experience

Begin with your job title, the name of your employer, and dates of employment. Indicate whether it was a full-time or a part-time job. List the details of your work and your field of responsibility. Highlight information that is relevant to the position for which you are applying. Describe how your skills have developed through your tasks and achievements. Summer jobs and shorter periods of employment performed prior to your professional career should be summarized.

Should there be any gaps in employment history, it is very important that you explain the reason for each gap in a reasonable manner. Also, for part-time employment, explain the reason why you chose not to work full-time.

Achievements/Accomplishments

You may briefly mention awards, special recognition, or promotions received during employment.

Special Skills

Proficiency in foreign languages and knowledge of specific computer programs should be noted.

Professional Affiliations

List any professional affiliations relevant to your focus area. Include information about your involvement in activities within the organization or any leadership roles.

Personal Interests

Briefly mention your personal interests such as sports activities, reading, touring, enjoying music, and so on.

References

The references you select should be connected to your academic background or professional experience, such as your professor at university or previous managers. These people should be well acquainted with you and your work performance.

RESUME PRESENTATION

Format and Layout

Your resume/CV is an indicator of your academic training, thinking process, and professional skills as well as your education and employment history. Therefore, a clear picture of these areas and other important experiences helps an employer to understand you better. A reverse chronologically arranged list with the afore-mentioned headings is best.

Start your resume/CV by describing your educational background, followed by the details of your professional experience. Please bear in mind the importance of writing your resume/CV in a clean, clear, and concise manner. A systematic statement utilizing a consistent approach to all the important components of the resume/CV is highly recommended.

Length

Your resume/CV should be two pages in length, or no longer than three pages.

Attachments

Grades, certificates, and letters of reference do not necessarily have to be included with your application, as you can present them at the interview. If you prefer to attach such documents, choose your most recent grades and a letter of reference from your current employer. To personalize an application with a small photo is becoming popular, especially when applying for a position at the junior level. Including a photo gives the reader a more vivid picture of the person and allows the reader to put a face with a name for future reference.

E-mail Applications

More and more companies in China place recruiting ads in their web sites and receive CVs at their e-mail addresses. In this case, always attach your resume to the letter/e-mail.

COVER LETTERS

To clearly explain to your future employer the kind of job in which you are interested, you should attach a personalized cover letter to your CV. Furthermore, you may attach grades, certificates, and letters of reference or recommendation, though doing so is not required. A cover letter of one page in A4 format is usually sufficient.

Content/Detail

Always start a cover letter with a phrase stating the position for which you are applying. Remember that the purpose of the letter is to raise the reader's interest, so try to let your personality influence the content. In other words, *be yourself.* Everything you say in the letter should also be found in your resume/CV. Begin by describing your current position, the work content, field of responsibility, organizational level, reporting line, and the name of the employer. Also, state the date when you started in your current position and your personal and professional development within the company.

If relevant, you can explain why you are applying for this job. Summarize your experiences and emphasize those which are connected to the position for which you are applying. Include details concerning your current personal situation: marital status, ability to relocate, availability to travel on business trips, and so on. Also, briefly describe your future professional goals.

JOB INFORMATION SOURCES

Newspapers

Daily papers, job market journals, and the like all contain employment ads. The most popular daily papers among job hunters are *China Daily*, *China Trade News*, *Beijing Youth Daily*, *Xinmin Evening News*, *Shanghai Daily*, *Southern Daily*, and *Guangzhou Daily*.

Note: Most newspapers cover the locality where the newspaper is based. You will find that these publications contain separate recruitment ads in both Chinese and English.

China Daily (English only, nationwide)
Phone: +86-10-6494 1104
E-mail: cads@chinadaily.com.cn

China Trade News (nationwide)
Phone: +86-10-6715 9851 (Beijing),
    +86- 21-6361 7878 (Shanghai)
E-mail: sales@51net.com (Beijing),
    shsales@51net.com (Shanghai)

Beijing Youth Daily (Beijing)
Phone: +86-10-6733 3716

Xinmin Evening News (Shanghai)
Phone: +86-21-5292 1234
E-mail: xmwb@xmwb.com.cn

Shanghai Daily
Phone: +86-21-5292 0167
E-mail: shdaily@public4.sta.net.cn

Southern Daily
Phone: +86-20-8737 3998
E-mail: xwxxzx@nanfangdaily.com.cn

Job Market (Shanghai)
Phone: +86-21-6443 8763
E-mail: jobmarkt@public2.sta.net.cn

Guangzhou Daily (Guangzhou)
Phone: +86-20-8188 7294

Job Fairs

In China, job fairs are often held in different cities where hiring needs are high. However, job opportunities offered at these fairs are usually not at senior levels. At a job fair, many companies set up recruiting booths where resumes are collected from the attendees.

Talent Exchange Center/Talent Market

In cities with significant foreign investment, especially in the coastal areas, Talent Exchange Centers/Talent Markets are the places where job openings are periodically announced.

Internet Sites

Online recruiting is still quite new in China. There are some multinational companies that are starting to recruit professionals through online recruiting web sites. The most popular employment web sites in China are www.zhaopin.com and www.HireChina.com.

WORK PERMITS/VISAS

Visas

A business or tourist visa is required for most foreign visitors.

Residence and Work Permits

Temporary residence and work permits are required for all non–mainland China citizens who want to work in China. Work permits are processed and approved at the Exit and Entry Management Section of the Public Security Bureau at the provincial or municipal level.

INTERVIEW ADVICE

▶ Most business organizations prefer not to receive telephone calls prior to deciding to interview. Once you have been interviewed, you may call the contact person to follow up on the status, but be careful to do so in a reasonable manner.

▶ At some large businesses and government organizations, decision making is a lengthy process. Be patient when you submit an application to a company.

▶ Avoid discussing salary and other parts of the compensation package in the early stages of the process. However, if requested, you should state your salary preference.

CULTURAL ADVICE

China is a country with thousands of years of history. Tradition advocates conformity, obedience, humbleness, and self-sacrifice, and does not encourage people to openly express themselves or aggressively pursue their own interests. This traditional influence is reflected in the hierarchical structures of many governmental and business organizations. With more and more multinational companies operating in China, Western values have been gradually introduced, but traditional influence still dominates the society as a whole. In addition:

▶ If you are applying for a job at a Chinese company, or at a Japanese-funded or Korean-funded company, it is wise to be low-profile. Acting too aggressive or overly ambitious is not always appreciated.

▶ Many Chinese people do not openly express their opinions. Do not take their silence as agreement.

▶ Chinese people take long vacations around the Chinese New Year (usually early February). It might be difficult to develop new business during this period.

▶ When you visit your Chinese friend's home, do not forget to take a gift.

▶ Chinese society is very seniority-oriented—pay careful attention to this tradition.

The Czech Republic

Kvetoslava Peerova, PricewaterhouseCoopers

COUNTRY OVERVIEW

The Czech Republic is a landlocked country in Central Europe, bordered by Austria, Germany, Poland, and the Slovak Republic. It covers 78,884 square kilometers. Its three regions, Bohemia, Moravia, and Silesia, are interconnected by a highly developed road and rail network. About 53 percent of the land is used for agriculture and 36 percent is covered by forest. It has a population of 10.3 million, with one-third living in five large cities (Praha, Brno, Ostrava, Plzen, and Olomouc). Prague is the capital, with about 1.3 million inhabitants. Approximately 85 percent of the population live in towns with more than 2,000 inhabitants.

Czechoslovakia is one of the independent states that came into existence in the wake of the Austro-Hungarian Empire's dissolution in 1918. Its democratic economy was already highly prosperous and developed. Nazi Germany occupied it from 1939 to 1945. In 1948, the Communist Party took control of the country and directed it toward the Soviet Union. The so-called Velvet Revolution in 1989 brought about great political and social change. The free elections of 1990 introduced a democratic parliament. The country began to develop a market economy and moved closer to the European Union. In 1993, the Czech and Slovak Federative Republic, known as Czechoslovakia, was peacefully transformed into two independent countries—the Czech Republic and the Slovak Republic. In 1996, the Czech Republic applied for full membership in the EU and in 1999 joined NATO. The Czech Republic has a democratic political system with a two-chamber parliament and a government led by a prime minister. The president, currently Václav Havel, is elected by the parliament. The Constitution guarantees equal rights for men and women, as well as for all members of ethnic and religious groups.

Under the previous regime, the country had the highest standard of living of all Communist countries (although low in comparison to neighboring Western countries). Currently, Czech GDP purchasing-power capacity per capita is 66.6 percent of the EU average. There are significant differences between Prague and the other regions. The national unemployment (unknown for decades) is growing rapidly and is expected to reach 9 percent. Inflation was 6 to 8 percent in 1999.

The Czech Republic is highly industrialized. Its principal industries are: the manufacture of machinery; chemicals and rubber; food and beverages; iron metallurgy; service industries, particularly tourism; and industries producing goods for export, such as glass and porcelain.

The official language is Czech, which, along with Polish and Slovak, belongs to the western Slavic languages. The older generation speaks German, and educated young people can communicate in English, which is used as the business language. The principal churches are the Roman Catholic, the Evangelical, and the Czech Hussite. Although church affiliations remain high, religious faith is not widespread. There is also a small Jewish community, primarily concentrated in Prague.

The Czech Republic has been a center of European culture for centuries, most notably in Prague, where some of Europe's most famous literary figures and composers, including Franz Kafka and Antonín Dvorák have lived. Popular sports are ice hockey, soccer, tennis, and skiing.

RESUME SPECIFICS

Personal Information

Indicate your year of birth, citizenship, marital status, number of children, home and e-mail addresses, and telephone number.

Education

Explain your focus areas during upper secondary school/high school, with reference to specific courses and programs. Also, state your graduation year and whether you have studied abroad. Continue with a description of your college/university education. State your graduation year, major/specialization, and grade. Briefly describe any student internships or awards received during studies.

Additional Education/Specialized Training

Any additional college/university courses should be mentioned in this context. Also, include courses or training in specialized areas, such as language, computer, or sales skills.

Work Experience

Start by listing your job title and name of the employer. Specify the employment dates and whether it was a full-time or a part-time job. Briefly describe your work and field of responsibility. Emphasize information that is relevant to the position for which you are applying. Summer jobs, and shorter periods of employment performed prior to your professional career, should be summarized. If there are any gaps in employment history, it is important that you explain the reason for each gap in reasonable detail.

Achievements

Any awards, special recognition, or promotions received during employment should be highlighted. Include information about your involvement with activities within the organization or any leadership roles.

Special Skills

Proficiency in foreign languages and knowledge of specific computer programs should be stated.

Note: Most employers in the Czech Republic require fluent Czech and English.

Personal Interests

> You may include activities with associations, clubs, or areas of personal interest. Briefly describe your personal interests and hobbies, such as sports activities, gardening, reading, politics, and so on.

RESUME PRESENTATION

Format and Layout

> Your resume/CV should present a clear picture of your education, internships, and employment, as well as other important experiences that might interest an employer, such as professional association memberships. A reverse chronologically arranged list with the above-mentioned headings is best.
>
> An introductory statement or paragraph describing your professional objectives is becoming popular. Start your resume/CV with personal information, followed by your educational background and details of your professional experience. Attach a small photo to allow the reader to put a face with a name for future reference.
>
> **Note:** Be aware that you may be required to have your resume/CV attested or verified by someone who can confirm the accuracy of the information.

Length

> Your resume/CV should be no longer than two pages.

Attachments

> Grades, certificates, and letters of reference do not necessarily have to be included with your application. You can present them at the interview.

E-mail Applications

> It is increasingly common for employers in the Czech Republic to accept applications via e-mail. In this case, always attach your resume to the letter/e-mail.

COVER LETTERS

> An employment application should always include a personalized cover letter and a complete resume. The one-page A4 letter format should contain information about how you heard about the company and/or position. Do not forget to state the title of the position you are applying for and to describe in detail the area of your interest. It is always good to mention why you are attracted to this specific job opportunity and what your relevant strengths are. Your date of availability and ability to relocate should be included in the cover letter. It is not appropriate to mention the expected salary in the job application letter. Include certificates, diplomas, and letters of reference only when these documents are requested in the advertisement.
>
> When writing a job application, always keep in mind that the documents you provide represent your personality, and that handwritten letters are not appreciated.

JOB INFORMATION SOURCES

Newspapers

> Nearly all Czech daily papers contain employment advertisements. They are primarily written in the Czech language, although some international companies

prefer to place advertisements written in English. The most interesting job offers are typically found in the nationwide newspaper, *MF Dnes*. The regional press offers positions within that region only.

MF Dnes (largest and most popular nationwide general newspaper; job opportunities section "Zamestnani" [employment] published on Tuesday, Thursday, and Saturday)
Phone: +420 2 220 62 111
E-mail: mfdnes@mafra.cz
Web site: www.idnes.cz (*Note:* Electronic version does not contain job offers.)

Hospodáijské Noviny (financial newspaper; lists managment positions and specialized jobs; job opportunities section "Kariera" [career] published on Monday)
Phone: +420 2 3307 1773
Web site: www.ihned.cz (contains job offers in section "Kariera")

The Prague Post (Prague's weekly English-language newspaper; job opportunities target native English speakers and foreigners living in Prague—language teachers and similar positions)
Phone: +420 2 9633 4400
Web site: www.praguepost.cz (contains job offers in section "We Are Hiring")

Special Publications

The *Prague Business Journal* "Book of Lists" is an annual reference guide with in-depth information about over 2,000 of the Czech Republic's leading companies in over 90 different business sectors. It provides information about potential employers, as well as an overview of recruitment firms. This publication is available for US$40 and can be ordered through the Internet: www.pbj.cz/pbj/about/subscribe.asp.

Chamber of Commerce

The chance of finding a job with the assistance of the chamber of commerce is limited. However, it might be able to provide you with useful information about important Czech industrial companies.

Chamber of Commerce of the Czech Republic (Hospodarska komora CR)
Seifertova 22
130 00 Praha 3
Czech Republic
Phone: +420 2 240 96 111
Fax: +420 2 240 96 222

Internet Sites

There are several sites on the Internet, specialized in job opportunities in the Czech Republic. These web sites sometimes also provide a brief presentation of preferred employers. The most popular Czech job sites are:

www.jobs.cz	www.jobshop.cz
www.profese.cz	www.jobmaster.cz
www.perspektiva.cz	www.jobatlas.cz
www.jobonline.cz	www.cvonline.cz
www.jobpilot.cz	www.infojob.cz
www.joblist.cz	www.academica.cz

Telephone Directory

The Czech Yellow Pages provide contacts for recruitment agencies in Section #626, "Personalni poradenstvi."

Country Employment Office

Information about the national employment bureau (Sprava Sluzeb Zamestnanosti) of the Ministry of Labor and Social Affairs and all Czech Labor Offices, along with job information and consulting services in the Czech language can be found at the web site www.mpsv.cz.

WORK PERMITS/VISAS

Visas

In general, foreign citizens may stay in the Czech Republic for a period ranging from 30 days to six months before they need to acquire a residency permit. Single-entry visas can be processed relatively quickly at Czech consular offices. Multiple-entry visas are available, but require a letter of introduction from a Czech business.

Work and Residence Permits

All foreigners coming to the Czech Republic to engage in paid employment, even for a short period, must obtain a work permit from the local Labor Office. The procedure for obtaining the permit is not very complicated. It is usually issued within one to two months. A written offer of employment must accompany the work permit application. A work permit is usually granted for up to one year and is renewable. All foreigners and their families must obtain a residence permit from the Foreign Police after they have received their work permit. The residence permit is usually issued within two months. Like the work permit, it is usually valid for one year and is renewable.

INTERVIEW ADVICE

- ▶ Show a reasonable level of energy and self-confidence. Being overly assertive, aggressive, or, on the other hand, overly humble is not recommended.
- ▶ Before a job interview, it is worthwhile to get information about the company that is interviewing you, and have questions prepared.
- ▶ Make sure to be on time for the interview. Telephone in case of any delay.
- ▶ Shake hands with the interviewer and smile. First impressions are very important.
- ▶ Be spontaneous without acting unnatural.
- ▶ Make sure that your responses are to the point. Support your answers with practical examples.
- ▶ When applying for a commercial position, show entrepreneurial drive and good business understanding.
- ▶ Wait to discuss the remuneration package until the interviewer brings it up.
- ▶ Show a high motivational level and maintain eye contact.
- ▶ Shake hands and thank the interviewer at the end of the session.
- ▶ Feel free to phone the contact person listed in the job advertisement for further details before sending in your curriculum vitae.

CULTURAL ADVICE

▶ Czechs tend to be nonconfrontational, flexible, and creative. They are known to be skillful, hardworking, and ingenious.

▶ Family and private life have always been very important to Czechs. Weekends are spent with the family at home or at the country house.

▶ Czechs are proud of being Czechs. They have great pride in their beer, their women, their sense of humor (rather sarcastic), and their "golden hands" (ability to create things from nothing or very little).

▶ Czechs are punctual in both professional and social life.

▶ Shaking hands is customary when meeting people and when parting, even if the parties already know each other well.

▶ It is important always to take business cards to meetings and to give a card to each person.

▶ Men usually hold doors open for women and tend to go out of their way to do so.

▶ When drinks are served, it is customary to wait for everyone to be served and then say to each person *"na zdravi"*—"To your health." Eye contact should be made with the person as the words are said. It is polite to wait for everyone to be served before eating and to wish everyone *"Bon appétit"* or *"dobrou chut"* before eating.

▶ The terms Pan (Mr.), Paní (Mrs.), and Slecna (Miss) are used. Slecna is used for single women under age 30 only; single women over 30 will usually be addressed as Paní.

▶ For those people with degrees in economics or technical subjects, the title Inzenyr/Inzenyrka (abbreviated to Ing.) is used. The title Doktor/Doktorka (Dr.) is used for lawyers and those with postgraduate degrees. If one is unsure of the qualifications of the person being contacted, it is usually advisable to address him or her as Inzenyr(ka) or Doktor(ka).

▶ The workday starts between 6:00 and 9:00 A.M. and ends between 3:00 and 6:00 P.M. The maximum number of hours per week that can be required of staff is 42.5 (though a reduction to 40 hours is currently being discussed). The maximum number of hours per day is nine.

▶ There are 10 official public holidays. The annual vacation allowance ranges from three to five weeks.

▶ The labor force is well educated and disciplined. Employer/employee relations are regulated by the Labor Code. Trade union members make up about 40 percent of the workforce; however, the unions' role has been perceived as little more than social.

▶ Average salaries in the Czech Republic are low compared with those in Western Europe.

Denmark

John Macfarlane, Mercuri Urval

COUNTRY OVERVIEW

Denmark is the southernmost Scandinavian country. It forms a gateway to the Baltic area for people and goods traveling east-west and vice versa. It is also the gateway to Scandinavia if you are traveling from south to north. This small country is made up of one large peninsula, called Jutland, and two large islands, Fynen and Zealand. The capital, Copenhagen, is located on the eastern coast of Zealand. There are hundreds of smaller islands in this nation of water and land, which is also one of the oldest monarchies in Europe. Denmark formally heads a union of Greenland and the Faeroe Isles which, for historic reasons, have been under Danish rule and influence for centuries. In Denmark proper there are five million inhabitants, 1.5 million of whom live in the greater Copenhagen area.

The Queen of Denmark, Margrethe II, is the head of state in this parliamentary democracy. There is a one-chamber parliament, a supreme court, and a government headed by a prime minister, called the Statsminister. Every four years (the maximum term of office) there are elections for parliament. The result is usually a coalition of either the right or the left—almost always dominated by centrist policies. Denmark has been a member of the European Union since 1972 and is a longtime member of NATO.

Many world-famous companies have their origins and headquarters in Denmark: LEGO, Danfoss, B&O (Bang & Olufsen), MÆrsk Shipping. Denmark has progressed from an agricultural to an industrial and information-age country in the past century.

The spoken language is Danish, which is closely related to both Swedish and Norwegian so that Scandinavians have no real difficulty communicating with one another. Most Danes speak English reasonably well—and many speak German also.

Denmark is a small, relatively uniform nation of middle-class people, with a very high standard of living (usually ranking number three or so in international listings). Like the other Scandinavian countries, Denmark has a high degree of social welfare and a high rate of taxation.

RESUME SPECIFICS

Education

Present a clear and complete overview of your education and the order in which each part was acquired. Also give the names/titles and the results of the exams you have taken.

Extracurricular Activities

Describe these in overview form with the length and degree of involvement and the type of competence you received from the experience. Make sure that this type of activity does not overshadow your educational or professional activities.

Awards/Honors

List all awards and honors received for achievements or outstanding performance in educational or professional endeavors.

Specialized Training

If you have any kind of additional training in other skill areas be sure to include them in this part of the CV. Specify if these skills are from evening classes or more formal education (e.g., computer skills, language skills, or the like).

Work Experience

List all dates and places of employment since leaving secondary school. Leave no unexplained gaps in this listing. Describe your job title and the type of work you performed. Note all promotions and increases in competence.

Note: You may list any military duty or volunteer jobs in the work experience overview.

Personal Information

Describe your hobbies, sports activities, and other interests, so that the reader may form a holistic impression of who you are. Again, make sure that this description does not appear to be more important than your educational or professional background.

Be sure that all the standard information is correct, easy to read and understand (i.e., your name, address, telephone number, e-mail). Also list your civil status (whether married or not, number of children, your age/date of birth, and your nationality).

References

While not compulsory, you may provide only a few names and explain their connection to you. Make sure that the relationship is a relatively recent one or the reference is someone who knows you very well.

RESUME PRESENTATION

Format and Layout

The CV should be a clear and easy to read and understand chronological listing of the aforementioned headings. Make sure to include all possibly relevant information, but do not boast or exaggerate.

Length

If possible, try to limit your CV to one A4 page. Companies receive many CVs, so the quicker the reader can get an overall picture of your qualifications, the better. Two pages should be considered the maximum length of any CV. If a longer explanation is required to understand your background, save it for the interview.

Attachments

You may want to attach written references, educational documents, or the like, though doing so is not strictly required. If you do attach anything, it should not be the original document; send a photocopy.

Photos

You may send a photo of yourself for a more personalized application. However, use your best judgment; send only portrait-quality photos and only if the reader will easily recognize you from this photo. Most people would probably benefit from not sending a photo.

E-mail Applications

E-mail applications are becoming more and more common. Two things can turn an e-mail application to your disadvantage: The formatting of your application may not go through with the text, giving a totally different appearance to your CV. Also, the personal signature will not be on your application.

Note: This is still an important part of the application in Denmark, so take care that your e-mail application has a signature!

COVER LETTERS

Any application should always include a customized cover letter, as well as a comprehensive resume.

The cover letter's main function is to give a personal introduction of yourself and to explain why you are submitting your application to this particular company. Take care to highlight the connection between your particular skills/experiences and the needs of the company in question (this may require some research). If there is a deadline for the submission of applications, do not be late. If there is any question of the recipient receiving your application after the deadline date, inquire if you may submit your application anyway.

Note: In Denmark it is sometimes permissible to send a faxed copy of your application as an interim solution, followed by a posted original application later on. However, be sure to have permission for this, as well as a specified recipient for the faxed application.

JOB INFORMATION SOURCES

Newspapers

Most dailies contain job advertisements, primarily on Fridays and Sundays. Also, look in trade and professional journals. The most important Danish newspapers are: *Berlingske Tidende*, *Børsen* and *Jyllands Posten*, which contain more than 90 percent of all advertised jobs.

Berlingske Tidende
Phone: +45 33 75 75 75
Fax: +45 33 75 20 20
Web site: www.berlingske.dk

Børsen
Phone: +45 33 32 01 02
Fax: +45 33 12 24 45
Web site: www.borsen.dk

Jyllands Posten
Phone: +45 87 38 35 35
Fax: +45 87 38 34 86
Web site: www.jp.dk

Internet Sites

The best way to link into job opportunities in Denmark is to search for "jobs" and/or "career" + dk. This should lead you to all the relevant links. The larger recruitment web sites in Denmark are www.job.dk, www.dkcareer.dk, and www.mercuri-urval.com.

Chamber of Commerce

Danish Chamber of Commerce
"Handelskammeret"
Phone: + 45 33 95 05 00
E-mail: handelskammeret@commerce.dk

WORK PERMITS/VISAS

The Danish state designates four categories of foreigners. First: People from Norway, Sweden, and Finland are treated as Danes with respect to residence and work, and require no special permits. You must, however, register your current address with the National Persons Register. Second: People from the European Union are automatically allowed to live and work in Denmark under application. (Only in a very few specific areas of work such as medical doctors or chartered accountants does one need special professional permission to work.) Third: People from countries where Denmark has a special agreement are allowed to apply for residence and work permits. These permissions are routinely granted upon application (contact your local Danish embassy for information on which countries are included). Fourth: People from the rest of the world are required to get a visa before entering Denmark. You must secure a sponsor who will promise to employ you for a specified term before applying (from abroad) for a work permit. For the special forms and further information, contact the following organizations or your local Danish embassy or consulate.

Visa Information
Danish Foreign Office
Phone: + 45 33 92 00 00
Fax: + 45 32 54 05 33

Work Permit Information
Udlaendingestyrelsen
(Control Board for Foreigners)
Phone: + 45 35 36 66 00
Fax: + 45 35 36 19 16

INTERVIEW ADVICE

▶ It is often wise to phone the company or institution before applying to make sure that the job is one you are qualified for and truly interested in.

▶ It is wise not to start discussing or inquiring into the salary issues of the job too early in the process (it is usually left until the second or third interview). However, if questioned on your salary expectations, you should have an opinion on this. You may want to give your present salary as a reference point.

▶ Denmark has many labor laws that give certain minimum rights to employees. Any contract that does not give the minimum specified by law is automatically deemed invalid, and the minimum is afforded to the employee.

▶ During the interview you are expected to show interest in the company and the job in question. Always try to research as much as possible beforehand. Questions about the company demonstrate a measure of interest, so always have some prepared.

▶ Most employers want their employees to have a certain amount of initiative and be able to think for themselves. Try to show or provide examples of such qualities if relevant to the job in question.

▶ Always dress for the occasion. It is better to overdress a little if in doubt.

▶ Always be on time, as Danes are a rather punctual people.

▶ Be advised that politics, religion, and sexual subjects should not be discussed in job interview contexts.

▶ You may easily find yourself invited to the home of a potential employer either before or after a contract is signed. Be natural and at ease and bring a small gift for the hostess (flowers or chocolate are appropriate). The gift need not be lavish; it could well be from your homeland. If you do not eat certain types of food or if you do not drink alcohol, discreetly advise your host beforehand.

Finland

Kirsi Paajanen, Mercuri Urval

COUNTRY OVERVIEW

Finland, the neighbor of Sweden, is one of the most northern countries in Europe. About one-third of the country lies north of the Arctic Circle. Together with Finland's 180,000 lakes, the forests form a vast and beautiful unspoiled landscape. The endless white nights in the summer draw tourists from around the globe to visit northern Finland in particular. As a nation, the Finns are justly proud of the unspoiled nature of their land. A favorite pastime is to enjoy the countryside either at holiday cottages or by boating. Finland has the longest border with Russia in Western Europe, making it an important gateway between East and West Europe. The capital of Finland is Helsinki, which houses about 10 percent of the five million population. Helsinki boasts a rich cultural and sports center.

Since 1917, Finland has been an independent, neutral, and democratic republic. The country is led by a president who is elected for a period of six years. Every four years, 200 MPs (members of parliament) are elected to the parliament. Since 1995, Finland has been a member country of the European Union and is currently the chairing country. Additionally, Finland is a member of the European Monetary Union.

Finland is officially a bilingual country, with Finnish being the main language while Swedish is spoken mainly in the coastal areas and in the archipelago. Most of the younger generation also have a fluent command of English. Lutheranism is the leading religion of the country.

Finnish women were the first in Europe to be granted the right to vote. This portrays equality, even today. Most women work outside the home, and a considerable number hold important posts in Finnish society.

Finland is a safe, stable, and basically middle-class society. It is a welfare state that offers some of the world's best education, social security, and health care systems; these, in turn, lead to heavy taxation. Finland is famous for its high technology and forest industry. The best-known Finnish companies are Nokia, UPM-Kymmene, Stora-Enso, and Fiskars (scissors).

RESUME SPECIFICS

Education

Explain your focus areas during upper secondary school/senior high school. State your graduation year and mention if you have studied abroad.

Continue with a description of your college/university education. State your graduation year, major, education title, and other relevant details.

Note: In Finland, students can select focus areas in their high school studies, such as physical education, music, mathematics, or art, similar to having a major in college.

Extracurricular Activities

If you have recently finished your studies, you may briefly describe any extracurricular activities in which you have participated.

Work Experience

Start with listing your job title, name of the employer, and the industry (field). Specify the employment dates and whether it was a full-time or a part-time job. Describe your field of responsibility, tasks, and relevant achievements. If you have just completed your studies, summer jobs and shorter periods of employment should be summarized. If there are any gaps in employment history, it is important that you explain the reason for each gap.

Achievements/Accomplishments

Any awards, special recognition, or promotions received during employment should be highlighted.

Special Skills

Proficiency in foreign languages and knowledge of specific computer programs should be noted.

Professional Affiliations

List any professional affiliations relevant to your focus area. Include information about your involvement with activities within the organization or any leadership roles.

Military Experience

Include information in your resume/CV about your military service (which is obligatory for males in Finland, and is even a possibility for women today!). State the focus of your training, your field of responsibility, and any managerial positions. Include the correct dates.

Personal Information

Describe your personal interests such as sports activities, gardening, reading, rebuilding old cars, politics, memberships in different clubs or associations, and so on. Do not exaggerate, as it is important to be believable. Family activities and hobbies may be mixed in with this section.

References

The references you select should be connected to your professional experience, such as previous managers. These people should be well acquainted with your work performance, and your association be rather recent in time.

RESUME PRESENTATION

Format and Layout

Your resume/CV should represent a clear picture of your education and employment, as well as other important experiences that might interest an employer, such as professional association memberships. A reverse chronologically arranged list with the aforementioned headings is best.

Note: Always begin your resume/CV by describing your educational background, followed by the details of your professional experience.

Length

Your resume/CV should be no longer than two pages.

Attachments

Grades, certificates, and letters of reference do not necessarily have to be included with your application, as you can present them at the interview. Any documents attached to your resume should be copies, not originals. You may personalize your application with a small photo, although it is not customary in Finland.

E-mail Applications

It is increasingly common that employers in Finland accept applications via e-mail.

COVER LETTERS

An application should always include a personalized cover letter and a complete resume. Furthermore, you may attach grades, certificates, and letters of reference or recommendations. A personal cover letter of one page is usually sufficient. A typed application in A4 format is preferred, but a handwritten letter is acceptable provided that the writing is legible.

Note: If you are unable to send in your application before the given deadline, you can always telephone or send in a short e-mail notice to express your interest and explain that your application will be late due to specific reasons (for example, travel abroad).

Content/Detail

Your cover letter should start with a phrase stating the position for which you are applying. Remember that the letter aims to raise the reader's interest, so try to let your personality influence the content. Everything you say in the letter should also be found in your resume/CV. Start by describing your current position, the work content, field of responsibility, organizational level/reporting structure, achievements, and the name of the employer.

Explain why you are applying for this job. Analyze your experiences and emphasize those which are connected to the position for which you are applying. If relevant, give information of your ability to relocate, availability to travel, and your future professional goals. If you are unemployed at present, you should state that in your cover letter.

JOB INFORMATION SOURCES

Daily papers, trade journals, and the like all contain recruitment employment ads. The most popular daily papers are *Helsingin Sanomat*, *Aamulehti*, *Turun Sanomat*, *Hufvudstadsbladet*, and *Kaleva*. Daily trade journals include: *Kauppalehti*, *Tekniikka & Talous*, and *IT Viikko*. The *Helsingin Sanomat* Sunday edition is a widely read source of information for job seekers from all over the country. Most recruitment ads are in Finnish (or in Swedish in *Hufvudstadsbladet*). However, you do find some individual ads in other languages, primarily in English.

Note: No newspaper covers the entire country.

Newspapers

Helsingin Sanomat (news of greater Helsinki area and southern Finland)
Phone: + 358 (0)9 1221
Web site: www.helsinginsanomat.fi/oikotie (a special Internet service for job seekers and employers)

Aamulehti (morning paper; greater Tampere area)
Phone: + 358 (0)3 266 6111
Web site: www.aamulehti.fi

Turun Sanomat (news of greater Turku area and Finnish-speaking western Finland)
Phone: + 358 (0)2 269 3311
Web site: www.turunsanomat.fi

Hufvudstadsbladet (Swedish newspaper)
Phone: + 358 (0)9 125 31
Web site: www.hbl.fi

Kauppalehti (commercial/business paper appearing five days a week)
Phone: + 358 (0)9 507 81
Web site: www.kauppalehti.fi

Tekniikka & Talous (trade journal targeted to engineers, technical people, and businesspeople)
Phone: + 358 (0)9 148 801
Web site: www.tekniikkatalous.fi

IT Viikko (new weekly journal for IT people)
Phone: + 358 (0)9 1201
Web site: www.itviikko.fi

Internet Sites

Through the Internet, companies usually advertise open positions on their web sites. The most popular employment web sites in Finland are:

www.uratie.net
www.jobline.net
www.helsinginsanomat.fi/oikotie
www.mercuri-urval.com
www.rekry.com
www.mol.fi

www.soneraplaza.net/tyopaikat
www.hel.fi
www.tyopaikat.net
www.cvonline.net
www.uranusfin.com

Please note that most information will be in Finnish.

Country Employment Office

Työvoimatoimisto has its own Internet site where you can find information about vacant positions. You can also visit the bureau in person at local offices in the greater Helsinki area. Refer to the Helsinki telephone directory under "työvoimatoimisto." The offices also organize training and education programs. Please note that it is recommended that you make an appointment in advance by phone.

Phone: + 358 (0)20 366 066 "work-line" (*työlinja*)
E-mail: työlinja@te-keskus.fi
Web site: www.mol.fi ("*työministeriön kotisivu*")

Telephone Directory

In the Finnish telephone directory Yellow Pages, you will find companies listed under the relevant heading. This can be a fruitful way to start looking for companies that interest you. In the telephone directory's business section (*Yritysnumerot*), all companies are listed in alphabetical order.

WORK PERMITS/VISAS

Visas

A business or permanent residence visa is required for most foreign visitors staying more than three months in Finland. For further information, see the web site www.uvi.fi.

Residence and Work Permits

Residence and work permits are required for most foreign citizens who want to work in Finland. Citizens from the other Nordic countries are excluded from this requirement. Citizens from EU or EEA countries also need an "EEA card." If you come from any other country, you will need both a residence and work permit. For further information, contact the Finnish embassy in your home country. Work permits can only be applied for after you have signed an employment contract. A written offer of employment must accompany the work permit application. Work permits are processed and approved by the Immigration Office, telephone number: +358 (0)9 476 5500; fax number: +358 (0)9 4765 5857.

INTERVIEW ADVICE

▶ Feel free to telephone the contact person listed in the recruitment advertisement for further details.

▶ Avoid discussing salary and other parts of the compensation package early in the process.

▶ Finns appreciate modesty. They prefer to talk about things in basic terms, saying what they mean. This straightforwardness is not considered to be impolite, nor does it mean a lack of interest. Finns do not naturally react verbally to your comments.

▶ Finns appreciate and want independence in their work. They also value honesty—a person's word is still considered as good as a written agreement and should be kept!

▶ Finland has strong trade unions. In many industries, the employee's rights are carefully regulated by specific labor laws and collective agreements.

▶ Most Finns still take their annual four to five weeks' summer vacation after Finnish midsummer (around June 21st), so it is difficult to conduct any new business or seek jobs from late June through the month of July. Christmas holidays also tend to be lengthy and may extend into early January.

CULTURAL ADVICE

▶ As in other Nordic countries, it is recommended that you show a modest and humble style and spirit. To appear aggressive, overconfident, or too ambitious is considered to be in poor taste.

▶ Finns are very punctual, both professionally and socially, and thus expect punctuality from others.

▶ In social circumstances, it is recommended to arrive at someone's home with a hostess gift (typically flowers or a bottle of wine). At restaurants, when the first drink is served, everyone toasts everyone else while looking them directly in the eye.

▶ Please note that driving under the influence of alcoholic beverages (0.5 percent) is strictly forbidden. There are severe penalties, should you be caught in such a circumstance.

France

Rose-Marie Ponsot, Mercuri Urval

COUNTRY OVERVIEW

France is in the western part of the European continent. It is at the crossroads of several civilizations and is bordered by the following well-defined natural borders: the North Sea, the Atlantic Ocean, the Mediterranean Sea, and the mountain ranges of the Pyrenees and of the Alps.

Despite efforts at decentralization—France has 22 administrative regions and 95 *départements*—the country is still highly centralized toward the country's capital, Paris. Of the 59 million inhabitants, 11 million are concentrated in the Paris region, and more than 73 percent of the population live in urban areas. There are three other large population areas with more than one million inhabitants: Lyons, Marseilles, and Lille.

France is a republic organized in the form of a parliamentary democracy. The president of the republic is elected by universal suffrage, as are the deputies who sit in the National Assembly. The president of the republic appoints the prime minister. French political life is governed by the right-left split. The country's primary economic sectors are hypermarkets/supermarkets, energy, and automobiles. Food processing and luxury goods are France's leading export sectors. France is the number one tourist destination in the world (72 million foreigners visited France in 1999).

For many years, French has been the language of diplomacy and of the aristocracy. Today, French is spoken by roughly 140 million people worldwide. Although English has replaced it as the universal language, French is still synonymous with culture.

RESUME SPECIFICS

Education

It is not necessary to mention the name of one's high school; only the high school diploma need be mentioned (the equivalent of France's baccalaureate degree). In the case of university-level education, candidates should mention the diploma obtained, the department and the specialization, the college or university, the city, and the year in which the diploma was obtained. Do not forget to list the beginning and ending dates of your studies.

Extracurricular Activities

You should mention only extracurricular activities in which you have had significant involvement (e.g., in which you achieved something specific or carried out concrete projects), provided that these activities are relevant to your career.

Awards/Honors

List university awards and honors, if applicable. Also, your final ranking in school should be mentioned.

Additional Education/Specialized Training

All additional education and training should be mentioned, as well as language and computer skills. You should indicate the specific skills acquired, the duration of the education or training, and the training organization.

Work Experience

Begin with dates, the name of the firm, the activity sector, the size (sales and number of employees), and location, followed by your job title. Then describe your main duties and responsibilities, along with skills and knowledge utilized. Include relevant figures: number of people managed, results obtained in terms of growth or sales, and so on.

Achievements/Accomplishments

As noted earlier, it is important to specify the results of your work. Also mention any professional distinctions—for example, "best salesperson of the year." It is also worthwhile to include your internal promotions.

Special Skills

You must indicate your level of expertise in foreign languages: basic, school knowledge, reading knowledge, writing knowledge, fluent, or professional use. Indicate your computer skills by specifying the languages and tools with which you are familiar.

Professional Affiliations

Professional affiliations should not be mentioned on your resume unless you are an active member of the group or unless you play a key role.

Military Experience

Military experience can be described when applying for very junior positions. Beyond this level, you should mention it only if you had an important role (i.e., if you were an officer).

Volunteer Experience

This is not a very common section in France. Here, too, you should include only information that is relevant; otherwise leave it out.

Personal Interests

You should describe only your true passions or those activities in which you are seriously involved (e.g., if you are an active member of a cultural group, sports association, or club). Avoid banal comments such as "reading, movies, swimming."

References

In France, it is very rare to include professional references on the resume itself. The recruiter will ask for them after the interview.

Personal Information

Indicate your personal information: name, address, telephone number, and e-mail address. Your date of birth or age and marital status (married or single, and number of children) are optional topics, but are often mentioned.

Miscellaneous

You can mention your salary and geographic mobility at the end of your resume, but this is not necessary.

RESUME PRESENTATION

Format

Your resume can be in chronological or reverse chronological order. If you wish to combine your experiences in the form of a summary, you must include a simplified chronological presentation. The reverse chronological order, which emphasizes one's most recent experience, is recommended by most professionals.

Layout

Begin with personal information (name, address, etc.). Next, list your professional experience followed by education, or education followed by professional experience. A candidate should begin with education only if it does not take up too much space. (For example: "Ph.D. in Analytical Chemistry, University of Paris, 1995.") If you have more than one diploma, or if you need to give more detail, provide these details after discussing your professional experience. These sections are followed by languages and skills, plus other personal information.

Length

Under no circumstances should the resume exceed two pages. Resumes for those with no experience, or those with only limited professional experience, should not exceed one page.

Attachments

Only a photograph need be attached, glued to, or printed on your resume. Never send references, recommendations, copies of diplomas, or *certificats de travail* (documents from a previous employer giving the dates and nature of employment) with a resume; the recruiter will ask for these after the interview if he or she wishes to pursue your candidacy. An exception may be made for those with scientific backgrounds, in which case a list of articles or publications can be enclosed.

E-mail Applications

Candidacies sent by e-mail are becoming increasingly more common. Send your resume with a cover letter with specific reference to the position for which you are applying, if you are responding to an ad. Send everything in an attached file (preferably in Word).

COVER LETTERS

Your resume should always be accompanied by a cover letter, which should not exceed one page.

In the cover letter, you should indicate your motivation in applying for the position at the company. Succinctly explain how your profile corresponds to the profile sought.

Note: In France, cover letters are traditionally handwritten, because many employers use handwriting analysis as a selection tool. However, typewritten letters are increasingly common with the use of the Internet and e-mail.

JOB INFORMATION SOURCES

Newspapers

In France, there are several types of newspapers that publish job offers: national and regional dailies, generalist and professional weeklies, and specialized reviews. This includes the following national dailies and weeklies:

Le Figaro (special job supplement called "Figaro Economie" is available with Monday's issue)
66 avenue Marceau
75008 Paris
Phone: 33 1 56 52 80 00
Fax: 33 1 56 52 21 87
Web site: www.cadremploi.fr

Le Monde (special job section is available with the Monday evening and Tuesday evening issues)
21 bis rue Claude Bernard
75005 Paris
Phone: 33 1 42 17 39 00
Fax: 33 1 42 17 39 36

Les Echos (economics and finance daily; job pages run on Tuesdays)
46 rue de la Boétie
75008 Paris
Phone: 33 1 49 53 65 65
Fax: 33 1 42 56 04 98
Web site: www.lesechos.fr

L'Express (generalist weekly, published on Thursdays)
17 rue de l'Arrivée
75015 Paris
Phone: 33 1 53 91 10 73
Fax: 33 1 53 91 10 06
Web site: www.cadresonline.com

L'Usine Nouvelle (industrial weekly, published on Thursdays)
12-14 rue de Médéric
75017 Paris
Phone: 33 1 56 79 41 66
Fax: 33 1 56 79 41 71

Regional Daily Press

Les Dernières Nouvelles d'Alsace
Rue de la Nuée Bleue
67000 Strasbourg
Phone: 33 89 37 79 00
Fax: 33 89 59 59 42
Web site: www.dna.emploi.net

Ouest France
10 rue du Breil
33 35051 Rennes Cedex 9
Phone: 33 2 99 32 60 00

Each region has its own local daily. Very often, the job pages are in the weekend issue. The jobs published are not for senior executives; they are usually local jobs. However, a few regional publications are essential reading for regional job searches: for example, Les Dernières Nouvelles d'Alsace for the Alsace region or Ouest France for Brittany.

Professional/Specialized Press

Le Moniteur (construction and civil engineering)
17 rue d'Uzes
75002 Paris
Phone: 33 1 40 13 38 03
Fax: 33 1 40 13 30 37
Web site: lemoniteurbtp.com

01 Informatique (computer specialists)
26 rue d'Oradour sur Glane
75015 Paris
Phone: 33 1 44 25 30 32
Fax: 33 1 45 57 63 72
Web site: www.01-informatique.com

Tour Hebdo (tourism)
1 avenue Edouard Belin
92500 Rueil Malmaison
Phone: 33 1 41 29 99 99
Fax: 33 1 41 29 97 93

Business Organizations

Chambre de Commerce et d'Industrie de Paris
27 avenue de Friedland
75382 Paris Cedex
Phone: 33 1 42 89 73 99
Fax: 33 1 42 89 71 20
Web site: www.ccip.fr

Internet Sites

As of fall 1999 there were more than 450 Internet job sites. Many are very small sites, although a few large generalist sites cover the entire market. Two large sites contain ads published in the press:

Cadremploi: www.cadremploi.fr
Cadremploi contains the ads from *Le Figaro* and a hundred recruitment and
   headhunting firms. Cadremploi is a partner of Careerpath.

Cadresonline: www.cadresonline.com
In partnership with press media, Cadresonline contains ads from *L'Express*, *Le
   Monde*, *L'Usine Nouvelle*, and *01 Informatique*.

France also boasts international sites such as Monster (www.monster.fr) and Career Mosaic (www.careermosaic.fr), and two large European sites, Jobline (www.jobline.fr) and Job&Adverts (www.job.fr.) The two largest recruitment sites are those of Mercuri Urval (www.mercuri-urval.com) and Michael Page (www.michaelpage.fr).

Country Employment Offices

In France, there are two governmental entities, Agence Nationale pour l'Emploi (ANPE) and Association pour l'Emplois des Cadres (APEC) that publish job offers. Visit their web sites at www.anpe.fr and www.apec.asso.fr.

WORK PERMITS/VISAS

Two types of authorizations are needed to work in France: *autorisation de séjour* (authorization to stay) and *autorisation de travail* (authorization to work).

Autorisation de Séjour

In order to stay up to three months, citizens of the following countries do not need a visa (they need only a valid passport): the 15 countries of the European Community, plus Andorra, Australia, Bermuda, Brazil, Brunei, Bulgaria, Canada, Chile, Costa Rica, Croatia, Cyprus, the Czech Republic, Guatemala, the Holy See, Hungary, Iceland, Israel, Liechtenstein, Malaysia, Malta, Mexico, Monaco, New Zealand, Norway, Paraguay, Poland, San Marino, Slovakia, Slovenia, Switzerland, the United States, and Uruguay. Citizens of all other countries need a visa.

A *visa de long séjour* (long-term visa) is needed to stay longer than three months. Applicants must apply for the long-term visa with their local consular authorities prior to their departure. They need to submit a "promise to hire" or an employment contract. Upon arrival in France, the applicant must apply for an *autorisation de séjour* with the prefecture of his or her place of residence to obtain the *carte de séjour* (residency card), which is renewable annually.

Autorisation de Travail

The employer is responsible for obtaining the working authorization from the ANPE (National Employment Agency) in France. The employer must justify why it wants to hire someone who is not French, although France is less protectionist than many other countries. Two types of working authorizations can be issued: a temporary authorization for less than nine months and an authorization for more than nine months.

More detailed information can be obtained from your local French embassy or consulate.

INTERVIEW ADVICE

▶ It is important to research the company to prepare for the interview. Most companies have Internet sites, which facilitate access to such information.

▶ It is recommended that you ask questions concerning the position during the interview. You should first ask how much time you have in the interview to present yourself.

▶ To avoid needlessly wasting time (yours and the recruiter's), you should find out about the position's compensation, location, and essential criteria, such as the need to speak a specific language.

▶ Be yourself. Do not oversell yourself, but do not underestimate yourself, either. Being natural and sincere always pays off.

▶ Do not attempt to justify your failures or your career mistakes. Do not feel guilty about periods of unemployment.

▶ Find out about the rest of the recruitment procedure: What are the next steps, how long will each step take, and whom will you meet?

▶ If you are not given the job, do not hesitate to ask why you were turned down.

CULTURAL ADVICE

▶ The French place a great deal of emphasis on hierarchy; they like titles and status. This hierarchy is often reflected in the layout of offices; the higher the floor, the closer one is to God.

▶ Working hours vary significantly and executives may work 10 hours or more (many work until 8:00 P.M. and later). Meetings are generally not well organized and rarely begin on time.

▶ The French do not like rigid rules. It is very difficult to get them to respect the ban on smoking in public places.

▶ There are few problems with male/female harassment in the workplace.

▶ The influence of the Catholic culture means that discussing money and business are taboo. The French do not like to talk directly about business and money; conversations about these subjects always take an indirect route.

▶ The French may seem cold at first. They do not start friendships easily, although once a friendship has been established, it is often long-lasting and genuine.

Germany

Ann Frances Kelly, Signium International

COUNTRY OVERVIEW

The Federal Republic of Germany (Bundesrepublik Deutschland) has a population of more than 80 million people and total size of almost 360,000 square kilometers. Located centrally on the continent of Europe, it is bordered by nine countries: Denmark, Poland, the Czech Republic, Austria, Switzerland, France, Luxembourg, Belgium, and the Netherlands. Germany's only coastline is in the north and northeast, where islands such as Rügen, Fehmarn, Sylt, Helgoland, and the North Friesland Islands are popular holiday retreats. Germany's huge landmass, with a wealth of forest, lake, and mountain landscapes, offers a further abundance of internationally renowned holiday regions.

The country is a federal democracy consisting, since reunification in 1990, of 13 federal states. The official head of state is the president, who is elected in five-year terms. Legislative power lies with the National Parliament, headed by the prime minister (Bundeskanzler), which is elected every four years. In addition, there are the federal state parliaments, which govern the individual states with a certain degree of autonomy.

The school system and curriculum vary slightly from state to state, with a minimum legal attendance requirement of 9 to 10 years. There are about 300 institutes of higher education spread across Germany, including approximately 80 universities. There is a 10-month obligatory military service for young males.

The official language of the country is German; however, there are a number of very strong regional dialects. Cultural traditions, as well as social behavior, also vary greatly across the states. English is commonly recognized as the primary foreign business language, although that does not necessarily mean that it is widely spoken. A good working knowledge of German is advisable when planning to live or work in the country for a long period.

Germany has a wealth of natural resources and is the second largest provider of milk and meat products in the EU. The country is also renowned for its industrial strength, and is the fourth largest industrial country in the world. Based on turnover volume, ranking of the strongest industries is as follows:

▶ Machine construction (including automobiles).
▶ Food and beverages.
▶ Chemicals.
▶ Electrotechnical industries.

▶ Mineral oil processing.

▶ Textiles and clothing.

RESUME SPECIFICS

It is important that the focus of the resume change with increasing business experience. The university graduate should pay attention to individual courses of study and extracurricular activities, whereas the young professional should place more emphasis on the highlights of career development. Despite broad guidelines governing structure and format, a resume should portray an individual statement in both content and presentation.

Education

Junior and secondary schools should be listed chronologically, with details of the years spent at each. Major courses of study during secondary education should be highlighted, and the degree attained (A-levels, high school diploma, leaving certificate, etc.) listed.

The description of college or university education should also include the dates and major courses taken, as well as graduation year and degree. Of particular relevance and interest are periods of study spent at foreign universities.

Extracurricular Activities

It is important to list items that encompass participation in student organizations, business/college cooperations, special events, or other unusual activities.

Awards/Honors

Prizes or special recognition of scholastic achievements should be highlighted.

Additional Education/Specialized Training

Courses, certification, additional training, or expertise in areas outside the standard curriculum should be mentioned and briefly described.

Work Experience

There should be a clear distinction in the CV between your part-time work and internships before or during college, and your full-time employment periods. In both cases, the name of the employer should be clearly stated and a brief description of the nature and size of the business given. Dates of employment should be included, as well as the position held and a description of the key areas of responsibility. Quantifiable parameters such as turnover, personnel, and project or team responsibility should be stated to give the reader a clear indication of the scope and nature of the role. When describing part-time or full-time employment, relevant business experience should be described in considerable detail. A brief description is adequate for explaining occasional summer jobs.

Achievements/Accomplishments

In addition to specifying areas of responsibility, it is important to highlight special projects, particular successes or achievements, or any corporate or external awards won during the course of employment; these give additional insight into the overall performance.

Special Skills

It is important to note foreign languages (and levels of language ability), and other specialized skills or areas of expertise, such as computers.

Professional Affiliations

Membership in trade associations or other relevant bodies should be noted, including offices held and active roles played therein.

Military Experience

Mandatory military service or alternative civil service periods should appear in the resume. A description of standard service is not necessary. Here, too, specialized training or achievements should be described, especially in the case of voluntary service over and above the norm.

Volunteer Experience

A brief mention of charitable, social, or other voluntary roles is sufficient.

Personal Information

A brief list of major hobbies and interests outside of studies or work is necessary. You may want to highlight particularly unusual hobbies or major athletic achievements.

References

References need be furnished only upon request and must not be listed in the initial resume. Should they be required, ideal references are current or former business partners, colleagues, or superiors who have had ample opportunity to evaluate and appraise personal and business performance.

RESUME PRESENTATION

Format and Layout

Your resume should be clearly structured and presented in four major sections:

1. Personal details: name, date of birth, marital status, and number of children, if any.
2. Educational background: primary, secondary, high school, and university education.
3. Employment history: part-time work, internships, and full-time business experience.
4. Extracurricular activities: affiliations, hobbies, and interests.

To make it easier for the reader, bold print, block capitals, or underlining should be used to highlight relevant specifics such as degree, name of employer, or position held.

Note: In Germany the resume should be presented in chronological order beginning with personal details, followed by education and terms of employment, and ending with the most current position.

It is important to remember that the CV is the door opener for a personal interview and that the graphic impression is just as important as the content. Poorly designed CVs, where the reader has difficulty instantly recognizing the most important points, may land in the out basket regardless of content. Therefore, select quality paper and a good printer. Construct the information in clear sections, highlighting relevant points. Avoid reams of text and stick to descriptive bullet points.

Length

With increasing business experience, it is necessary to have a longer CV. In general, for new graduates or young professionals a CV of approximately two pages is quite adequate. It is not necessary to fill space with irrelevant information if your resume turns out to be shorter.

Attachments

A full application in Germany consists of a cover letter and a detailed resume, including if necessary one or two extra pages giving details of a particularly complex project or period of employment.

Note: *Zeugnisse* are other documents that are generally part of a full application. Similar to references and provided by employers in Germany after each term of employment or period within a term of employment, *Zeugnisse* give details of the employment dates, the role and responsibility encompassed in the position, as well as judgment of and commentary on personal and professional performance. *Zeugnisse*, if available, should be included for each relevant term of employment, beginning with the most recent.

Copies of university and school diplomas or degrees should also be enclosed, as well as certificates from any other special courses or training. A photo may be included, but should be recent, of good quality, and not too extravagant in size or pose.

Note: Some potential employers may prefer to receive a short resume initially. In this case it is sufficient to send a letter and CV; other documents can be provided at a later date. If responding to a job advertisement, be careful to see whether or not a comprehensive application package is necessary.

E-mail Applications

E-mail applications are becoming more common. In this case, it is sufficient to provide a cover letter, as well as a detailed resume, without attachments.

COVER LETTERS

Content/Detail/Length

A cover letter should accompany a resume. In the past, this letter was handwritten to provide a sample of the applicant's handwriting. Today it is extremely uncommon, and also unsuitable, to provide handwritten documentation. The letter should be printed on good paper and should not be more than one page in length. It is not necessary to summarize the entire CV, but rather to highlight particular points the applicant wants to emphasize or which may not come across clearly in the CV. In the same vein, the applicant should explain any irregularities in the resume (e.g., periods without employment or perhaps a particularly short period with a particular company). The applicant should also clearly state the level of the position he or she is interested in, geographical preferences, or, if applying for a specific position, the reasons why this position would be a good match. The applicant may include current or desired salary level in the cover letter, and must include this information if it is so requested in the job advertisement.

As with the resume, it is important to remember that the letter should be structured and to the point, and should highlight the writer's individuality (without being too offbeat or experimental). The cover letter should give the reader a clear impression of the applicant's current situation. Clearly state what your intentions are (e.g., looking for a first career step after university, interested in moving out of the current position or industry, etc.). If your current term of employment has already been terminated, this should be clearly stated. Surprising the interviewer with such details at a later stage will not be beneficial.

JOB INFORMATION SOURCES

Newspapers

Because of the size of the market, there is an abundance of regional newspapers with good job advertising sections. Depending on location preference and business level, this is a good place to start looking. On a national basis, the *FAZ* (*Frankfurter Allgemeine Zeitung*) is probably the most widely circulated newspaper offering a wide range of professional positions (up to general management level) in the Saturday edition. Only a small minority of advertisements are published in English.

Frankfurter Allgemeine Zeitung
Hellerhofstrabe 2-4
60327 Frankfurt
Phone: +49 (0) 69-75910
Web site: www.faz.de

Trade Publications

The German market offers a wide range of trade publications for almost every imaginable industry and industry niche. Many of these also have an advertising section for specialists. There are two major publications in which such magazines are classified by industry and title:

▶ *Handbuch für Pressevertrieb—Neumann-Verlag* (Directory for Press Publications; Neumann Publishing), Hamburg; phone: + 49 (0) 40-565031.

▶ *Stamm Leitfaden durch Presse und Werbung—Stammverlag* (*Stamm Guide to Press and Advertising*; Stamm Publishing), Essen; phone: + 49 (0) 2 01 843000.

Internet Sites

Job search through the Internet is fast emerging as a common means of identifying positions. Due to the expansive nature of the market, new sites are appearing all the time. A few of the most common sites used today are:

www.arbeitsamt.de (national employment office).
www.berufswelt.de (newspaper *Die Welt*).
www.heise.de (IT industry).
www.stellenmarkt.de (general).
www.wdr.de (general).

www.absolvent.de (for recent graduates).
www.deutscher-stellenmarkt.de (general).
www.dv-job.de (general).
www.mamas.de (general).

Business Organizations

Each major city has its own chamber of commerce (Industrie- und Handelskammer) that can provide information on individual firms, industries, and groups of industries. The six largest are:

Industrie- und Handelskammer Berlin
Phone: + 49 (0) 30-315100

Industrie- und Handelskammer Frankfurt
Phone: + 49 (0) 69-21970
Web site: www.ihk.de/frankfurt-main

Industrie- und Handelskammer Düsseldorf
Phone: + 49 (0) 211-35570
Web site: www.duesseldorf.ihk.de

Industrie- und Handelskammer Hamburg
Phone: + 49 (0) 40-36138401
Web site: www.handelskammer.de/hamburg

Industrie- und Handelskammer Köln
Phone: + 49 (0) 221-16400
Web site: ihk-koeln.de

Industrie- und Handelskammer München und Oberbayern
Phone: + 49 (0) 89-51160
Web site: www.muenchen.ihk.de

Almost every field of industry and profession is represented by a trade body in Germany. However, nonmembers can find it extremely difficult to obtain more than perfunctory information.

Country Employment Office

The Country Employment Office (Arbeitsamt), with offices in every city, is reachable through the Internet at www.arbeitsamt.de. For professionals, however, the Arbeitsamt is not a major avenue for job search.

WORK PERMITS/VISAS

For EU residents, visas are not required in Germany. However, work and residence permits must be applied for. These can be obtained at every local Ausländeramt (registry office for foreign residents). It is necessary to provide personal identification and a fixed address and to have a lot of time and patience. Work and residence permits are issued easily enough for the first three months. Once full-time employment can be established, the permits have to be renewed only sporadically, or not at all.

For non-EU residents, the procedure can be more complicated and varies extensively with land of origin. It is advisable to be well informed and prepared before trying to take up residence in Germany.

INTERVIEW ADVICE

▶ Be punctual! Calculate traffic jams, train delays, and other difficulties into the time you will need to arrive punctually for your interview. If you are unavoidably delayed, call and give sufficient notice. There are not many good excuses for being late for an interview.

▶ Be well dressed for the interview! Regardless of the industry or personal taste, one should take care to make more of an effort for the interview situation. Once you have been hired, your clothing style can be adapted to the environment, but do not assume that casual dress will be acceptable beforehand.

▶ Be informed! Read up on the company you are interviewing with.

▶ Ask relevant questions! Do not be afraid to ask questions about any issues that may be of particular relevance, interest, or concern to you. Show that you have put some thought into your application and ask questions concerning structure, colleagues, reporting lines, and so on. Initially try to avoid asking questions regarding the number of holidays or exact hours of work. Also, be careful to listen. The interviewer will want to tell you about the job and the company, and it is better not to interrupt.

▶ Show interest! There is no harm in letting people know that you are definitely interested in the position. Playing too hard to get can very often backfire.

CULTURAL ADVICE

▶ Punctuality in business and social circumstances is a must, and arriving late for a gathering is never very acceptable.

▶ Germans never pop around uninvited. Even when visiting close friends or family, it is considered appropriate to call first.

▶ When invited to dinner, it is common to have a small gift for the host or hostess. This must not be extravagant, but to come empty-handed could be embarrassing.

▶ It is considered impolite to take a drink at a social gathering before the toast has been spoken. In a very informal situation, this faux pas may cost you a round of drinks.

▶ When invited to a person's home it is usual to expect *Kaffee und Kuchen* (coffee and cake) if invited during the course of the afternoon. An evening invitation, unless explicitly stated otherwise, usually includes an evening meal.

Hong Kong

Fiona Yung, PricewaterhouseCoopers

COUNTRY OVERVIEW

Hong Kong, situated on the South China coast of the People's Republic of China (PRC), consists of Hong Kong Island (78 square kilometers), Kowloon (47 square kilometers), the New Territories (824 square kilometers), and Lantau Island (144 square kilometers). In practice, the name Hong Kong is used to identify both Hong Kong Island and the territory as a whole. The Central District on Hong Kong Island is the chief financial and commercial area. On the mainland, in Kowloon and the adjacent areas, are commercial, industrial, and residential areas, major wharves, and container berths. The new Hong Kong International Airport is located at Chek Lap Kok on Lantau Island.

Hong Kong became a Special Administrative Region (SAR) of the People's Republic of China on July 1, 1997, after more than a century of British rule. The 1984 Sino-British Joint Declaration and the Basic Law guarantee the territory a high degree of autonomy under the "one country, two systems" formula.

The government of the Hong Kong SAR is the executive authority of the region and is headed by the chief executive, Tung Chee Wah. The Executive Council assists the chief executive with policy making. The Legislative Council legislates, approves public expenditures and monitors the performance of the administration.

Hong Kong is strategically located in the fast-growing Asia-Pacific region and is considered the gateway to business opportunities in the PRC. With a total population of over 6.5 million people and land area of only 1,095 square kilometers, Hong Kong is one of the most densely populated places in the world. There are two official languages in Hong Kong, English and Cantonese, both of which are used with equal status in all types of communications. Cantonese (the dialect of the southern part of mainland China) is spoken by nearly all the Chinese population. English is widely spoken in the commercial and financial circles. After the transfer of sovereignty, many people now speak Putonghua (Mandarin), the official language of the PRC.

Hong Kong is a sophisticated banking and financial center, has a free-trade economy, and has an excellent infrastructure. The currency, linked to the U.S. dollar, is stable.

RESUME SPECIFICS

Education

Including the name of the secondary/high school is optional. It is important to provide details of undergraduate and graduate degrees, date of graduation for each degree, name and country of the university, and the major selected. If the university was not attended on a full-time basis, it is common to explain whether it was a part-time or distance-learning program.

Extracurricular Activities

If you have participated in any extracurricular activity at your university, or volunteer work involving the business community or charitable organizations, make sure they are included.

Specialized Training

External courses completed should be mentioned, especially if they are relevant to the position you are seeking.

Professional Qualifications/Membership

Memberships in professional associations and organizations are important, especially for positions in finance, accounting, securities and banking, engineering, and other professional sectors. In addition to professional qualifications, memberships in other business associations are useful information.

Awards/Honors

All awards and honors attained should be listed. These can range from graduating with an honors degree from a university to an award for outstanding performance recognized by a company.

Work Experience

For each employment, state the name of the company, location/country, all positions held (with the appropriate dates), and a short paragraph describing the company's business nature and activities. If the company is the subsidiary or affiliate of a group, also mention the name of the parent or holding company. List your job duties and responsibilities in bullet-point format. This should be a responsibility overview rather than a detailed outline of the job description. Recent jobs should be described in a more comprehensive and detailed format. Earlier/shorter employment can be summarized.

Note: For your current or most recent position, explain the reasons for wanting to leave. If there are any gaps in your employment history, give an explanation for the break in your career. Always be truthful and do not put down any false dates. Also mention any employment that is on a part-time or contract basis, and provide an explanation for not holding a permanent position.

Achievements

Organizational recommendations, technical achievements, articles published, and systems improved should all be mentioned. Wherever possible these should be illustrated with facts and figures. Achievements should be briefly and crisply stated. They should specify the results of the impact on the organization. Avoid being too general and making vague claims—such as "improving efficiency"—without supplying a quantified measurement.

Special Skills

Fluency in languages should be noted as well as technical expertise in specific computerized hardware and software applications.

Personal Information

Under Hong Kong's Employment and Privacy Ordinance, personal details such as age, marital status, number of children, etc., cannot be asked during an interview. It is therefore useful if these personal issues are included for the reader in the resume. Hobbies and sports activities can be mentioned briefly.

References

A reference from your present company is important, especially if you have been with the company for a long period. This can be obtained after you resign.

Note: A minimum of two references from those who were your immediate supervisors should be provided. Checking references is important and can be expected by most employers in Hong Kong.

RESUME PRESENTATION

Format and Layout

Always make your resume easy to read by bolding the headings and leaving spaces between paragraphs (white space is always attractive). Put a return address, daytime and nighttime contact numbers, and a mobile phone number to make it easy for the recruiter to find you. In Hong Kong, it is best to use a chronologically arranged list of your past and current employers and positions held. As interviewers are accustomed to the chronological sequence, a functional resume will have a negative impact. Highlight promotions and achievements and give reasons for leaving prior employment. If there are gaps in your career history, be prepared to explain them.

Length

As a general rule, if you have less than 10 years' experience, your resume should not be longer than two pages. If you have more than 10 years' experience, keep the length of your resume to three pages or less.

Attachments

Certificates and reference letters do not have to be included with your application. However, originals should be brought with you to the interview.

Note: In Hong Kong, employers are not allowed to ask for a photo to be submitted with your resume. However, if you wish to send a photo, make sure it is a professionally taken passport-size portrait.

E-mail Applications

In Hong Kong, e-mail applications are becoming more and more common. If the employer displays his or her e-mail address in the advertisement, feel free to apply via this method. Make sure that your resume is written in a commonly used word processing program like Microsoft Word.

COVER LETTERS

Always include a cover letter with each application you send out. Write the letter from the reader's perspective. Say what needs to be said and no more. Personalize the letter by confirming the recipient's name, title, and gender to get more attention instead of merely addressing it to the "The Manager" of the department. Your resume is the goods, but the letter is the package and must reflect quality.

Content/Detail

In the cover letter, start with stating the position for which you are applying. Highlight your skills and background and why you are the suitable candidate. Analyze, prioritize, and address all requirements and criteria. Use short words, short sentences, and short paragraphs, and avoid negative words and phrases. Cover letters should be neatly typed on one A4-size page using quality business stationery.

JOB INFORMATION SOURCES

Newspapers

In Hong Kong, recruitment classified ads can be divided into two categories, English and Chinese. For English advertisements, the most widely read newspaper is *South China Morning Post*. The largest recruitment section is published on Saturday, which is the most popular day to advertise. *The Asian Wall Street Journal* also has a classified section and appointments are often based within the Asia region. For advertisements in Chinese newspapers, the *Hong Kong Economic Times*, *Apple Daily*, and *Oriental Daily* each have a well-developed classified section.

South China Morning Post
Morning Post Centre
22 Dai Fat Street
Tai Po Industrial Estate
Tai Po, New Territories
Phone: (852) 2680-8819
Fax: (852) 2689-8851
E-mail: clsad@scmp.com
Web site: www.scmp.com

The Asian Wall Street Journal
Dow Jones Publishing Company
   (Asia) Inc.
25/F, Central Plaza
18 Harbour Road
G.P.O. Box 9825
Hong Kong
Phone: (852) 2573-7121
Fax: (852) 2834-5291

Hongkong Wen Wei Po
Unit 8, 1/F, Newport Centre
Phase 2
116 Ma Tau Kok Road

Tokwawan, Kowloon
Phone: (852) 2802-0862
Fax: (852) 2802-2393

Hong Kong Economic Times
Unit 910-2 Kodak House II
321 Java Road
North Point, Hong Kong
Phone: (852) 2880-2888
Fax: (852) 2572-6931

Apple Daily Limited
No. 8 Chun Ying Street
TKO Industrial Estate West
Tseung Kwan O
Hong Kong
Phone: (852) 2752-3040
Fax: (852) 2990-7227

Oriental Daily
Oriental Press Group Ltd.
Oriental Press Centre
Wang Tai Road
Kowloon Bay, Hong Kong
Phone: (852) 2795 1111
Fax: (852) 2795 3322

Hong Kong Standard Newspapers Ltd.
4/F, Sing Tao Building
1 Wang Kwong Road
Kowloon Bay
Kowloon, Hong Kong
Phone: (852) 2798-2798
Fax: (852) 2795-3009
E-mail: Standard@hkstandard.com

Newspaper Sites
www.scmp.com
www.appledaily.com.hk
www.careertimes.com.hk
www.orientaldaily.com.hk

Internet Sites

A majority of the blue-chip exchange-listed companies in Hong Kong have their own web sites posting career opportunities. If you are interested in a specific blue-chip/multinational company, it will be worth your while to check the web sites of these companies first.

In Hong Kong, there are currently two major Internet employment web sites in operation: JobsDB and JobAsia. The level of positions posted on these sites is usually junior to middle management. For more senior positions, it is best to check the web sites of the international search and selection firms. *South China Morning Post* also places its weekly employment classified ads on the Internet.

Recruitment Sites
www.jobsdb.com
www.jobsasia.com

Search and Selection Sites
www.pwcglobal.com/hk/eng/about/svcs/ex-search/index.html

Chambers of Commerce

British Chamber of Commerce
1401-2 Tung Wai Commercial Building
111 Gloucester Road
Wanchai, Hong Kong
Phone: (852) 2824-2211
Fax: (852) 2824-1333
E-mail: jilly@britcham.com
Web site: www.britcham.com

The American Chamber of Commerce in Hong Kong
1904 Bank of America Tower
12 Harcourt Road
Central, Hong Kong
Phone: (852) 2526-0165
Fax: (852) 2810-1289/2877-6941
E-mail: amcham@amcham.org.hk
Web site: www.amcham.org.hk

The Canadian Chamber of Commerce
Suite 1003-4 Kinwick Centre
32 Hollywood Road
Central, Hong Kong
Phone: (852) 2110-8700
Fax: (852) 2110-8701
E-mail: canada@cancham.org

The Australian Chamber of Commerce in Hong Kong
4/F, Lucky Building
39 Wellington Street
Central, Hong Kong
Phone: (852) 2522-5054
Fax: (852) 2877-0860
E-mail: austcham@austcham.com.hk
Web site: www.austcham.com.hk

WORK PERMITS/VISAS

Visas

If you are coming to Hong Kong for a short duration as a visitor, you are not required to apply for a visitor visa prior to arrival. However, if you want to work in Hong Kong, either paid or unpaid, regardless of the length of employment, you need to apply for and secure a Hong Kong employment visa. Applications should be made while you are resident outside Hong Kong. Your spouse and children can obtain dependent visa status. These visa applications should similarly be made prior to arrival in Hong Kong. Failure to do so is an offense under the Hong Kong Immigration Ordinance.

You must prove that your services and/or expertise are unique and such that the employer cannot find someone locally in Hong Kong to fill the position. In the case of an intracompany transfer, this requirement is usually satisfied based on your having worked in the overseas affiliate office. In this situation, you are presumed to have intrinsic knowledge of the operation, internal administration, and culture of the company (i.e., the type of knowledge that is not readily available in Hong Kong).

Note: The employment visa is employer-specific. You may not take up employment with another employer in Hong Kong, regardless of whether your visa is still valid, until approval is obtained from the Hong Kong Immigration Department.

INTERVIEW ADVICE

▶ Before attending the interview, study the company's background. Be sure you understand the nature of the job and find out what skills and experience are required.
▶ Identify in advance your own strengths and weaknesses, likes and dislikes (via self-assessment, consultants, family, and friends). Think of possible questions and practice the answers in role-playing situations. Here are some tips you should follow at the interview:

Dress appropriately and bring along paper and pen.

Be on time, be on time, be on time.

Switch off your mobile phone or pager.

Know the interviewer's name and position and the correct pronunciation of his or her name.

Be polite, relaxed, and courteous to the interviewer, as well as the secretary, receptionist, and assistant.

Give a firm handshake and be aware of body language. Do not forget to maintain eye contact and smile.

Listen to the questions carefully and make sure you understand. If a question is not clear, ask—don't guess.

Be responsive to questions and avoid closed-ended answers.

Be enthusiastic; show excitement and interest.

Ask appropriate, open-ended questions.

At the end of the interview, ask for the next step.

Thank the interviewer for his or her time and interest.

▶ Do not ask about the salary unless the interviewer raises the issue first. You should not show interest only in the compensation. Employers in Hong Kong are more concerned with stability, commitment to the job, and your genuine interest in long-term career development with the company.

CULTURAL ADVICE

▶ Traditionally, the people of Hong Kong had little leisure time, given that many worked six days a week. Today, the trend is toward a shorter work-week, increasing the amount of leisure time available. Since the majority of people live in concentrated, high-rise environments, outdoor activities are popular. However, given the population density, Hong Kong's popular parks and beaches can become extremely crowded on weekends and holidays. There is great enthusiasm for horse racing, with two race meetings every week, normally on Wednesday evenings and Saturday afternoons.

▶ Soccer, rugby, golf, tennis, and basketball are popular, as are indoor sports such as squash and bowling. Water sports are possible most of the year, but the waters surrounding Hong Kong are becoming increasingly polluted, resulting in the closure of some of the beaches to swimmers.

▶ Eating out is very popular with both the local and foreign communities. Hong Kong boasts a large number of restaurants offering many types of cuisine. Given the relatively small living accommodations, most entertaining is done outside the home, in private clubs or restaurants.

Hungary

Krisztina Csóka, PricewaterhouseCoopers

COUNTRY OVERVIEW

The Republic of Hungary is located in Central Europe. It shares its borders with Austria, Slovakia, the Ukraine, Romania, Serbia, Croatia, and Slovenia. Hungary lies in the Carpathian basin and is divided into three parts by two rivers flowing north to south, the Danube and its tributary, the Tisza. One-fifth of the population lives in Budapest, which is divided by the river Danube into the Buda side and the Pest side.

After World War II, Hungary became part of the Soviet bloc. At that time, the government introduced a program of nationalization, industrialization, and planned economy based on the Soviet pattern. In 1989, the Constitution was completely rewritten, and Hungary returned to democracy. That year also saw the start of the privatization process of state-owned organizations, as well as the grant of a free hand to private investments, with no distinction between domestic and foreign ownership. This gave the newly elected democratic government (1990) a basis on which to rebuild market economy structures. This process was supported by a strong and continuous inflow of foreign investments. Budapest and western Hungary have benefited the most from foreign investment. Although eastern Hungary suffers from its poor links to the Western European transport system, continuous upgrades to the road network are improving this situation. The telecommunication infrastructure is also being continuously extended and upgraded.

Multinational companies are present in most sectors of the Hungarian economy. In recent years, many have expanded their operations by increasing production capacity and, in a number of cases, establishing research facilities. The latter take advantage of the country's skilled, educated labor force, which is competitively priced compared with Western European pay levels.

Hungary is a member of the United Nations and many of its subordinate organizations. It is also a member of the World Trade Organization (WTO), the World Bank, NATO, and Central European Free Trade Agreement (CEFTA), together with Bulgaria, the Czech Republic, Poland, Romania, Slovakia, and Slovenia. (CEFTA is an organization founded in 1991 for the coordination and harmonization of the development of trade relationships between some of the former Eastern European socialist countries.) Hungary's application for EU membership has been accepted by the European Commission. However, formal admission is unlikely before 2003.

RESUME SPECIFICS

In the past few years, the Anglo-Saxon type of CV writing has become preferable to the handwritten "novel" format. The CV should be no longer than two pages. This saves time and focuses on the essence of what the candidate wishes to say about himself or herself in a few substantial sentences. Since the CV gives the first and sometimes even the determining impression of the author, be sensitive about emphasizing information that is relevant to the position for which you are applying.

Note: Even if a photo is not requested, sending a photo is becoming more and more accepted. It helps the interviewer to have a photo to remember the person after meeting with many candidates.

Education

Always begin your CV with your educational background. If you are a new graduate, explain the areas you majored in during upper secondary school/high school, and state your graduation year. It is important to indicate the major, the year of graduation, degree (B.A., M.Sc., etc.), education title (economist, engineer, etc.) postgraduate degree (if any), or, if it is in progress, the expected graduation year. Also state if you have studied abroad. Briefly describe any student internship and your diploma work. If you already have several years of work experience, do not devote too much space to describing your education. In that case, it is sufficient just to state your university, year of graduation, your major, and your degree.

Extracurricular Activities

Note: In Hungary, you do not describe your student activities, especially if you graduated before 1989.

Work Experience during College/University

If you have a few years of professional experience from your university years, devote the majority of your CV to emphasizing this experience. Practical professional experience is considered to be a great plus. Describe your summer jobs and any other employment performed prior to your graduation under this section. Do not mix this experience with the professional work experience section.

Awards/Honors

If you are a new graduate, list awards and honors received for scholastic achievement. If you already have two to three years of work experience, keep this section to a minimum.

Specialized Training

The specialized training section of your CV should be used if you have participated in company training, developed certain skills, or have special knowledge.

Professional Work Experience

List the name of your current employer, starting date of employment, and job title. Give the details of your responsibilities and reporting structure in a bullet-point format. If you have held other positions in this company, state them. Indicate the dates and your responsibilities to enable the reader to understand how your skills have developed through your tasks and achievements and how rapidly you were promoted. Emphasize information relevant to the position for which you are applying. The more experience you have, the less space you need to devote to discussing earlier jobs.

Note: In Hungary the work experience you had before 1989 should be listed, but not described.

Achievements/Accomplishments

These should not be described in a separate section. List them under the bullet points of the work experience sections.

Special Skills

Command of foreign languages and the level of proficiency should be indicated. There are accepted levels of fluency that should be used—fluent, advanced, intermediate. Certificates are not important in Hungary. If the knowledge of a specific language is important for the position, you will be interviewed in that language. Your interview performance is what will matter, not your diploma work. Indicate the level of your computer literacy, listing the programs with which you are familiar. State whether you have a driver's license.

Professional Affiliations

Do not include your professional affiliations in your CV. Describe them in the cover letter.

Military Experience

Military service is important only if you entered service after starting your first job and it caused a break in your career (i.e., as an explanation for a nine-month gap in your work history). Otherwise, indicate only if you have successfully completed this requirement.

Volunteer Experience

Volunteer activities are generally not included.

Personal Information

Describe your personal interests such as sports activities, gardening, reading, and traveling. Besides your name, address, marital status, and telephone number, it is important to indicate your date of birth and nationality. Always give a telephone number where you may be reached during business hours.

References

Your references do not necessarily have to be included in your application. Merely indicate "upon request" on your CV.

RESUME PRESENTATION

Format and Layout

Your CV should represent a clear picture of your education and employment. Always start with your educational background and work experience. These two sections should be the focus of your CV. Be sure that your name, address, telephone number, and e-mail address are indicated in the heading of the first page. Always use reverse chronological format, with your most recent experience listed first.

Length

Your resume/CV should be no longer than two pages.

Attachments

Attaching references or recommendations is not necessary; you provide them in a later phase. Photos are appreciated as a way to put a face with the name.

Note: School transcripts need be attached only if your work experience is less than three to four years. You can send photocopies of your diplomas.

E-mail Applications

It is becoming more common to send applications via e-mail. The CV should always be a separate attachment in the e-mail.

COVER LETTERS

An application should also contain a typed, personalized cover letter of one page. Just like the CV, the cover letter should raise the interest of the reader. It is advisable to indicate your address and telephone number on this document as well. Handwritten letters are not appreciated.

Content/Detail

Explain why you are applying for this job. If it was not advertised, say where you heard about the vacancy. Indicate the reasons why you feel you should make a career change and what kind of responsibilities, atmosphere, and so on you are looking for. You can mention why you think that this position would advance your career. Focus on your strengths, experiences, and skills connected to the position for which you are applying. If you are unemployed at present, you should state that in the letter. Keep the letter short. Do not duplicate your CV: just highlight your strengths.

JOB INFORMATION SOURCES

Newspapers and Magazines

Daily papers, weekly business and economics magazines, and trade journals contain employment ads. Some of them are in English. The most popular daily paper is *Népszabadság*, and the most popular weekly magazines are *HVG* and *Figyelÿ*. All of these publications cover the entire country.

Népszabadság
Phone: +36 1 250 1680
Web site: www.nepszabadsag.hu

HVG
Phone: +36 1 436 2020
E-mail: hirdet@hvg.hu
Web site: www.hvg.hu

Figyelÿ
Phone: +36 1 437 1414
E-mail: figyelo@vnubp.hu
Web site: www.figyelo.hu

Budapest Business Journal
1055 Budapest
Szent István krt. 11
Phone: 36 1 374 3344
Fax: 36 1 374 3345
Web site: www.bbj.hu

Chambers of Commerce

German-Hungarian Chamber of Commerce and Industry
1143 Budapest
Stefánia út 99
Phone: 36 1 467-2140
Fax: 36 1 363-2427

American Chamber of Commerce in Hungary
1052 Budapest
Deák F. u. 10.
Phone: 36 1 266-9880
Fax: 36 1 266-9888

British Chamber of Commerce in Hungary
1054 Budapest
Bank u. 6.
Phone: 36 1 302-5200
Fax: 36 1 302-5201

French–Hungarian Chamber of Commerce
1056 Budapest
Váci u. 51.
Phone: 36 1 318-8513
Fax: 36 1 338-4174

Canadian Chamber of Commerce in Hungary
1052 Budapest
Aranykéz u. 2.
Phone: 36 1 318-4152
Fax: 36 1 318-4712

Internet Sites

Major multinational companies and recruitment companies place their employment ads on their own Internet sites. Other sites include:

www.jobline.hu
www.multijob.hu
www.jobpilot.hu

Trade Journals/Telephone Directory

The Hungarian Yellow Pages lists all companies under trade headings. This might be a helpful way to start to look for a job. There is also a publication of the *Budapest Business Journal* called the "Book of Lists," where you can find all of the major companies listed under the relevant heading, including the top recruitment firms operating in Hungary.

Budapest Business Journal
1055 Budapest
Szent István krt. 11.
Phone: 36 1 374 3344
Fax: 36 1 374 3345
Web site: www.bbj.hu

WORK PERMITS/VISAS

Visas

A business or permanent residence visa is required for most foreign visitors staying more than three months.

Residence and Work Permits

Hungarian companies are obliged by law to apply for permits to employ foreigners to carry out their work in Hungary. The permit should be obtained before commencement of the employment. The employee must provide a certificate of professional qualification and a medical certificate. Once the work permit is obtained, the employee must apply for a work visa (TM4). Family members should also apply for family member visas on the basis of the work visa. The visa is valid for only 14 days after crossing the border. It must be converted into a residence permit within this time limit to take up legal residence in Hungary. An initial permit is issued for one year; it must then be renewed annually, along with the work permit. Accompanying family members will need to obtain family member residence permits.

INTERVIEW AND CULTURAL ADVICE

▶ Office hierarchies are vertically structured in Hungary, similar to the structure of American-owned companies. A free hand in decision making is valued in higher positions. You are expected to be a team player and to be decisive.

▶ It is wise to avoid discussing salary, and other parts of the compensation package early in the process. However, when it comes time to discuss this issue, you should be clear about your expectations and state the gross annual salary amount. Other parts of the compensation package (bonus, car, mobile phone, postgraduate study loans, etc.) should be discussed at this stage as well.

▶ It is wise to be open toward the company and future possibilities, but not to be overambitious. It is expected that you will ask questions of the interviewer, but remember that primarily you are the one to be asked. To make negative remarks about previous employers is considered to be in poor taste.

▶ In Hungary you are always expected to be on time, behave in a humble way, and dress appropriately. Do not be too extroverted. Attempt to have a moderate personality.

▶ Hungarians generally take their annual vacations in July and August or between Christmas and early January. It is difficult to conduct new business during those times.

India

Atul Kumar, Amrop International

COUNTRY OVERVIEW

India, a peninsula in the southwestern tip of Asia, is large (1.2 million square miles), and among the most densely populated countries in the world, with a population of about 984 million. The climate is warm, and temperatures in the summer can reach as high as 50°C. The primary business cities are Delhi, Mumbai, Chennai, Bangalore, Hyderabad, and Calcutta.

India is a democracy led by a parliament that is elected every five years. Until recently, India had a socialist economy. However, in the past six years, it has opened its markets for global investments. Personal tax rates range from 30 percent to 35 percent.

India is a country with many languages and over 100 dialects, though Hindi is probably the most commonly known language. The business language of the country is English, and most company managers are fairly fluent. India is an industrialized nation, though it remains one of the largest agricultural economies in the world. A large part of the population continues to live below the poverty line. In recent times, India has become one of the most exciting destinations for investments by global companies.

RESUME SPECIFICS

Residential Address

List your current residential address and all contact telephone numbers.

Family Details

Mention your marital status, whether your spouse is working and where, number of children, and their ages.

Education

Explain your focus areas during college, with reference to specific courses and programs. Also, state your graduation year and if you have studied abroad. List the name of college or university from which the degree has been obtained. Continue with a description of your postgraduate education. State your graduation year, major and education title, and the institute from which the degree has been obtained. Briefly describe any student internship or diploma work: length of time, number of credits, and references.

Extracurricular Activities

Describe any extracurricular activities in which you participated, such as arranging different types of student activities, working within the student administration, and so forth.

Awards/Honors

List any awards or honors received for scholastic achievement or outstanding performance in other areas.

Specialized Training

Describe any specialized training received either during college or in-house while employed. Indicate training received, duration, training institution, and year training took place.

Special Skills

Proficiency in foreign languages and knowledge of specific computer programs should be noted.

Professional Affiliations

List any professional affiliations relevant to your focus area. Include information about your involvement with activities within the organization or any leadership roles.

Work Experience

Start with listing your job title and name of the employer. Specify the employment dates and whether it was a full-time or part-time job. Give the details of your work and your field of responsibility. Emphasize information that is relevant to the position for which you are applying. Explain how your skills have developed through your tasks and achievements. Describe the business environment, specific challenges or responsibilities, and achievements during your tenure with the organization. Summer jobs and shorter periods of employment performed prior to your professional career should be summarized.

If there are any gaps in employment history, it is important that you explain the reason for each gap in reasonable detail. Also, for part-time employment, explain the reason why you chose not to work full-time.

References

The references you select should be connected to your professional experience, such as previous managers. These people should be well acquainted with your work performance and be rather recent in time.

RESUME PRESENTATION

Format and Layout

Your resume/CV should represent a clear picture of your education, internships, and employment, as well as other important experiences that might interest an employer, such as professional memberships. A chronologically arranged list with the aforementioned headings is best.

Note: Always begin your resume/CV by describing your educational background, followed by the details of your professional experience.

Attachments

Grades, certificates, and letters of reference do not have to be included with your application, as you can present them at the interview. To personalize an application with a small photo is becoming more and more accepted. Including a photo gives the reader a more vivid picture of the person and allows the reader to put a face with a name for future reference.

E-mail Applications

It is increasingly common that employers accept, appreciate, and prioritize applications received via e-mail. In this case, always attach your resume to the letter/e-mail.

COVER LETTERS

An application should always include a personalized cover letter and a complete resume. Furthermore, you may attach copies of grades, certificates, and letters of reference or recommendations, though it is not typically required at this stage. A typed application in A4 format and one page in length is preferred.

Content/Detail

Your cover letter should start with a paragraph on the competencies that you have acquired in your career and should highlight some of the more noteworthy experiences that you have had in relevant industries. Everything you say in the letter should also be found in your resume/CV. Start by describing your current position, the work content, field of responsibility, organizational level/reporting structure, and the name of the employer. Also, state the date when you entered your current position and your personal and professional development within the company. It helps to provide a brief explanation about the key achievements of your major assignments.

JOB INFORMATION SOURCES

Newspapers

Daily papers, trade journals, and the like all contain employment ads. The most common daily papers are: *Times of India*, the *Hindustan Times*, and *The Hindu*. The *Economic Times* is an important newspaper focused on the business news in the country. All newspapers have web sites.

Times of India
Phone: 011-3719416
Fax: 011-3323346, 011-3715832

Economic Times
Phone: 011- 3312277
Fax: 011-3323346, 011-3715832

Hindustan Times
Phone: 011-3361234, 011-3704597
Fax: 011-3704589, 011-3704600

Asian Age
Phone: 011-6255113, 011-6253137
Fax: 011-6251179
E-mail: letters@asianage.co.in

Pioneer
Phone: 011-3755271, 011-3755272
Fax: 011-3755275

Indian Express
Phone: 011-331111
Fax: 011-3716037
E-mail: letters-delhi@express2.indexp.co.in

Statesman
Phone: 011-3315911, 011-3312152
Fax: 011-3315295
E-mail: sman@nd.vsnl.net.in

Note: Although all of the newspapers are available throughout the country, they have multiple publication centers and the content varies depending on the publication location.

Internet Sites

Job listings are available typically for junior/middle management positions at www.naukri.com. Most multinational organizations provide listings of job opportunities for India on their own web sites.

Industry/Business Organizations

Confederation of Indian Industry (CII)
Phone: 011-4629994-7
Fax: 011-4626149
E-mail: cii@co.cii.ernet.in

FICCI (Federation of Indian Chambers of Commerce and Industry)
Phone: 011-3738760-70
Fax: 011-3320714, 011-3721504
E-mail: ficcifb@nds.vsnl.net.in

NASSCOM (National Association of Software and Service Companies)
Phone: 011-6885474, 011-6110101 Ext. 2109
Fax: 011-6885475
E-mail: nasscom@nasscom.ernet.in

ASSOCHAM (Associated Chambers of Commerce and Industry)
Phone: 011-6292310-13
Fax: 011-6292319, 011-6451981
E-mail: assocham@sansad.nic.in

WORK PERMITS/VISAS

Visas

A business or permanent residence visa is required for most foreign visitors staying more than three months.

Residence and Work Permits

Job candidates require visas and work permits issued by the Ministry of External Affairs. Though visas can be applied for by individuals, work permits need to be applied for by the employer.

INTERVIEW ADVICE

▶ Business attire is expected during an interview, which typically can last between one to three hours.
▶ It is a good idea to leave extra time available, as multiple meetings can be organized at short notice.
▶ Candidates should expect a discussion about desired compensation in the first or the second meeting and should be prepared to indicate the level of desired compensation.

CULTURAL ADVICE

▶ It is wise to demonstrate a collaborative and humble style during a meeting.

▶ It is beneficial to understand the many cultures that exist within India. There are differences in culture in the north, south, west, and east regions of the country. It is helpful to have an understanding of the organizations that dominate these regions, their background and history.

▶ In certain sectors, like manufacturing, it is advisable to consider the cultural differences between management and those employees who work on the shop floor.

Indonesia

PricewaterhouseCoopers

COUNTRY OVERVIEW

Indonesia is the largest archipelago and fourth most populous nation in the world with over 200 million people. It comprises five main islands—Java, Sumatra, Sulawesi, Kalimantan (southern Borneo), and Irian Jaya (western New Guinea)—as well as about 30 smaller archipelagos totalling 13,667 islands, of which approximately 6,000 are inhabited.

Jakarta, in west Java, is the capital of Indonesia and the seat of government. It is Indonesia's largest city, with a population of around 10 million. The People's Consultative Assembly is the country's highest policy-making body. It elects the president and vice president for five-year terms and establishes the broad outlines of state policy. The Asian economic crisis, which began in late 1997, hit Indonesia especially hard and exacerbated a political crisis. In October 1999 a new government was elected, which has paved the way for improving the social and economic conditions in Indonesia in a journey toward more openness and democracy.

While about 365 languages and dialects are spoken, the majority of Indonesians understand the national language, Bahasa Indonesia. However, most Indonesians are comfortable in engaging in a business or social conversation in English. Dutch and Chinese are also commonly spoken within the Indonesian business community. Although predominantly Moslem, Indonesia is not an Islamic state, and Christianity, Buddhism, Hinduism, and Confucianism are also embraced.

Indonesia has one of the lowest wage rates in Asia, but there are considerable differences among industries and locations. The industry sectors in Indonesia are very wide, encompassing agriculture, manufacturing, trading, finance and banking, crude oil and gas, mining, transportation, communication, and other services. Many companies of global importance are represented in Indonesia. The telecommunications sector as well as the manufacturing sector are anticipated to expand in the coming years.

RESUME SPECIFICS

Education

It is important to describe your university/college education, stating your specific major and the years studied. Continue with a description of your secondary education. Indicate your degree, the institution that awarded it, the year, and your focus area of study. If you are light on professional experience but strong in educational background, you may wish to list the courses you completed that have a direct bearing on the job, and any related courses that may add strength to your qualifications.

Note: In Indonesia, there is often a preference to select nationals who have had overseas education. However, this is not the case with all companies.

Extracurricular Activities

Describe any extracurricular activities in which you participated. While none is likely to qualify as education or experience, your participation (especially if you held office) says something about your preference for and effectiveness in mixing with people. Simply identifying yourself as *a doer* could help persuade the employer that you have, for example, the ability to deal effectively with all media.

Awards/Honors

List any awards or honors received for scholastic achievement or for outstanding performance in other areas.

Additional Education/Specialized Training

Any additional college/university courses should be mentioned in this context. Also, include courses or training in specialized areas, such as information technology, management, and/or marketing and sales.

Work Experience

List the jobs you have held, starting with your present position and working backward. Describe the specific duties of each job. Focus on any relevant experience you have. Describe how your skills have developed through your tasks and achievements. Summer jobs and shorter periods of employment performed prior to your professional career should be summarized.

If there are any gaps in employment history, it is important that you explain the reason for each gap in reasonable detail. Also, for part-time employment, explain the reason why you chose not to work full-time.

Achievements/Accomplishments

Any awards, special recognition, or promotions received during employment should be highlighted.

Special Skills

List any specific or particular technical skills (e.g., computer, licenses, equipment, psychological testing accreditation).

Note: It is critical for candidates to apply in English; proficiency in both oral and written English is deemed necessary for most professional positions.

Professional Affiliations

List any professional affiliations relevant to your focus area. Include information on your involvement with activities within the organization or any leadership roles.

Military Experience

It is not compulsory for people to undertake military training in Indonesia. This is done on a voluntary basis.

Volunteer Experience

Any volunteer experience that you have initiated or participated in should be described, such as activities with associations, clubs, or areas of personal interest (connected to your children's school, sports, charity, etc.).

Personal Information

In some resumes you will see headings such as: "special interests and achievements," "brief personal history," "statement of philosophy," and the like. If you have something really important to say under these headings, by all means go ahead and say it.

Note: At one time, it was standard practice to include a heading called "personal data," which included such information as date of birth, marital status, and so on. You may do this if you wish, but the current trend is to omit such data entirely. The information you supplied earlier in the resume will reveal all the employer needs or should want to know.

References

List three or four references, giving their official titles, names, positions, affiliations, addresses, and, if possible, their contact numbers. Your most important references will be those for whom you have worked—supervisors, managers, and executives.

RESUME PRESENTATION

Format and Layout

Although somewhat formal in setup—mainly for quick reading and reference purposes—the resume is essentially a sales instrument. You should emphasize those events and accomplishments that make you look attractive to a prospective employer. It should not be a razzle-dazzle document but neither should it be a condensed biographical sketch of your life and work. It should be an interesting profile showcasing your best side. Every good resume should contain four basic parts:

1. Heading: your name, address, telephone number, and e-mail address. The position you are applying for also is important information.
2. Education: degrees, major courses taken, special training, and so on.
3. Experience: descriptions of the jobs you've held.
4. References: a short list of people whom an employer can contact for information about you.

Length

Your resume/CV should be no longer than two to three pages.

Attachments

Grades, certificates, and letters of reference do not necessarily have to be included with your application, as you can present them at the interview. If you prefer to attach such documents, choose your most recent grades and a letter of reference from your current employer.

Note: Any documents attached to your resume should be the original documents, not copies, as these will be returned to you.

There is a tendency for applicants here to attach a recent passport-sized photograph to the resume. However, this is not mandatory.

E-mail Applications

It is increasingly common that employers in Indonesia accept and appreciate applications via e-mail. In this case, always attach your resume to the letter/e-mail.

COVER LETTERS

▶ Observe the three Cs—your letter should be clear, concise, and convincing.

▶ Outline your major points and plan the format of the letter before you begin to write.

▶ Type your letter. Avoid lined, strongly colored, or other unusual paper; use business-quality stationery.

▶ Edit your letter several times, getting rid of all unnecessary words and checking spelling and grammar carefully.

Content/Detail

The main objective of both documents (cover letter and resume) is to obtain an interview; few people are hired sight unseen, no matter how impressive the written description of their qualifications. You have achieved your objective if you are invited to come for an interview; it means that you looked good enough on paper to be seriously considered for the position.

A good application letter contains the following elements. Do not simply repeat what is in your resume.

▶ How you learned about the vacancy if appropriate.

▶ A brief statement as to why you are interested in the job and why you believe you qualify for it.

▶ A request for a personal interview.

▶ Information about where you can be reached.

JOB INFORMATION SOURCES

Newspapers

With relatively few English speakers and the lack of sophistication in the media industry, most companies rely on newspapers to advertise their vacancies. Multinationals essentially advertise in English, irrespective of the local papers the ads are placed in. There is no specific classified section in these newspapers.

Of significance is the *Kompas* newspaper, which has nationwide coverage. Other common papers include *Bisnis Indonesia*, *Media Indonesia*, and *Suara Pembaruan*. The latter two include vacancies for middle- and lower-level positions.

The most popular English newspaper, which covers most of the prominent cities in Indonesia, is *The Jakarta Post*. Companies seeking expatriates would generally advertise their vacancies here.

Kompas
Jl. Palmerah Barat no. 29-31
Jakarta Barat
Phone: (62-21) 534 7710, 20, 30/530 2200
Fax: (62-21) 548 6085
Web site: www.kompas.co.id

Bisnis Indonesia
Wisma Bisnis Indonesia, floors 5 and 6
Jl. S. Parman Kav. 12-13
Slipi Jakarta 11480
Phone: (62-21) 530 4016
(switchboard)/530 5868 (advertising)
Fax: (62-21) 530 5869
Web site: www.bisnis.com

Media Indonesia
Jl. Pilar Mas Raya Kav. A/D
Kompleks Delta Kedoya
Jakarta Barat
Phone: (62-21) 581 2088 (Press 9 for
assistance)/549 1656
Fax: (62-21) 581 2102
Web site: www.mediaindo.co.id

Suara Pembaruan
Jl. Dewi Sartika no. 136 D
Jakarta Timur 13630
Phone: (62-21) 801 3208 (ext. 102)
Fax: (62-21) 800 7262
Web site: www.suarapembaruan.com

The Jakarta Post
Jl. Palmerah Selatan 15
Jakarta 10270
Phone: (62-21) 530 0476, 77, 78/530
6971
Fax: (62-21) 549 2685
Web site: www.jakartapost.com

Chamber of Commerce/Trade Organizations

The Chamber of Commerce of Indonesia does not provide employment services. It is a point of contact for investment decisions and trade practices.

Chamber of Commerce and Industry (Kadin Indonesia)
Menara Kadin Indonesia, floor 29
Jl. HR. Rasuna Said Blok X-5, Kav. 02-03
Jakarta 12950
Phone: (62-21) 527 4484-5
Fax: (62-21) 527 4486
E-mail: adm_dj@indonesia.kadin.net.id
dirtu@indonesia.kadin.net.id

World Trade Centers Association
World Trade Center Jakarta
World Trade Center Building, floor 2
Jl. Jend. Sudirman Kav. 29-31
Jakarta 12920
Phone: (62-21) 521 1125, (62-21) 252 1126
Fax: (62-21) 252 2152
Web site: www.wtcjk.or.id

Internet Sites

Through the Internet, companies usually advertise open positions on their web sites. It may be worthwhile to look for companies in your field of interest. Recently launched and most visited sites include www.jobsdb.com and www.karir.com. The most popular employment web sites can be identified in the Indonesian Yellow Pages. To access this online, you can visit www.yellowpages.co.id.

Popular portals also recommended to locate companies and other concerns include:

www.satunet.com
www.astaga.com
www.indoexchange.com

Telephone Directory

In the Indonesian telephone directory Yellow Pages (www.yellowpages.co.id), you will find companies listed under the relevant trade headings. This can be a fruitful way to start looking for companies that interest you.

Country Employment Office

It is not common for candidates to look to the Country Employment Office for employment assistance. Multinational companies tend to look to either executive search firms or recruitment agencies or may seek to advertise their vacancies in the newspapers.

Using Employment Agencies and Recruitment Consultants

Employment agencies, recruitment consultants, and search firms are all part of the established job market. There are several directories that list the employment agencies, executive recruiters, and search firms in Jakarta and other important cities. Employment agencies generally handle positions at the middle and entry level of the job market. You may also look in your newspapers for recruiter advertisements.

Reputable search firms include:

PricewaterhouseCoopers	www.pwcglobal.com
John Clements	www.johnclements.com
Egon Zehnder	www.egonzehnder.com
Korn Ferry	www.kornferry.com
Tasa Consulting	www.tasa.co.id
Boyden International	www.boyden.co.id

WORK PERMITS/VISAS

Visas

A visa is required for a visit to Indonesia of any duration. Tourists and business visitors from 29 countries—the other Association of Southeast Asian Nations (ASEAN) countries, EU member countries, Australia, Canada, Iceland, Japan, New Zealand, Norway, Switzerland, and the United States—may obtain free visas upon arrival if they have a return ticket and the period of their stay does not exceed two months. Visitors from other countries can obtain a social-visit visa before arrival. Such a visa is valid up to one month.

Most companies employing expatriates bear the immigration cost. The normal fee to obtain a multiple exit-reentry visa (valid for six months) would be approximately US$100 for one person, assuming that the Indonesian company provides a sponsor—valid for *kartu ijin menetap/sementara* (KIM/S) holder.

Residence and Work Permits

Temporary resident visas are valid for six months to one year and are issued exclusively to experts required for national development. Noncitizens are not allowed to work in Indonesia unless they have a work permit.

The Indonesian foreign and domestic investment laws allow the employment of expatriate personnel in positions that cannot be filled by Indonesian nationals. The number of positions available for expatriates has been reduced by the government in recent years in an attempt to increase the use of Indonesian nationals. Permits will be issued only to companies having government approval. These permits are valid for one year, or for a shorter term, to allow for irregular visits by an expatriate working in Indonesia. A non-PMA (foreign-owned company) or PMDN (locally owned company) is also allowed to employ expatriates after it has obtained an operating license (*surat ijin usaha pedagangan*—SIUP).

It is not unusual for a work permit application to take two or three months for approval. Extension permits are available. To be employed, foreigners must also be in possession of an entry permit (*kartu ijin menetap/sementara*—KIM/S) and a police certificate card (*surat tanda melapor diri*—STMD).

INTERVIEW ADVICE

▶ Do not forget that the person interviewing you may also feel stressed. Try to make the interview as relaxed as possible. The easier the interview, the more positive points you will score. Indeed, an interview is very much like a game: For every positive point you put on the board, it takes only one negative to knock it off. For every negative you put on the board, it takes 10 positives to retrieve the situation.

▶ One key to taking much of the stress out of the interview situation is *preparation*. If you know what you can do, what you like to do, and what kind of contribution you can make to an employer, then no question can lessen your self-confidence.

▶ In an interview, eye contact is necessary to show interest and concentration.

▶ Dress at a level of formality that shows you understand the importance of the situation and respect for the person you are meeting.

▶ Take notes during the conversation, recording both questions and responses. If names come up that are difficult to understand, ask for them to be spelled out.

▶ You may phone the contact person listed in the employment advertisement before sending in your application, for further details, or just to introduce yourself. However, do not persistently telephone for the status of the recruitment process.

CULTURAL ADVICE

▶ Indonesians are polite people. Upon meeting and leaving, it is customary to shake hands with both men and women. A business guest will often be served a drink and should not reach for the drink until the host gestures to do so. It is polite to at least sample the drink or any food offered. Indonesians avoid use of the left hand when offering food and other objects because it is regarded as the unclean hand; it is also rude to point with a finger. Indonesian cultural values do not include some of the elements common in the Western societies.

▶ Indonesians show considerable respect for status, position, and age. It is considered important to be formal and polite in the presence of one's elders and superiors and to show due respect. Social acceptance and connections with socially acceptable persons may have significant influence on your business success. In fact, personal friends and contacts may prove more important in a business relationship than the quality of a product or service.

▶ The concept of social hierarchy is important in Indonesian society. Inequalities and status differences tend to be seen positively. Senior levels of hierarchy demand respect, and it is common for middlemen or go-betweens to be used when dealing with persons who are of lower status or not of Indonesian origin. The operation of status hierarchy is important in facilitating business transactions. There is a tendency for middle levels of the social hierarchy to overstate their status. Manual labor is perceived as having low status, and this may lead to lack of attention to physical detail (quality control).

▶ Business relationships may develop on the basis of family connections and ethnic ties. Indonesians have a general feeling of moral obligation toward their general family and members of the same ethnic group. As a result, in business dealings and employment policies preference may be given on the basis of such relationships, even though this may not be the better alternative from a business point of view. Those doing business should be aware of the need to consider and respect the traditional roles of different ethnic groups and appreciate the value of the family.

▶ Generally, Indonesians prefer to avoid disharmony or conflict and to preserve their own and other people's dignity. This characteristic can prove frustrating for Westerners because people may avoid admitting openly that they lack certain knowledge, that they are wrong, or that they are unable to complete a business transaction. This characteristic is reflected in the general reluctance to make changes. Initiative may be stifled to the point where direction is expected from other persons, and enforcing employee discipline may prove difficult.

▶ Indonesia does not have a strong union movement by Western standards. Collective labor agreements are an effective method of establishing industrial harmony in the Indonesian environment. Collective bargaining agreements are valid for a maximum of three years. Awareness of employee rights is increasing.

▶ The annual leave period is prescribed by law. Employees are entitled to a minimum period of 12 working days with full wages after 12 months' continuous service. Public holidays include Islamic holidays and national days. There are 12 main public holidays in Indonesia. Compensatory time off is not normally provided if a holiday falls on a Sunday.

Italy

Annamaria Carrozza, Mercuri Urval

COUNTRY OVERVIEW

Located in southern Europe, Italy is a peninsula extending into the central Mediterranean Sea. With a total area of 116,303 square miles and a population of 57 million, Italy has the fifth highest population density in Europe—about 490 persons per square mile. The coastline measures more than 4,720 miles, so that the sea plays a major role in the Italian economy, climate, and way of life. Italy is largely homogeneous linguistically and religiously, but is diverse culturally, economically, and politically with a deep gap between the north and south areas. Although Roman Catholicism is the major religion—99 percent of the people are nominally Catholic—all religious faiths are provided equal freedom under the constitution. Rome, with 2.7 million inhabitants, is the capital. It is a city known throughout the world. Since the first century A.D., when it was at the heart of the Roman Empire, Rome has been the center of tourism, ancient art, and cultural Italian life. The Pope, the temporal head of the Roman Catholic Church, is sovereign pontiff of Vatican City. Other major cities include Turin, Naples, and Milan, where most of the country's economic activities take place.

Italy has been a democratic republic since 1946. The Italian state is highly centralized. The constitution establishes a bicameral parliament, a separate judiciary, and an executive branch composed of the Council of Ministers, which is headed by the President of the Council (prime minister). The President of the Republic is elected by the parliament.

Since World War II, the Italian economy has changed from one based on agriculture to a ranking industrial economy, with approximately the same per capita output as France and the United Kingdom. This basically capitalistic economy is still divided into a developed industrial north, dominated by private companies, and a less developed agricultural south, with large public enterprises. Most of the raw materials needed by industry and over 75 percent of the energy requirements must be imported. Services are the most important component of the gross domestic product (more than 60 percent). Key sectors of industry are automobiles, machinery, chemicals, textiles, and shoes. These are represented by large multinational companies, such as Fiat and Pirelli—and, in fashion and design, by Benetton, Armani, and Ferragamo. Italy belongs to the Group of Seven (G-7) industrialized nations; it is a member of the European Union and the Organization for Economic Cooperation and Development (OECD).

The official language of the country is Italian, derived from Latin. There are numerous dialects, some of which show French, German, Spanish, or Arabic influence. Most members of the middle and upper classes can speak English.

The standard of living of the professional classes and of upper and middle management is high, similar to that of other developed countries. However, unemployment remains high, especially in the south. Women and young people have significantly higher rates of unemployment than do men. A rigid labor market serves as a disincentive to job creation. There is a significant underground economy absorbing substantial numbers of people, who work for low wages and without social benefits and protection. Currently, the best job opportunities are to be found in the computer and IT sectors.

RESUME SPECIFICS

Education

Start by discussing your high school or secondary school experience. Carefully list the type of school, the name and the town, the year you started, and the year you graduated. Always specify the grades that you received. If you attended a private school, which is not typical in Italy, explain something about it (with a focus on specific courses and programs). When explaining your university studies, specify the focus area you selected and the title of your thesis (including the name of the professor you worked with). Mention if you graduated within the minimum number of years required for your degree (normally four). If you have studied abroad (which is generally appreciated), note when, where, and the length of time.

Extracurricular Activities

Briefly describe any interesting involvement with organizing or promoting cultural or social activities. List any major success in extracurricular activities, including sports. Discuss this issue briefly at the end of your CV.

Note: If you are involved in religious or political organizations, do not specify which side you are on.

Awards/Honors

List only the special awards and honors you received that mean something on a national or international level. Do not write about minor accomplishments.

Additional Education/Specialized Training

Mention additional courses and training. Do not forget to specify the institute, the duration of the course, attendance dates, and the focus areas you concentrated on. Computer, languages, and sales are usually the most interesting for the Italian market.

Work Experience

Write the month and year you started work and the month and year you left the job. State the name of the company and a brief description of its business focus. Indicate if it is a national or multinational company, where the headquarters is located, how many people worked in your division, and what the turnover was. Then list your job title and responsibilities in the company: if you managed people, if you were involved in international projects, if your work required traveling or dealing directly with clients, if you worked in a team, and so on. Highlight special achievements, such as the budget you developed, especially if you are in the sales field. If you changed jobs often in a brief time, or if there are any gaps in your career, you need to give some explanation. Specify if it was a short-term or a part-time contract.

Achievements/Accomplishments

List any acknowledgment or recognition for special achievements or accomplishments.

Special Skills

In Italy, foreign languages are of great interest to employers. Clearly and honestly explain the level at which you speak and write. It is no use to pretend on this point. Some Italian people say that they have good English when they know almost nothing at all. Fluency is what you need to work and to manage business relations in English.

Also, always specify your computer skills and your level of confidence with using the Internet, which is of growing interest and importance.

Note: If you are a foreigner applying for a job in Italy, you will almost always need to be fluent in Italian. Proficiency and TOEFL (Test of English as a Foreign Language) certifications are well-known language tests in Italy.

Professional Affiliations

List only if relevant.

Military Experience

A man should state if he has already performed his military service, which is mandatory in Italy. Note whether you had a managerial or technical position, or if you chose the civil service.

Volunteer Experience

Mention your volunteer experiences, especially those activities performed during your studies.

Personal Information

Do not forget to include where and when you were born, if you are married, and if you have children. Be sure to list your address and a telephone number where you can be easily reached. Include your e-mail address, if you have one. Specify where you want to be contacted. You may add a short note about your hobbies, sports, and other interests.

References

It is not necessary to list references on your CV. However, if you do, list the names of your former supervisors or those familiar with your professional experience. Do not list friends, relatives, or professors. Be sure that the person you mention is informed that he or she could be contacted and has a positive opinion about you.

RESUME PRESENTATION

Format and Layout

Analyzing the overall structure and style of a resume can tell a lot about a candidate's ability to effectively organize and communicate a set of facts. A well-structured resume should be concise. It should summarize the applicant's relevant qualifications and work experience, and those that meet the required levels. It should contain educational and career histories in reverse chronological order to emphasize your most recent activities, and should highlight your most relevant skills. Make sure that your resume presents your information in a logical and easily digestible form. Be careful to avoid any mistakes in spelling.

Length

Your CV should be no longer than two pages.

Attachments

Do not attach certificates, letters of reference, or recommendations to your resume if not requested to do so. It is better to present them at the interview.

Note: In Italy, it is not considered to be good form to attach a photo, especially for high-level positions. Attach a photo only if requested.

E-mail Applications

Applications via e-mail are not very common in Italy. However, they are welcome, especially for IT positions. In any case, be sure the company can process your e-mail.

Note: It is more common in Italy to send applications by fax.

Other

Note: According to Italian law 675/96, you should grant permission for your personal data to be used. Write a special notation with reference to this law and sign it on the original resume/CV.

COVER LETTERS

Content/Detail

It is very polite, and it is appreciated, if you include a personalized cover letter with your resume. Discuss the position for which you are applying. Highlight your strong points that match the needs of the position. Explain the main reason for your interest in the position.

Note: Many Italian companies appreciate receiving a handwritten cover letter, because they use it to analyze the individual style of writing.

Length

The cover letter should never be longer than a half page. It should be very impressive and easy to read.

JOB INFORMATION SOURCES

Newspapers

Different newspapers and trade magazines contain employment ads. The *Corriere della Sera* is the leader in job market ads. Other relevant daily papers are *Il Sole 24 Ore*, *La Repubblica*, *La Stampa*, and *La Gazzetta del Mezzogiorno*. Trade publications focus on very specific areas.

Advertisements are generally in Italian only, except in cases where another language is a requirement for the position. You can also find a selection of ads on the web site of the newspaper.

Corriere della Sera (news of today; covers the entire country; job ads on Fridays)
Phone: +39-2-290-6339
Fax: +39-2-29009668
E-mail: dimafoni@rcs.it

Il Sole 24 Ore (financial/business/industry news; covers the entire country; job ads on Mondays and Wednesdays)
Phone: +39-2-30223770
E-mail: system@ ilsole24ore.it

La Repubblica (news of today; covers the entire country; job ads on Thursdays)
Phone: +39-2-57494639
E-mail: m.prusciano@manzoni.it

La Stampa (news of today; covers the north/west areas)
Phone: +39-11-5638111
Web site: www.lastampa.it

La Gazzetta del Mezzogiorno (news of today; covers the south area; job ads on Fridays
Phone: +39-2-24424422
Fax: +39-2-24424550

Internet Sites

Major companies usually advertise open positions on their own web sites. You can search in www.mercuri-urval.com, too. The largest daily papers also place their employment ads on the Internet.

Company Directories

There are four very good directories where you can find all the companies listed in Italy, with detailed information:

- ▶ *Career Book* (published by *La Repubblica*).
- ▶ *Guida Monaci* (published by Monaci).
- ▶ *Kompass* (published by Kompass).
- ▶ *Dun's 10,000* (published by Dun & Bradstreet).

WORK PERMITS/VISAS

Citizens of European Union countries do not need work permits. For other nationalities, the Italian employer must request permission to hire the foreign employee from the Provveditorato del Lavoro (the Department of Labor). Once the permission has been granted, the employer sends the approval form to the new employee. The new employee must then submit the work approval form to the Italian embassy/consulate in his or her home country in order to apply for a visa. A residence permit is issued by the quaestorship (the local neighborhood authorities) once the employee actually resides in Italy.

INTERVIEW ADVICE

▶ Italians expect candidates not to be too casual in dress. Remember, you are interviewing for a professional position. Dress in business attire. Be on time.

▶ Have your thoughts and several questions well organized in advance.

▶ Do talk about yourself. When asked a question, do not just answer yes or no. However, stick to the question asked. Take the opportunity to provide specific examples of how you handled situations in the past.

▶ Let the interviewer direct the conversation. Do not act too familiar with him or her. A kind of hierarchy is still recognized in Italian organizations.

▶ Learn about the employer. Read the recruiting literature and the annual reports. Study product lines, services, sales, earnings, business strategies, culture, and values.

▶ Do not discuss salary early in the process. If requested, you should be open about your current salary.

CULTURAL ADVICE

▶ Body language is noticed, used, and appreciated in Italy. People are open and tactile: Personal space is less than in northern Europe, for example. The interviewer does not feel invaded if you sit or stand quite close. However, you are not expected to touch the interviewer's arm or shoulder if he or she is a stranger.

▶ Make frequent and continuous eye contact. Shake hands firmly and warmly. Maintain a relaxed sitting position. Try to imitate the posture of your interviewer. Appear confident.

▶ Work ends quite late in the afternoon. Appointments can be scheduled at 7:00 P.M., which is normal—and you are expected to agree.

▶ August is holiday time for almost every company in Italy. It will be almost impossible to conduct new business during this period.

Japan

Birgitta Lofving and Charlotte Kennedy-Takahashi,
Oak Associates

COUNTRY OVERVIEW

Japan consists of four major islands and thousands of smaller islands and is located in the northeast part of Asia. Approximately 125 million people live in an area of 377,812 square kilometers (145,874 square miles)—about the size of California. More than 75 percent of the land area is mountains, with Mount Fuji as the highest peak at 3,776 meters above sea level. Tokyo is located on the largest island, Honshu, which has 80 percent of the nation's population. More than 25 million people live within the Tokyo/Yokohama metropolitan area, with about five million in the Osaka/Kobe area.

Japan is a democracy with a parliamentary form of government. The head of government is the prime minister, who is elected by Japan's parliament, the National Diet. Elections to the Lower House are held at least once every four years. Upper House elections are every three years, at which time half the membership is elected. The role of the Emperor is essentially symbolic. A well-educated and capable bureaucracy, which is managed by the ministries, serves the country. However, this group is slow to reform or to change.

Shinto and Buddhism are the major religions of Japan. Few Japanese actively pursue a religion today, except for ceremonial occasions. Nevertheless, Confucianism has a strong influence on the Japanese mind. Approximately 1 percent of the population practice Christianity.

Japanese is the national language. The written language includes three different types of alphabets: *kanji* (deriving from the Chinese characters), *hiragana* (a syllabary for Japanese words), and *katakana* (non-Japanese words). English is the primary foreign language and is taught in schools.

Japanese society is in the middle of social change as a result of 10 years of economic recession. Personal values, Japanese management, government regulations, business style, and growth in internationalism are creating a new face for Japan. Japan has the largest unemployment figures since World War II despite economic initiatives; however, governmental efforts are providing new opportunities for growth in the service industry, technology, and small business. The country has a low crime rate and safe streets, but steep increases in crime have occurred in the past several years, as well as illegal drug consumption.

Japan has 47 prefectures, which are all in the same time zone: nine hours ahead of Greenwich mean time (GMT) and 14 hours ahead of eastern standard time (EST). Japan does not observe daylight saving time.

RESUME SPECIFICS

Note: The following information reflects the practices in virtually every Japanese work environment and, in part, in international companies in Japan, which have both Japanese and international practices.

There is a major difference in content between an English-written resume in Japan and the traditional Japanese *rirekisho*. The English-written resume is influenced by foreign companies' requirements and is much like an American-style resume. The *rirekisho* is divided into two parts, (1) personal information and (2) job experience. The primary purpose of the Japanese resume is to explain your education and whether you come from an environment that gives you a propensity for long-term success in a company.

Unless noted to the contrary, the following advice refers to the English-style resume.

Experience Profile

Make a summary of your strengths and professional experience. If possible, this should be specifically related to the job you are applying for.

Education

Mention the highest level of education—degree, major and minor, graduation year, and name of university.

Note: Education and the prestige of the educational institution are major criteria for job selection in Japan, for Japanese and foreigners alike. However, the standard for foreigners may be slightly lower.

Additional Education/Specialized Training

List additional education and specialized training, computer courses, language training, and certificates for specialties from organizational and government-approved sources.

Work Experience

List the names of employers, dates of employment, and job title(s). Include each company's field and the focus of its business. Also give information about whether you worked full-time or part-time, field of responsibility, and teamwork experience. Be sure to correctly list dates of employment.

Achievements/Accomplishments

Be precise about your achievements, describing your success in concrete terms.

Special Skills

Languages

Specify your level(s) of knowledge, not simply your years of study in foreign languages. If relevant, give the results of the Japanese tests for Japanese language levels. Companies that hire foreigners usually require bilingual skills, with one language being Japanese. If you do not know any Japanese, there are still some areas in which you would be able to find a job—computers, banking, and English teaching.

Computers

List your knowledge of programming languages and applications: specify PC or Macintosh. People with advanced computer software skills are very much sought after in Japan.

Professional Affiliations

List memberships in any professional associations, networking organizations, and so on that are relevant to the job or professional field.

Personal Information

For the English-style resume you should mention nationality, age, and marital status. (Age is very important in Japan.)

Note: The Japanese resume (rirekisho) includes information about age, gender, family members, hobbies, club memberships, and nationality (if non-Japanese). This information is used to get an overview of the candidate and to check public records of family, school, police, and so on to prove the honesty and good standing of the applicant.

Those who are older (35 to 45) generally have an advantage, as it is believed that they are more reliable and mature; young professionals generally do no have or are not given authority and are not expected to provide leadership at a young age. They are expected to prove they can work hard and are loyal to their work group as they enter the work force. This is based on old cultural Japanese values to respect the knowledge of experienced and seasoned members of society and that young people must pass through rites of development in the company. It is also based on the practicality that few young people receive the type of college education that provides immediate specialization or knowledge to immediately take responsibility in a business area (such as occurs in the American business environment). In addition, it is a generally-held opinion that most Japanese females do not mature until 30. There has been a moderate breakdown in these ageisms, but they are still deeply ingrained—age equals respect. It becomes a major topic of conversation when someone under 50 takes a key management position in a large firm.

References

References may include a former manager or colleague, since a current manager might not know that you are looking for a new job. State what relationship you have to the designated reference. Do not include anyone you have not asked to give references.

Note: Having a Japanese reference is a great advantage. The level of respect of the contact will enhance the level of trust accorded to you. However, Japanese do not easily permit their names to be used, as it will tarnish their image if it does not work out.

RESUME PRESENTATION

Format and Layout

Start your English-style resume with a summary, including your experience profile, which includes sales points concerning your background. Follow with a list of your working experience, educational background, and special skills. Use reverse chronological order (i.e., start with your most recent experience).

If possible, use both styles of resumes. If you do not know Japanese and are approaching a Japanese company, you may have your English resume translated into Japanese. However, when applying for a job at an international department of a Japanese company, an English-style resume is accepted.

Note: Usually resumes are written in both English and Japanese. The English-style resume is generally one to two pages long and should be neatly typed on bond paper. The Japanese *rirekisho* is handwritten on a specific two-page form, which can be purchased in stationery shops. A photo is attached. When writing dates in Japanese, the year is written in the Japanese way, with the Emperor's name and the specific year of his rule.

Attachments

Usually no attachments are sent with the application, except for the photo with the Japanese resume. It is not common to send recommendation letters from previous employers with the application, but this might change in the future. Such letters are usually submitted at a later time during the interview process.

E-mail Applications

The use of e-mail applications varies depending on the company you are approaching. When applying for a job in newly established and modern companies, e-mail applications are acceptable. However, many large Japanese companies receive a large number of e-mail resumes, and you might want to use another approach to avoid being lost in the shuffle.

COVER LETTERS

If preferred, a cover letter that states your objectives, what kind of position you are looking for, and why you should be interviewed may be included. When responding to an advertisement, refer to the content of the ad when describing your strengths.

Note: A cover letter is not usually part of an application, as it commonly includes a summary of skills and objectives, which are already noted on a Japanese resume. A short note with a reference to a previous phone conversation is sufficient.

JOB INFORMATION SOURCES

Newspapers and Magazines

Japan Times (English) has a special Job Advertisement section on Mondays (web site: www.japantimes.co.jp).

B-ing and *Tech B-ing* (both Japanese) contain job advertisements, the latter for technical positions (Japanese web site: www.recruit.co.jp/r-staffing).

Computing Japan is the only English-language computer magazine in Japan. This magazine also contains advertisements for computer positions (web site: www.cjmag.co.jp/jobs.html).

Chambers of Commerce

The American Chamber of Commerce in Japan publishes *ACCJ News*, where job seekers can place their resumes for a fee. There is also an on-line service for resumes.

American Chamber of Commerce in Japan
Phone: +81 3 3433 5381
Fax: +81 3 3436 1446
Web site: www.accj.or.jp

Other chambers of commerce:

Australian and New Zealand Chamber
of Commerce in Japan
Phone: +81 3 5214 0710
Fax: +81 3 5214 0712
Web site: www2.gol.com/users/anzccj

Canadian Chamber of Commerce in
Japan
Phone: +81 3 3224 7824
Fax: +81 3 3224 7825
Web site: www.cccj.or.jp

British Chamber of Commerce in Japan
Phone: +81 3 3267 1901
Fax: +81 3 3267 1903

Japan Chamber of Commerce
Phone: +81 3 3283 7851
Fax: +81 3 3216 6497
Web site: www.jccj.or.jp/home-e.html

Networking Organizations

In Japan, networking is important. There are many organizations where you can
meet other business professionals and get to know about job opportunities. Here
is a list:

Kaisha Society
Phone: +81 3 5562 0382
Web site: www.kaisha.gol.com/main-
fr.html

Foreign Executive Women (FEW)
Phone: +81 3 5449 3865
Web site: www.few.gol.com

Japan Webgrrls
Web site: www.inj.ac/webgrrls

Foreign Correspondents' Club in Japan
Phone: +81 3 3211 3161
Fax: +81 3 3211 3168

Forum for Corporate Communications
Phone: +81 3 3299 1719

Internet Sites

Two large, general employment sites are: www.monster.com and www.workin-
japan.com.

Oak Associates K.K. (www.oakassociates.co.jp), a human resources consulting company, actively recruits Japanese-English bilingual staff for non-Japanese
companies in Japan. The firm assists foreign technical and professional staff to locate positions that are in line with client needs. Career consulting is also available
for those who want to know how to adapt their skills to Japan or to build cross-
cultural work competencies.

The web site www.asianet.com lists jobs for candidates who are bilingual
(English plus Japanese, Chinese, or Korean). Many of the openings are in Japan,
and most of the jobs are in the financial or technical fields. The Newsletter at
www.ohayosensei.com lists teaching jobs in Japan.

Other

The Japan Exchange and Teaching (JET) Program is designed to invite foreign
young professionals to Japan and to provide them with opportunities to teach
language and sports at junior and senior high schools all over Japan, or to engage
in international exchange activities with local governments. For more information: www.mofa.go.jp/j_info/visit/jet/index.html.

Note: When approaching a Japanese company, it is very helpful to have a Japanese contact who can introduce you to a company. The level of this person's status
will affect your application.

WORK PERMITS/VISAS

To be able to work in Japan, you will need a valid passport from your home country and a work visa from the Justice Ministry of Japan. Visas are obtained through a certificate of eligibility system. First, you need to find a company to agree to hire you and to provide the required documents. Next you need to contact the Japanese embassy or consulate in your country and complete the application (a cost of 4,000 yen). Of course, you can travel to Japan to interview on a tourist visa, but must return to your home country to get the eligibility certificate, which will be forwarded to the Japanese embassy/consulate. To get a work visa in Japan, you must have a university degree. Basically, foreigners are allowed to work only in positions that do not take work away from the Japanese or which will provide new technology or education to the Japanese people.

If you are in Japan on a student visa, or as an accompanying spouse with a dependent visa, you are allowed to work a maximum of 25 hours per week with special permission from the Immigration Bureau. If you want to work full-time, you must give up your dependent visa and get a regular work visa. As a student, you cannot work full-time.

Visas are issued for one to three years, depending on the status of residence, which is determined by the Japanese government. Approximately one month before your visa expires, you must go to the Immigration Bureau to apply for a visa extension if you wish to continue your stay in Japan.

Once you have received a work visa, if you leave Japan temporarily, you will need a reentry permit (issued at the Immigration Bureau—3,000 yen for single reentry permit and 6,000 yen for multiple reentries for the term of the visa). If you do not have this permit when you leave Japan, you will lose your visa status.

Any foreigner who stays in Japan for more than 90 days must report to the local authorities to receive a Certificate of Alien Registration. This is as important as your passport. You are required to carry this certificate with you all the time while in Japan. You do not need to carry your passport upon receipt of this certificate.

You will be deported if you work without a proper visa. Always check for up-to-date requirements, as they change over time.

INTERVIEW ADVICE

▶ Before the interview, get a map showing the location of the meeting place—as a reference or to show to the taxi driver, since locations can be difficult to find in complicated urban areas.

▶ Be on time; plan to arrive 15 minutes early.

▶ The business card (*meishi*) plays an important role by formalizing the introduction process and establishing the status of the parties. How you use these cards will be a good indicator of whether you know how to function in Japanese business society.

▶ Business attire should be conservative. Men usually wear somber gray or blue suits. Women's attire is somewhat dressier in Japan than in many Western countries. Suits and smart accessories are appropriate.

- ▶ Japanese companies will be impressed by a Japanese-written resume, especially if written by you.
- ▶ Expect many people to be involved in the interviewing process. It is a group decision.
- ▶ Usually there are many personal questions asked in the interview. Questions—for example, about your parents—should be courteously and briefly answered.
- ▶ Speak clearly and slowly in English, if you are not a Japanese speaker.
- ▶ Listen carefully, and always wait for the interviewer to finish speaking. It is very rude to interrupt.
- ▶ Do not brag or exaggerate.
- ▶ Personality, especially demonstration of good communication capabilities, is often as important as your credentials.
- ▶ Emphasize and demonstrate that you are a team player.

Note: The purpose of interviews held by Japanese companies is usually not to determine a candidate for a particular position, but rather to determine if the applicant will fit into the company.

CULTURAL ADVICE

- ▶ Generally, Japanese admire hard work, team focus, extra efforts, ability to keep an even temper, openness, obedience, and willingness to learn. While young people are changing and becoming more interested in hobbies and vacations, it is still these traditional values that bring recognition from an employer.
- ▶ Japanese do not like to make mistakes, as it will reflect badly on the group.
- ▶ Expect to work long hours; the workplace is a society/family and extends beyond the confines of work.
- ▶ National laws allow for seven days paid holiday during the first year, with additional days with each subsequent year. The local governments in big cities have local labor offices that will consult with foreigners who have concerns about labor issues—contracts, labor unions, pay levels, discrimination, and others.
- ▶ Respect those senior to you in the company. Hierarchy and seniority are also reflected in the language.
- ▶ Remember that long-term business relations are very important.
- ▶ Be flexible and maintain a sense of humor.
- ▶ Take language lessons. An effort to learn—especially a successful effort—will be appreciated.
- ▶ Social life includes going to restaurants and pubs, rarely to someone's home.

For further information on cultural advice, visit web sites www.insite-tokyo.com and www.livinginjapan.com.

Republic of Korea

Kang-Shik Koh and Peter Manlik, Signium International

COUNTRY OVERVIEW

The Republic of Korea, usually referred to as South Korea or just Korea, is located south of the 38th parallel on the Korean peninsula. It is bordered by the Democratic People's Republic of Korea or North Korea to the north. The surface, about the size of Hungary or Portugal, is mountainous with about 65 percent covered with forests and woodlands. Koreans love their mountains, and flock out in crowds every weekend. Approximately 80 percent of the population of nearly 47 million live in urban areas. Korea has one of the world's highest population densities, with about 470 inhabitants per square kilometer. The capital, Seoul, located in the northwest part of the country, has about 11 million inhabitants. The second most important city is Pusan in the southeast, which is Korea's major port. The climate shows four distinct seasons, with cold but dry winters and tropical, humid summers.

Koreans are very proud of their nearly 5,000-year history. At one time, the ethnic Korean kingdoms reached far into Manchuria and Mongolia. The last kingdom ended with the Chosun Dynasty in 1910 when the Japanese annexed the Korean peninsula. Freed after the end of World War II, the peninsula was divided, and South Korea became an independent republic in 1948 after general elections supervised by the United Nations. The president, also directly elected, heads the government. Korea has had eight presidents to date. However, from 1961 to 1979 it was under a military regime. Recent governments have institutionalized the democratic processes further and made strong efforts to improve relations with Communist North Korea.

South Korea is a market economy. The country has experienced an unprecedented economic growth during the past three decades. It has successfully transformed itself from a typical backward economy to one of the so-called newly industrialized countries (NICs). Its success stems mainly from its export-oriented economic policies. Another driving force in this transformation is the strong educational system. Koreans have become increasingly well educated, with university education being the rule, nowadays often completed with graduate studies.

Supported by the government, the Korean economic power has traditionally been concentrated in a few huge Korean conglomerates, known as *chaebols* (e.g., Hyundai, Samsung, Daewoo, LG (Lucky-Goldstar), etc.). Forced by the Asian economic crisis in 1997–1998, these groups had to undergo rigorous staff reductions and sell-off measures to secure their financial future. This resulted in many new foreign investments and a much more active labor market. Although still far from perfect, the Korean social system includes medical insurance, industrial accident insurance, employment insurance, and national pension and retirement benefits. Income taxes are moderate at the lower salary levels, but increase progressively at the higher salary levels.

The Korean language is related to Japanese, Mongolian, Hungarian, Finnish, and Turkish. The Korean alphabet consists of 24 letters. Called *Hangul*, it is easily learned in just a few hours. Chinese characters are still in use, but their popularity is decreasing. Although English is commonly taught from elementary school on, the ability of the average Korean to communicate in English is poor, except in foreign-invested companies. From the total religious population (about 50 percent of all Koreans), about 45 percent are Buddhists and 52 percent are Christians.

RESUME SPECIFICS

Personal Data

State your full name, present address, and contact numbers for telephone, cellular phone, and e-mail; date of birth, place of birth, and nationality; marital status and family size.

Note: If you are Korean, also mention your resident number and whether you are the eldest child in your family. It is good if a photograph is attached.

Education

List all institutions attended from high school/secondary school onward. Mention high school name, place, and graduation year and the focus of your studies, if applicable. State the name of the college or university attended, place and graduation year, your major, and the title of your degree.

List any additional professional courses leading to certificates, diplomas, licenses, or authorizations, with length of time attended and place of instruction.

Extracurricular Activities

Describe any student activities you were engaged in or any other activity of merit that demonstrates your interests and abilities.

Awards/Honors

List awards and honors in chronological order along with descriptions. Indicate if you have received any award or scholarship for outstanding performance during studies.

Additional Education/Specialized Training

Any further training not mentioned under education, should be noted here—for example, various professional or management courses not leading to any diploma or license, as well as language and computer training.

Work Experience

List work experience in reverse chronological order, beginning with the most recent. For each job, state first the employment's start and end, with year and month, then the job title and the employer. Describe the job by detailing your responsibilities and achievements. Make sure that your description is relevant to the job. Explain the number of subordinates you managed, if applicable.

Do not leave any unexplained gaps in your work history. Also mention short-term employment and periods of unemployment.

Achievements/Accomplishments

List achievements and accomplishments in chronological order—any award, prize, or recognition you received for outstanding achievements during employment.

Special Skills

Any particular knowledge or skill gained (e.g., proficiency in languages, computer or equipment knowledge, driving or machine operator license, etc.) should be specified in this category.

Professional Affiliations

Note any memberships in professional or social affiliations relevant to the job for which you are applying.

Military Experience

State the exact period of your military experience, the unit, your duties, and your leadership responsibilities.

Volunteer Experience

In this section, mention any role you held, or hold, in clubs, charities, professional affiliates, or groups, especially those that enhance your contact sphere and managerial experience.

Personal Information

Briefly describe your hobbies and personal interests.

Note: It is of interest to show what you do to counteract stress from your job, to widen your intellectual or cultural view, or to find balance in your life.

References

References are usually not given at an early stage. However, you should be prepared in advance to submit them with short notice at a later time. Choose persons who were your former managers or colleagues, your clients, or influential people or opinion leaders.

RESUME PRESENTATION

Format and Layout

The Korean standard is written on a special form that can be bought in a stationery shop or produced in a spreadsheet program. The average Korean company expects this format from Korean applicants. It contains fixed fields for personal data and is completed in a chronological sequence (oldest first).

For the English application there is no real standard. However, the most common and recommended format should contain the following sequence of blocks: personal data, education, experience, others (languages, special courses, etc.). The sequence of information is usually in reverse chronological order (i.e., the most recent school and the most recent experience first). Arrange the information under bold headings for easy reading.

Note: There are two different resume/CV formats: one for applications in Korean and another one for applications in English. Koreans who are applying for a job with a foreign company often send both.

Length

A length of no more than two to three pages is recommended.

Attachments

Certificates, testimonies, or references are usually not attached to the application. You can present them at the interviews. If you attach items, make sure that they are copies, not originals. The companies do not return applications or attachments.

Note: Photos are required with the Korean application but not with the English version. However, it is still recommended that you attach a photo to give the application a more personal touch and to help the interviewer remember you.

E-mail Applications

It is more and more common to send applications by e-mail. If the resume is sent as an attachment, there is the risk that the receiver may not be able to open your attached file. Therefore, it is advisable to copy the resume directly into the text, although the formatting will be lost.

If your resume is a Word file, you can also send the file as an attachment. Then the receiver can select the method that suits him or her best for accessing the information.

Other

Note: For applicants with no or brief (less than one year) experience, it is common to prepare a separate one-page write-up entitled "Self-Introduction" (in Korean, "Jagi Sogeseo") in addition to the resume. This should describe the environment in which you grew up, the reasons for the selection of your schools and education, your interests and personal strengths, as well as your long-term goals.

COVER LETTERS

Although not always done, your application should be sent with a short cover letter, no longer than one page in length. The letter should be typed.

Content/Detail

This letter should spell out what position you are applying for and where you learned about the vacancy (if applicable). Summarize your experience and mention your long-term career objectives. You can mention why you think the position is a fit for you by emphasizing some of your characteristics. Salary expectation and availability should be mentioned only if requested, and then in very general terms. Do not give away your negotiation power at an early stage.

JOB INFORMATION SOURCES

Newspapers

The two English-language newspapers, *The Korea Herald* and *The Korea Times*, seldom have job advertisements. However, since the Asian economic crisis in

1997–1998, both papers have started to assist applicants by placing job-seeking advertisements.

The Korea Herald, Seoul (daily)
Column name: Job Link
Phone: +82 2 727 0007
E-mail: mischo@koreaherald.co.kr
Web site: www.koreaherald.co.kr

The Korea Times, Seoul (daily)
Column name: Times Marketplace
Phone: +82 2 724 2346
E-mail: ktnotice@hotmail.com
Web site: www.koreatimes.co.kr

Daily general, economic, and technical papers are all in Korean and publish some job advertisements. Printed ads have dropped to a minimum due to the introduction of Internet job sites.

Chosun Ilbo, Seoul (daily)
Phone: +82 2 724 5114
Web site: www.chosun.com

Dong Ah Ilbo, Seoul (daily)
Phone: +82 2 361 0114
Web site: www.donga.com

Chambers of Commerce

The major industrial countries maintain either independent chambers of commerce or have a trade section attached to their embassies through which very valuable assistance can be obtained (e.g., company directories, distribution of lists of applicants, etc.). All of this information is in English.

American Chamber of Commerce
Phone: +82 2 753 6471
Fax: +82 2 755 6577
E-mail: info@amchamkorea.org
Web site: www.amchamkorea.org

British Chamber of Commerce
Phone: +82 2 720 9406
Fax: +82 2 720 9411
E-mail: bcck@uriel.net
Web site: www.bcck.or.kr

European Chamber of Commerce
Phone: +82 2 2253 5631
Fax: +82 2 2253 5635
E-mail: eucck@eucck.org
Web site: www.eucck.org

French Chamber of Commerce and
  Industry
Phone: +82 2 2268 9505
Fax: +82 2 2268 9508
E-mail: fccik@nuri.net

Korean German Chamber of
  Commerce
Phone: +82 2 3780 4600
Fax: +82 2 3780 4637
E-mail: kgcci@kgcci.com
Web site: www.kgcci.com

Canadian Chamber of Commerce
Phone: +82 2 757 2776
Fax: +82 2 754 3623
E-mail: limeunkyoung@cec.or.kr

Internet Sites

Many open positions are advertised on the Internet, with the majority listed in Korean. The most popular web sites are: www.scout.co.kr, www.incruit.co.kr, www.recruit.co.kr, and www.mk.co.kr. Newly added sites with links in Korean are: job.combase.co.kr and www.joblink.co.kr.

Other web sites with links in English include:

English Teaching Positions (ESL)
http://eslcafe.com/jobs/korea
http://www.teachkorea.com
http://www.global-reach.net

General
asia-net.com
www.bilingula-jobs.com
www.info-tank.co.kr
www.finacialjobnet.com/kr.htm

Directories

Korea Telecom also issues Yellow Pages for foreigners in the English language, which can be useful for contacting companies. Contact them by telephone at +82 2 725 0411 or at their web site www.yellowpages.co.kr.

Executive Search Firms

The use of executive search firms has become particularly popular among foreign-invested companies in Korea. Therefore, it might be meaningful to send them your application if you have reached a qualified specialist and/or managerial level in your career. A background of working with multinational firms or with Korean firms with international affiliations is desirable.

Country Employment Office

There are government manpower agencies; these are primarily for blue-collar workers.

WORK PERMITS/VISAS

Visas

Visitors can stay either 15 or 90 days without a visa, depending on their nationalities.

Residence and Work Permits

A permanent work visa is required to work legally in Korea. You can apply either abroad at a Korean embassy or consulate, or in Korea. In the latter case, if the visa is approved, you receive a visa confirmation in Korea but you have to collect the visa at a Korean embassy or consulate abroad.

The possibility of receiving a Korean work permit is limited. There are two main alternatives:

1. You are hired through the parent company abroad and dispatched to Korea. In this case, the Korean authorities approve the visa almost automatically without any deeper queries.

2. You are hired by a company in Korea. In this case, the company has to prove that they need you because of your unique merits that cannot be found among Korean nationals. There are a number of qualified positions that specifically require foreigners for one reason or another. However, these positions may not be easy to find.

INTERVIEW ADVICE

▶ Although the Asian economic crisis in 1997–1998 has spurred a basic change, a typical Korean company and a typical Western company are still very different. A foreign-invested company with Western management located in Korea is usually somewhere in between.

▶ In spite of the widespread Christian and Buddhist beliefs, Confucian ethics still dominate Korean thinking—the respect for age, for the parents, for the teacher, and for the employer are important issues. Things are changing slowly, and the so-called seniority principle (hierarchy according to age) in companies is being replaced by a Western performance-based hierarchy of thinking.

▶ Previously, smaller Korean companies recruited new employees from the employees' own network. Larger companies recruited on campus and through newspaper advertisements. Today, the use of the Internet and search firms (headhunters) is gaining in importance.

▶ In traditional Korean companies, decisions are not made in teams. The highest boss makes a decision on the basis of the information he has and informs the levels under him. Young Koreans, and Koreans who work in foreign companies, expect a more Western style of teamwork.

▶ Koreans are very diligent and work long hours. There are two big holiday periods, the Lunar New Year (usually in February) and Thanksgiving (usually in September). During those periods, everyone takes off and joins their entire families in their hometowns. Annual leave (vacation) and the legal one day off per month are usually not fully taken.

Note: Due to the absence of a pension system in the past, in Korea, the eldest son has to take care of the parents in their retirement. This duty can be burdensome and limit his ability to relocate to other places.

CULTURAL ADVICE

▶ Be humble and natural. As a foreigner, you are expected to behave differently but, at the same time, show interest in the country and its traditions. Ask about and try to understand the differences between Korean and Western culture. Normal Western politeness is usually a good approach.

▶ Koreans present their business cards with both hands, directly into the hands of the recipient. Do not simply put the card on the table.

▶ When visiting a restaurant in a group, Koreans never pay their bills individually. The person who is highest in rank pays and can then, but often does not, collect the money from the colleagues.

▶ In the Korean organization, everyone is classified in a hierarchic title system. Managers are called by their full names and titles if superior or elder, with a suffix expressing respect. It is accepted that foreigners simply say Mr., Mrs., or Ms. before the family name when addressing Koreans.

Latin America

Victor P. Viglino, Latin America Search Associates (LASA)

COUNTRY OVERVIEW

Latin America refers to a region that comprises Mexico, the Caribbean, and all the countries of South America. There are approximately 26 countries in the region with a total population of about 500 million people and a gross domestic product in the neighborhood of US$1.7 trillion.

Spanish is spoken in most Latin American countries with the exception of Brazil, where Portuguese is the primary language, and other smaller countries where English is spoken.

Most of the better-known multinational companies have subsidiaries throughout Latin America. The countries with the most foreign economic activity are Argentina, Brazil, Chile, Colombia, Mexico, and Venezuela. There are also a number of large local companies that are publicly traded on the stock exchanges in these countries. Because there are 26 countries in Latin America there are 26 different job markets.

The job market is divided into three sectors:

1. The public sector includes local, state, and federal governments, which account for approximately 22 percent of the workforce.

2. The corporate sector, which can be defined as large companies that are quoted on the major stock exchanges, accounts for about 25 percent of the workforce.

3. The private sector is made up of all small, medium, and large privately owned companies, independent professionals, and so on. This sector accounts for approximately 53 percent of the job market.

RESUME SPECIFICS

When preparing a resume for a position in Latin America, one should understand that the greatest employment opportunities for expatriates are likely be the subsidiaries of international companies or large local public companies. Because English is the international business language, the resume should be written in English, as well as Spanish or Portuguese, if so requested. The average resume length is two to three pages.

Keep in mind that a curriculum vitae (CV) is a selling tool or brochure and not merely a detailed autobiography. In writing a CV, the applicant should be advertising the advantages of his or her services. A curriculum vitae should include important items such as your name, address, contact telephone numbers, e-mail, and so on. It should also highlight your education, as well as languages spoken. Work experience should be outlined in reverse chronological order with the most recent one listed first. It is important to describe the business of the employer, the company's products or activities, as well as the positions you have occupied. Make sure that the scope of the position is described, such as the amount of sales, responsibility, or the number of people supervised. List the major accomplishments of each position. Availability to relocate or travel should also be mentioned.

COVER LETTERS

Your cover letter should be only one page in length, and should succinctly describe your work experience, as well as the type of position you are seeking. Specifically request a personal interview. Follow up the letter with a telephone call.

If responding to an advertisement, be sure to follow the instructions outlined in the ad. Do your homework to determine to whom the letter and CV should be addressed. Generally, you should address it to the human resources manager and/or the potential hiring manager. Also, take the time to tailor your CV to the company you are approaching. Do not be afraid to send your CV out again a few weeks after the first mailing, perhaps this time to different executives within the target company.

JOB INFORMATION SOURCES

Internet Sites

In addition to the internationally known portals, such as America Online (AOL), Yahoo!, and so on, many new Internet sites have started up that target the Spanish-speaking audience. Some of these are:

www.español.yahoo.com
www.ole.es
www.elsitio.com
www.yupi.com
www.starmedia.com
www.quepasa.com

Malaysia

May T. Lim, Signium International

COUNTRY OVERVIEW

Malaysia is a tropical paradise situated seven degrees north of the equator in the heart of Southeast Asia. It comprises peninsular Malaysia and the two states of Sabah and Sarawak on the island of Borneo. Together, they cover a total area of 329,758 square kilometers. The climate is warm and humid throughout the year, with cooler temperatures in the hill resorts. Temperatures range from 21°C to 32°C. Malaysia is eight hours ahead of Greenwich mean time and 16 hours ahead of the U.S. Pacific standard time.

Malaysia is a multiracial country with a population of approximately 21.3 million consisting of Malays, Chinese, and Indians and a very diverse group of indigenous people in Sabah and Sarawak. Bahasa Melayu is the national language, but English is widely used. Although Islam is the official religion, Buddhism, Hinduism, Christianity, and other religions are practiced freely.

Malaysia is made up of 13 states and two federal territories—Kuala Lumpur (the capital), and Labuan, an island off the coast of Sabah. Nine of the states have hereditary rulers, from which the Supreme Head of State, the *Yang Di-Pertuan Agong* (king) is elected every five years. The government is a parliamentary democracy, with a constitutional monarch as head of state. A prime minister serves as head of the government and of the Cabinet of Ministers.

Malaysia has an open economy that welcomes foreign investors in a wide range of manufacturing and related support service sectors. International companies feel comfortable working in a business environment that is geared toward information technology and where legal and accounting practices are derived from the British system.

Manufacturing forms the largest single component of Malaysia's economy. This sector has progressed from import-substitution and labor-intensive industries to export-oriented, high technology, and capital-intensive industries. Today, Malaysia is one of the world's leading exporters of semiconductors, audio and video products, room air conditioners, and products manufactured from the natural resources of rubber, palm, timber, and petroleum.

RESUME SPECIFICS

Education

List schools, colleges, and/or universities attended, stating year of graduation, major, and certificate obtained.

Extracurricular Activities

> Describe any extracurricular activity in which you participated.

Awards/Honors

> List any awards or honors received for scholastic achievement or outstanding performance in other areas.

Additional Education/Specialized Training

> Any additional college or university courses or training in specialized areas should be mentioned here.

Work Experience

> List names of employers, job titles, employment dates, details of work, and responsibilities held. Emphasize information that is relevant to the position for which you are applying.

Achievements/Accomplishments

> Any awards, special recognition, or promotions received during employment should be highlighted.

Special Skills

> Proficiency in foreign languages and knowledge of specific computer programs should be noted.

Professional Affiliations

> List any professional affiliations relevant to your focus area. Include information about your activities within the organization and any leadership roles.

Military Experience

> Include information about your military service, if applicable. State the focus of your training, responsibilities, and any managerial positions. Include dates and location of service.

Volunteer Experience

> Any volunteer experience that you have initiated or participated in should be described. This section may include activities with associations, clubs, or areas of personal interest.

Personal Information

> Describe personal interests; list marital status, age, gender, and any other relevant information.

References

> These should be either character or professional references. These people should be acquainted with your work performance and your character, and be rather recent in time.

RESUME PRESENTATION

Format

Your resume should present a clear picture of your education, employment, and important experiences that might interest an employer. The information can be arranged either chronologically (oldest experience first), reverse chronologically (most recent experience first), or functionally (grouped by experience).

Layout

Your resume should begin with a description of your educational background, followed by your work experience and other details, and should end with your list of references.

Length

Your resume should be no longer than two pages.

Attachments

Certificates, transcripts, and letters of reference need not be included with your application unless specifically requested. Otherwise, these can be presented at the interview. Any documents attached to your resume should be copies, not originals.

A small photo may be included with the resume, as this allows the reader to put a face with a name for future reference.

E-mail Applications

This is becoming increasingly acceptable to employers. Always attach your resume with your letter/e-mail. Video recordings are not recommended.

COVER LETTERS

Content/Detail

An application should always include a personalized cover letter and a complete resume. Your letter should start by stating the position for which you are applying. Explain your interest in the job and emphasize relevant experiences.

Length

A personal cover letter of one page is usually sufficient, typed in A4 format.

Note: A handwritten letter is acceptable, provided that the writing is legible.

JOB INFORMATION SOURCES

Newspapers

The daily newspapers in Malaysia come in three languages: Malay, English, and Mandarin. All of them contain employment ads.

- ▶ *New Straits Times* (English); web site: www.nstpi.com.my
- ▶ *China Press* (Mandarin)
- ▶ *The Star* (English); web site: www.thestar.com.my
- ▶ *The Malay Mail* (English)

- *Nanyang Siang Pao* (Mandarin)
- *Sin Chew Jit Poh* (Mandarin)
- *Utusan Melayu* (Malay)

Internet Sites

Companies usually advertise open positions on their own web sites. It would be worthwhile to look for companies in your field of interest for job openings.

Telephone Directory

The telephone directory Yellow Pages list companies under the relevant trade heading. This can be a good way to start looking for companies that interest you.

WORK PERMITS/VISAS

Visitors must be in possession of valid passports or other internationally recognized travel documents endorsed for traveling in Malaysia. The documents must be valid for a period of at least six months beyond the time of stay allowed in Malaysia.

Visa Exemption

No visas are required for citizens of British Commonwealth countries (except Bangladesh, India, Pakistan, and Sri Lanka), British Protected Persons, or citizens of the Republic of Ireland, Switzerland, Netherlands, San Marino, and Liechtenstein.

Three-Month Visa-Free Visit

Citizens of Albania, Algeria, Argentina, Austria, Bahrain, Belgium, Bosnia, Czech Republic, Denmark, Egypt, Finland, France, Germany, Hungary, Iceland, Italy, Japan, Jordan, Kuwait, Lebanon, Luxembourg, Morocco, Norway, Oman, Qatar, Saudi Arabia, Slovakia, South Korea, Spain, Sweden, Tunisia, Turkey, Turkmenistan, United Arab Emirates, United States, and Yemen are eligible for three-month visa-free visits.

One-Month Visa-Free Visit

Applicable to citizens of ASEAN countries.

Residence and Work Permits

Residence and work permits are required for all foreign citizens who want to work in Malaysia. Work permits can be applied for only after you have signed an employment contract. A written offer of employment must accompany the work permit application. As regulations may change from time to time, it is advisable to check with the nearest Malaysian embassy with regard to visa and work permit applications.

INTERVIEW ADVICE

- Feel free to telephone the contact person listed in the employment advertisement before sending in your application for further details or just to introduce yourself. However, do not persistently telephone for the status of the recruitment process.
- It is wise to avoid discussing salary and other parts of the compensation package early in the process. However, if requested, you should state your salary requirements.

CULTURAL ADVICE

▶ To brag or appear aggressive or overly ambitious may be considered rude. It is wiser to be modest and tactful.

▶ There are severe penalties for drug possession or drug use, and for driving with any amount of liquor in your system.

▶ In Malaysia's multiracial society, it is important to be sensitive to racial and cultural customs and traditions.

▶ Religious differences must be respected and observed.

Mexico

José Hernandez

COUNTRY OVERVIEW

There are currently more than 90 million inhabitants in Mexico, and an annual growth rate of 2.2 percent. Approximately 61 percent of the population is mestizo (mixture of Spanish and native blood), 30 percent are pure native, and about 9 percent are of European descent. Mexico City in Distrito Federal (D.F.) is the capital city. Monterrey, Guadalajara, Queretaro, and Toluca are also important industrial cities.

Three powers—executive, legislative, and judicial—constitute the Mexican government. The federal government is headed by a president (executive power), elected by the people. Every Mexican has the right to vote at 18. The president leads the country for a six-year period.

Because almost all of the Mexican population is Catholic, religion plays an important role in the history and culture of the country. The official language of the country is Spanish. Yet, in some rural areas, dialects like Nahuatl, Maya, Otomi, Mixteco, and Zapoteco are still spoken. Staff at most business organizations and tourist facilities speak and understand English. The peso is the official currency in Mexico. Business offices are open normally from 8:00 A.M. to 6:00 P.M. five days a week.

RESUME SPECIFICS

Personal Information

Always begin your resume/CV with your personal presentation: name, place of birth, birth date, civil status, address, telephone, and e-mail.

Objectives

Describe your professional objectives such as career goals, type of position that you would like to obtain, and so forth.

Education

Begin with listing your education levels, starting with the title of the degree, name of the university, location, dates, and so on. If you have a second degree such as a master's, describe it. List any additional training in this section.

Work Experience

List all of your work experience in chronological order. Give the details, area of responsibility, positions, special tasks or projects executed, and important achievements and results.

Special Skills

> Proficiency in foreign languages and knowledge of specific computer programs should be highlighted.

Attachments

> Any extra documents attached to your resume should be photocopies.

Length

> Your resume/CV can be five or six pages in length up to a maximum of 10.

BUSINESS ORGANIZATIONS

> Cámara Nacional de Comercio de la Ciudad de México
> Paseo de la Reforma 42-3
> Mexico D.F.
> Phone: 52+5705-0549
>
> World Trade Center Mexico City
> Montecito 38-34 Col. Nápoles
> Mexico D.F.
> Phone: 52+5682-9822, 5682-9581
>
> World Trade Center Guadalajara
> Av. de las Rosas No. 2965. Col. Miravalle
> Guadalajara, Jalisco
> Phone: 52+3671-0000

JOB INFORMATION SOURCES

Internet Sites

> The key Internet sites for job openings are:
>
> www.laborum.com.mx
> www.banir.com.mx
> www.el-universal.com.mx
> www.wtcmexico.com

CULTURAL ADVICE

> ▶ It is important to understand that the differences between doing business in Mexico and in other countries are more subtle and perhaps more complicated than initial impressions might indicate.
> ▶ Class distinctions are marked, and position within Mexican society is important in daily social and business life. Mexican executives are interested in rank and status, which include attendance at the right schools, churches, and so on, and which provide important lifelong ties. The use of titles is common, and rank in a company is important.
> ▶ Relationships are accorded high priority by Mexicans, both professional and familial. In a business setting, establishing the relationship will often take priority over the business itself, especially when meeting a new colleague.

▶ Mexicans are very hospitable people. However, this more relaxed attitude should not be misunderstood. It does not mean that Mexicans don't care. On the contrary, it simply means that they have other priorities.

Business Protocol

▶ Be on time for your appointment, but expect your Mexican counterparts to be 15 to 30 minutes late. Do not complain about their lateness. Mexicans believe people are more important than time schedules.

▶ During a meeting, be prepared for interruptions such as telephone calls and people dropping in. Never show your irritation at these delays.

▶ If you are a newcomer to the Mexican market, be prepared to make small talk to develop the relationship before a Mexican will make a commitment.

▶ Conversation is important; your job and home country, travel, and arts and literature are good topics.

▶ Always use a person's title: Doctor, Ingeniero (Engineer), Arquitecto (Architect), or Licenciado (abbreviated Lic., designating a person with a bachelor's degree). Titles should be included on business cards. Refer to a secretary as Señorita, regardless of her age or marital status. Do not use first names until your Mexican counterpart initiates it.

▶ Mexicans are very appreciative and kind to those who attempt to speak Spanish. To avoid embarrassment, be sure to check questionable words and phrases with a fluent associate.

▶ If you expect to work in Mexico over a long period of time, Spanish lessons are a worthwhile investment.

Business Attire

▶ Conservative business dress is appropriate. For men, dark suits, ties, and black shoes are the norm. Leave your jacket on and your tie fastened during a meeting unless your host suggests that you relax a little. Women in business generally stick to dark suits or nice dresses, with makeup and heels.

▶ Mexicans are very status conscious, even down to their watches, and will most certainly observe what you are wearing.

Netherlands

Cor Hoeboer, Mercuri Urval

COUNTRY OVERVIEW

The Netherlands, also known as Holland, borders on the east side with Germany, on the south with Belgium, and on the north and west with the North Sea. The official language is Dutch. Most people speak English, and other languages, such as German and French, are also spoken by a large number of people.

Approximately 16 million people live in this small country of a little over 40 million square meters. This makes the Netherlands one of the most densely populated countries in the world. Almost all areas in the Netherlands are cultivated to make the most use of every available square inch. A large part of the country lies below sea level and has been conquered in a hard-fought battle with the sea. Some people jokingly say: "God created the world and the Dutch created their own country." Even today, the process of gaining land through the creation of so-called polders continues.

The capital of the Netherlands is Amsterdam, a beautiful city with a historic center that still shows the wealth and prosperity of Holland in the seventeenth century. Long canals and monumental historic buildings all lie within walking distance. Amsterdam has always been a city where people of all kinds live together in a modern and liberal way. The Netherlands is a constitutional monarchy with (at present) a queen as the head of state. She plays a symbolic role in Dutch politics. The real political power lies with parliament, which is democratically elected every four years. From the parliament, an executive government is formed on the basis of the outcome of the parliamentary elections. The head of the Dutch government is the prime minister, who is supported by a number of advisory ministers.

To many Dutch, the Netherlands has two main areas: the Randstad and the rest of the Netherlands. The Randstad consists of Rotterdam (the largest seaport in the world), The Hague (the seat of government), Amsterdam (which has one of the largest airports in Europe), and Utrecht (in the center of the Netherlands). In these cities, and in the towns between them, the great majority of jobs are to be had. This area is very densely populated and the influences of other cultures have turned it into a multicultural environment. The rest of the Netherlands, however, is by no means backward. It is only less densely populated and less influenced by other cultures. Industrial development and know-how are spread equally throughout all areas of the Netherlands.

The Netherlands, one of the founders of the European Union, is a market economy with an extensive social welfare system. There is a heartfelt feeling among the Dutch that there is a societal duty to take care of the less fortunate. Medical care and a basic income are considered inalienable rights for everyone. There are strong rules in the Netherlands against discrimination based on sex, race, religion, and age, and all people are considered and treated as equal. The current economic climate in the Netherlands is very good. The number of job vacancies is very high and, for certain types of jobs, exceeds the number of people available in the market.

RESUME SPECIFICS

In general, write a tailor-made resume for each application. Elaborate on the experience you have that is relevant to that particular job.

Education

Provide the relevant data in your educational history in a clear and concise way:

- ▶ When did you start your education?
- ▶ Did you finish it, and if so when and how (diploma, title, certificate)?
- ▶ What were the subjects in which you majored or received your degree?
- ▶ Describe your practical training or student internships briefly, stating assignments and when and where each was performed.

Extracurricular Activities

Describe your extracurricular activities. Do not make this list too long—make sure that you mention only the activities that point to certain personal skills (e.g., organizing, leading, initiating, etc.).

Awards/Honors

List any awards and honors received for scholastic achievement or outstanding performance in other areas.

Note: Do not boast! The Dutch do not like people who brag too much about their achievements.

Additional Education/Specialized Training

Additional courses or training in specialized areas should be mentioned in this context. Mention only those courses and training that are relevant for the position for which you are applying.

Work Experience

Start with specifying the employment dates, then give your job title and the name of the employer. Specify whether your position was a full- or a part-time job. Provide a clear and concise picture of your duties and responsibilities. Give some insight into the results that you achieved. Describe how your skills have developed. If you had more than one position with the same employer, list the other job(s) in a separate paragraph. Emphasize the information that is relevant to the position for which you are applying. Explain gaps in your track record. Do not go into them too deeply, but try to show how they were relevant for your development.

Achievements/Accomplishments

Your achievements and accomplishments should be integrated into the description of your work experience (except when they lie outside your job or the responsibilities of your position; then they should be mentioned separately in a subsection).

Special Skills

Special skills, such as languages and knowledge of specific computer programs, should be noted separately to give the person who reads the CV a quick insight into your skills.

Professional Affiliations

List involvement with organizations, such as membership in the work council, special interest groups, and so on.

Military Experience

If service in the military is mandatory, you should mention the focus of your training, the field of responsibility, and, if relevant, the leadership experience acquired.

Volunteer Experience

If you are actively involved in associations, clubs, or areas of personal interest connected to schools, charities, sports, and so on, mention these briefly. Also briefly describe the volunteer experience that you have acquired.

Personal information

Mention your hobbies, but do not elaborate on them too much.

References

Mention only references connected with your work experience. References should preferably be your (ex)managers or at least be people who are well-acquainted with your work. The names provided should be recent in time. Ask in advance for their permission to be listed as references. Alternatively, you can also state that references will be provided upon request.

RESUME PRESENTATION

Format and Layout

Send your letter to the person mentioned in the ad or to the personnel department. Remember that the purpose of your resume is to give your future employer a clear picture of your personal, educational, and professional experience. Your information should be easy to read. Be complete, but do not include too much detail. Recognize that your reader probably has many more CVs to read.

Always begin your CV with your name, address, telephone number, e-mail address, marital status, and nationality. After this, list your educational background followed by your professional career, both listed in chronological order. End your CV by describing personal details and references.

Length

Your resume should be no longer than two or three pages.

Attachments

Grades, certificates, and letters of reference need not be included with your application. If you want to include them, do not send originals since they can get lost. If you wish, you may include a picture with your application.

Note: For more advanced positions, photos are considered to be inappropriate.

E-mail Applications

It is more and more common for applications to be sent via e-mail. Treat the e-mail just as you would a normal application (i.e., send both an application letter and an attached CV). Video letters, CD-ROMs or other forms of presentation should be used only if they are appropriate for the type of job applied for.

COVER LETTERS

Always include a personalized cover letter with your resume. Do not send handwritten letters unless specifically requested. A personal cover letter of approximately one page is normal. The format of the letter should be A4.

Content/Detail

Start your cover letter by noting the position for which you are applying. Make the letter a personal one; your reader wants to get an impression of the individual with whom he or she is dealing. Begin with a brief description of your present position, your present employer, and the field in which you work. Explain why you are applying—what motivates your application. Show the link between your present position and the one for which you are applying. Explain why you believe that you are a suitable candidate. Realize that you have only one chance to get the reader's attention, so try to catch your audience. Be original, but do not try to be funny. Be yourself, be specific—and be sincere. Do not brag.

JOB INFORMATION SOURCES

The majority of job vacancies are published in the daily newspapers, both regional and national, on Saturday. Other places where you can find a large number of employment ads are trade journals and the special recruitment publications.

Newspapers

The most popular national newspapers are:

Dagblad de Telegraaf
Basisweg 30
1043 AP Amsterdam
Phone: (+31)20 5859111
Web site: www.telegraaf.nl

Algemeen Dagblad
Marten Meesweg 35
3068 AV Rotterdam
Phone: (+31)10 4067211
Web site: www.ad.nl

de Volkskrant
Perscombinatie
Wibautstraat 131
1091 GL Amsterdam
Phone: (+31)20 5629222
Web site: www.volkskrant.nl

NRC Handelsblad
Marten Meesweg 35
3068AV Rotterdam
Phone: (+31)10 4067211
Web site: www.nrc.nl

Recruitment Publication

A publication specializing in recruitment ads is:

Intermediair (higher and academic-level age: up to and including age 45)
VNU Business Publications
Rijnsburgstraat 11
1059 AT Amsterdam
Phone: (+31)20 4875487
Web site: www.intermediair.nl

Trade Journals

If you want to make use of these you will have to do some research. Try to find them through the Dutch chambers of commerce or through your own national trade organizations.

Internet Sites

Most recruitment ads are also found on the Internet. Ads are usually placed in Dutch. Some sites are:

www.jobnews.nl
www.IT-jobworld.nl
www.mercuri-urval.com

Country Employment Offices

The Dutch employment bureau can also help you to get started. Local addresses can be found at the web site of the Arbeidsbureau (www.arbeidsbureau.nl).

WORK PERMITS/VISAS

Residence Permits/Employment Permits

All foreigners who want to get a job in the Netherlands must obtain a residence permit for themselves and their families. Depending on your nationality, a residence permit is needed either before entering the country or after arrival. Check which procedure to follow with the Dutch embassy in your country. To apply for a residence permit, the person filing the application should submit a letter stating the terms of employment. If you are from a country outside the European Union or the European Economic Area, you also need an employment permit before you can start working in the Netherlands. If you do not have an employment permit, it is impossible to obtain a residence permit. The two are closely connected.

Again, for further details, check with your local Dutch embassy or see the web site www.bz.minbuza.nl.

Note: You should be privately insured for medical expenses.

INTERVIEW ADVICE

- ▶ A normal recruitment and selection process consists of a number of interviews often followed by an assessment and finalized with a meeting in which the terms and conditions are discussed.
- ▶ Feel free to call the contact person for further details, but only if you want to obtain or give specific information.
- ▶ Prepare yourself for the interview. Check the Internet for information about the company and, if possible, about the job.
- ▶ Ask questions, but do not take the lead.
- ▶ Show that you are successful on your own but also that you function well as part of a team.
- ▶ Prepare a statement regarding your motivation for the job; have a clear idea of what you want to achieve in the new position.
- ▶ Do not start salary discussions too early in the process. The only reason for discussing salaries during a first interview is to establish whether there is a basis to continue the process.
- ▶ Be assertive but do not be too aggressive. Do not brag.
- ▶ Show ambition and motivation, but too much ambition is deadly.
- ▶ The style of communication in the Netherlands is quite direct. Be prepared to receive pointed, and sometimes personal, questions. Answer them in a clear and direct way.
- ▶ Be on time. Prepare for the possibility of traffic jams during your journey to the interview.
- ▶ Show your professionalism, but be modest about it.
- ▶ Expect people to give their opinions freely. Show respect for their ideas, but do not hesitate to give your own.

Norway

Sven Iversen, Amrop International

COUNTRY OVERVIEW

Norway is one of the five Nordic nations that lie within the northern stretches of the European continent. The country is long and narrow, with more than 30 percent of the land covered by forests, rivers, and lakes, and nearly half covered by mountain ranges.

There are about 4.3 million Norwegians. Though most live in urban areas, they still enjoy uncrowded surroundings. Oslo is Norway's capital with a population of approximately half a million people. In addition to being the seat of government, Oslo is the business and cultural capital of the nation. Other major cities include Bergen, Trondheim, Stavanger, and Tromsø.

Norway is a constitutional monarchy that adopted its own constitution on May 17, 1814. Although the king has no real political power, the Royal Family enjoys a strong position among the Norwegian people. The country is a democracy, led by a parliament elected every four years, and an executive government, with a prime minister and advisory ministers. The prime minister is the head of Norway's government. Norway has a market economy, with an extensive social welfare system.

Norwegian per capita income ranks among the world's highest. North Sea oil and gas fields are one of the cornerstones of the Norwegian economy. Other major industries in Norway include fisheries, pulp and paper, forestry, mining, manufacturing, and shipping.

Norway is a member of NATO and an associate member of the West European Union. Through the United Nations, where Norwegian Trygve Lie was the first Secretary General, Norway works at many levels. Norwegians participate in many of the UN peacekeeping forces. Norway also seeks to create peace in other ways, and has played a vital role in a number of peace processes in unstable corners of the world. For several decades, Norway has cooperated extensively on political and practical issues with the other Nordic countries. Nordic nationals have been able to travel freely within the Nordic countries without a passport for many years, and the Nordic countries have a common labor market and comprehensive cooperation in the sphere of social welfare. In 1960, Norway became a member of the European Free Trade Association (EFTA). In 1994, the EU and EFTA countries established the European Economic Area (EEA), but the same year a narrow majority of the population voted against joining the European Union.

The country has two official Norwegian language-forms that are quite similar. The principal language is Bokmål, which developed from urban dialects and has historically been influenced by Danish. Nynorsk, the other language, is strongly influenced by dialects spoken in the districts. Approximately 16 percent of the young attend schools where Nynorsk is the primary language. However, most Norwegians are very comfortable engaging in a business or social conversation in English.

RESUME SPECIFICS

Education

Explain your focus areas during upper secondary school/high school, with reference to specific courses and programs. Also, state your graduation year and if you have studied abroad. Continue with a description of your college/university education. State your graduation year, major, and education title. Briefly describe any student internship or diploma work: length of time, number of credits, and references.

Extracurricular Activities

Describe any extracurricular activities in which you participated, such as arranging different types of student activities, working within the student administration, and so on.

Awards/Honors

List any awards and honors received for scholastic achievement or outstanding performance in other areas.

Additional Education/Specialized Training

Any additional college or university courses should be mentioned in this context. Also, include courses or training in specialized areas, such as languages, computers, or sales.

Work Experience

List your job titles and names of the employers in a reverse chronological order. Specify the employment dates and whether each was a full-time or a part-time job. Give the details of your work and your fields of responsibility. Emphasize information that is relevant to the position for which you are applying. Summer jobs and shorter periods of employment performed prior to your professional career should be summarized.

If there are gaps in employment history, it is important that you explain the reason for each gap in reasonable detail. Also, for part-time employment, explain the reason why you chose not to work full-time.

Achievements/Accomplishments

Any awards, special recognition, or promotions received during employment should be highlighted.

Special Skills

Proficiency in foreign languages and knowledge of specific computer programs should be noted.

Professional Affiliations

List any professional affiliations relevant to your focus area. Include information about your involvement with activities within the organization or any leadership roles.

Military Experience

Include information in your resume/CV about your military service (which is mandatory in Norway).

Volunteer Experience

Any previous or current honorary post should be described. These may include activities with associations, clubs, or areas of personal interest.

Personal Information

List your personal interests such as sports activities, gardening, reading, rebuilding old cars, politics, and so on. There is no need to go into detail. Family activities and hobbies may be mixed in with this section.

References

The references you select should be connected to your professional experience, such as previous managers. These people should be well acquainted with your work performance, and be rather recent in time. It should be noted whether or not these references can be contacted without your prior consent.

RESUME PRESENTATION

Format and Layout

Your resume/CV should represent a clear picture of your education, internships, and employment, as well as other important experiences that might interest an employer, such as professional association memberships. A reverse chronologically arranged list with the aforementioned headings is best. CVs arranged by function are not used in Norway.

Note: Always begin your resume/CV by describing your educational background, followed by the details of your professional experience.

Length

Your resume/CV should be no longer than two pages.

Attachments

Grades, certificates, and letters of reference do not have to be included with your application, unless specifically requested. If you prefer to attach such documents, choose your most recent grades and a letter of reference from your current employer.

Note: Any documents attached to your resume should be copies, as these documents in most cases will not be returned to you. Any thesis papers or diploma work should not be sent initially.

To personalize an application with a small photo is becoming more and more accepted. Including a photo gives the reader a more vivid picture of the person and allows the reader to put a face with a name for future reference.

E-mail Applications

It is increasingly more common that employers in Norway accept, appreciate, and prioritize applications via e-mail. In this case, always attach your resume to the letter/e-mail. Do not send your application on a floppy disk. Video recordings are usually not recommended.

Other

Note: It is recommended that you have copies of grades, certificates, or letters of reference certified or verified by an official person.

COVER LETTERS

An application should always include a personalized cover letter and complete resume. Grades, certificates, and letters of reference or recommendations should not be attached unless specified in the employment ad.

A personal cover letter of one page is usually sufficient. A typed application in A4 format is preferred; however, a handwritten letter is acceptable, provided that the writing is legible.

Content/Detail

The cover letter has one important objective—to get an opportunity to meet the employer. Your cover letter should start with a phrase stating the position for which you are applying. Remember that the letter aims to raise the reader's interest, so try to let your personality influence the content. Allow the reader to see your personality, motivation, intellectual strength, and ability to communicate. Everything you say in the letter should also be found in your resume/CV. Briefly describe your current position. Also, state the date when you entered your current position and your personal and professional development within the company. Explain why you are applying for this job. Given the limited space you have in a cover letter, there is no need to describe your background in detail, as this information is provided in the resume/CV.

Note: If you are unemployed at present, you should state that in the letter.

JOB INFORMATION SOURCES

Newspapers

Daily papers, trade journals, and the like all contain employment ads. The most popular daily papers are *Dagens Naeringsliv, Aftenposten, Adresseavisen, Bergens Tidende, Stavanger Aftenblad,* and *Nordlys.* No Norwegian newspaper has a complete supplement of recruitment ads in any language but Norwegian. However, you do find that these publications contain separate ads in different languages, primarily in English.

Dagens Naeringsliv (covers all of Norway)
Phone: +47 22 00 10 00

Aftenposten (all of Norway)
Phone: +47 22 86 30 00

Note: *Aftenposten* is the number one employment ad paper in Norway and lists ads from all parts of the country.

Bergens Tidende (daily news of Bergen and the west coast area)
Phone: +47 55 21 45 00

Adresseavisen (covers Trondheim and the central area)
Phone: +47 72 50 00 00

Stavanger Aftenblad (Stavanger and the west coast area)
Phone: +47 51 50 00 00

Nordlys (Tromso and the northern area)
Phone: +47 77 62 35 00

Chamber of Commerce

Oslo Chamber of Commerce
Box 2874 Solli
N-0230 Oslo
Phone: +47 22 55 74 00
Fax: +47 22 55 89 53
E-mail: chamber@online.no

Internet Sites

Through the Internet, companies usually advertise open positions on their web sites. It may be worthwhile to look for companies in your field of interest. The most popular employment web sites in Norway are:

www.stepstone.no (the largest commercial site).
www.aetat.no.
www.jobworld.no (IT-related jobs).
www.jobline.no.
www.finn.no (lists all jobs advertised in the major daily newspapers including
   Aftenposten).
www.topjobs.no.

Telephone Directory

In the Norwegian telephone directory Yellow Pages (www.gulesider.no), you will find companies listed under the relevant trade headings. This can be a fruitful way to start looking for companies that interest you. In the Pink Pages, all companies are listed in alphabetical order.

Country Employment Office

The Norwegian Employment Service, Arbeidsmarkedsetaten, lists all open jobs on its web site, www.aetat.no.

Note: This web site also gives useful information tips about working and living in Norway.

WORK PERMITS/VISAS

Visas

A business or permanent residence visa is required for most foreign visitors staying more than three months.

Note: Applications for visas are made on a special form that may be obtained from the Norwegian mission in the applicant's country of residence.

Residence and Work Permits

When entering Norway, you must have a passport or identity papers that are recognized by the Norwegian authorities as valid travel documents. European Economic Area nationals and members of their families who wish to stay in Norway for more than three months must have residence permits. You do not need a residence permit if, as an EEA national, you work in Norway but retain a place of residence in your country of origin and return home once a week on the average.

If you wish to obtain a residence permit in Norway, you may contact either the police or a Norwegian foreign service mission abroad. You will be given an application form with instructions specifying which documents you should enclose with your application. If you have not obtained a residence permit through a Norwegian foreign service mission (embassy or consulate), you must register with the Norwegian police within three months of your arrival in Norway. If a residence permit has already been granted, or if you normally return to your home in another EEA country at least once a week, you must register with the police within one week of your arrival in Norway.

If you intend to work in Norway, you must submit documentation from your employer stating that you are employed (proof of employment—*ansettelsesbevis*). A form for this purpose is available from the police or any Norwegian foreign service mission. An employed person may normally be accompanied by family members: spouse, children, and/or parents. A residence permit is normally valid for five years. A residence permit may be extended if the grounds on which it was granted still apply. Family members are granted residence permits for the same period of time as the principal person. If you are granted leave of residence in Norway, you will receive a special residence document that confirms this. This permit is issued by the police.

The police or Norwegian foreign service mission will supply further details on request.

For further information, please contact:

Directorate of Immigration
P.O. Box 8108
Department N-0032
Oslo, Norway

INTERVIEW ADVICE

▶ Knowledge of the Norwegian language is a prerequisite for obtaining most jobs in Norway. However, for certain categories within the technical sector and some positions in the hotel and restaurant industry, a good command of English may suffice. If you have received a job offer in Norway, you are entitled to free Norwegian language tuition offered by the municipal authorities.

▶ Feel free to telephone the contact person listed in the employment advertisement before sending in your application, for further details, or just to introduce yourself. However, do not persistently telephone for the status of the recruitment process.

▶ Be prepared for the interview—read available information about the company. If you have a basic knowledge of the company, you will appear more confident in the interview.

▶ It is wise to avoid discussing salary and other parts of the compensation package early in the process. However, if requested, you should state your salary preference.

▶ Norway has a history of strong trade unions, which means that the employee's rights are carefully regulated by labor laws and collective agreements. For example, the minimum regulated vacation by law is four weeks per year.

CULTURAL ADVICE

▶ To other Europeans, Norwegians can seem inscrutable: worldly, but isolated; liberated, yet morally square. As a people they are tight-knit, but as individuals they can be aloof to one another. On close inspection, Norwegians are less homogeneous than their reputation suggests.

▶ Norwegians are thinkers and weighers of opinion. Neither anger nor joy slips out uncontrolled. Forming an opinion or making an important decision takes time. This goes for individuals as well as companies and government. Once a stand is taken, the Norwegians are sometimes viewed as stubborn.

▶ In international business negotiations, Norwegians roll with the flow better than they used to. Honest to a fault, some may point out the negatives of their own proposal in greater detail than the positives. They also tend to lay their cards on the table openly, and to react skeptically when a foreign counterpart uses more discreet or circular approaches. For most Norwegians, business is business, not an art or way of life.

▶ Norwegians are notorious readers—no country publishes more books per inhabitant. In addition, more than 200 newspapers are published, and the average household subscribes to two of them.

Philippines

Ellen N. Escalona, Signium International ZMG

COUNTRY OVERVIEW

The Philippine archipelago lies in Southeast Asia. Its position has led to its becoming a cultural crossroads that forged the unique cultural and racial blend known to the world as Filipino. The archipelago numbers some 7,100 islands, 11 of which make up 94 percent of the Philippine landmass. Two of these islands, Luzon and Mindanao, together with the cluster of the Visayan Islands that separate them, represent the three principal regions of the archipelago. These three regions are represented by the three stars on the Philippine flag. Topographically, the Philippines are broken up by the sea, which gives the country one of the longest coastlines of any nation in the world. Most Filipinos live on or near the coast.

The Republic of the Philippines has a population of 75 million with about 15 percent living in Manila, the capital city. It is the only Catholic country in Asia. Over 90 percent of the population claims to follow the Catholic faith. The largest of the minority religious groups are the Muslims, who live chiefly on Mindanao and in the Sulu archipelago.

The geography and history of the country have produced a multiplicity of languages, some 80 dialects in total. Tagalog is the national language, but English remains the language of commerce, government, international relations, and education.

It is hot and humid year-round. The weather can be roughly divided into the dry season (January to June) and the wet season (July to December).

The country likes to promote itself as the place where "Asia wears a smile" and the locals are, by and large, exceptionally friendly and helpful.

RESUME SPECIFICS

Education

Indicate the university/school you graduated from, the year, and the area(s) you majored in. Also include special courses that were taken. Do not explain information that is already implied. If you are a college graduate, there is no reason to describe your high school education.

Extracurricular Activities

State the extracurricular activities you participated in, the position(s) you held, and the duration, duties, and responsibilities.

Awards/Honors

Indicate academic awards and honors received—citations and other commendations.

Specialized Training

List special training courses and other job-specific seminars attended.

Work Experience

Start with describing your most recent position, and work back. Devote the most attention to recent employment; detail only the last four or five positions from the past 10 years. It is not necessary to show every position change with the same employer. Give a brief synopsis of your actual work experience. If you have had no work experience, or a very spotty record, leave out the employment synopsis entirely (but be prepared to talk about it at the interview).

Achievements/Accomplishments

Include awards or recognition received during employment. If you have written any books or articles and/or worked on easily recognizable products, indicate these as well.

Special Skills

Describe proficiency in foreign languages, expertise in computer programs, and other highly specialized competencies.

Professional Affiliations

List professional affiliations and other pertinent information about your involvement with such organization(s).

Personal Information

Include date of birth, civil status, and all your contact information. Do not include personal information such as weight, sex, health, children's names, church affiliations, social clubs, and so on.

References

Omit names and contact information of references. You can provide this information later if requested. "References provided on request" is assumed. Should you be asked to provide references, attach a separate sheet with their names and contact numbers. References should be people with whom you have worked who can attest to your character and work habits. They must be able to give corroborating information about your work performance and achievements.

RESUME PRESENTATION

Format and Layout

Clearly outline your work experience, education, and other important experiences. There are different ways of presenting your CV, but the reverse chronological format is preferred. Avoid using fancy fonts to emphasize certain sections. Instead, highlight key information in boldface or by underlining.

Length

Resumes should be no longer than two pages. Even if you have held numerous jobs and have several degrees, you should condense the information so that it attracts the employer's interest immediately. If the information is redundant, the impact is diluted, and the employer's attention will waver.

E-mail Applications

E-mail is evolving to be among the quickest and most convenient ways to send an application. Typically, a Word attachment follows the letter/main body of the e-mail text.

COVER LETTERS

A cover letter is a personal communication, generally typed on quality paper stock. Choose white, ivory, or off-white paper. Avoid tinted paper.

Content/Detail

The cover letter should address a particular person by name, demonstrate that you know something about that organization, and show how your skills would meet its needs. State the position you are applying for, your significant experience in that particular field, and how you could fit into the organization. Attachments such as transcripts of records, certificates, and letters of recommendation may be sent together with the application.

JOB INFORMATION SOURCES

Newspapers

Newspapers are the major source of information regarding job openings in the Philippines. Among the leading newspapers are: *Manila Bulletin*, *The Philippine Daily Inquirer (PDI)*, and *The Philippine Star*.

Note: No one newspaper covers the entire country. Each province carries a local publication.

PDI is considered the number one paper in terms of readership, but *Manila Bulletin* boasts the largest number of employment ads in its weekend supplement. Newspaper web sites:

Manila Bulletin	www.classifiedads.com.ph
	www.mb.com.ph
The Philippine Daily Inquirer	www.inquirer.net
The Philippine Star	www.philstar.com

Internet Sites

The more well-known employment web sites are www.trabaho.com, www.jobstreet.com, www.inquirer.net, www.headhunter.net, and www.jobsDB.com.ph. The leading newspapers also post employment ads on the Internet. In addition, the site www.asiadragons.com/philippines contains general information on business, finance, employment, education, government, arts and culture, and so on.

Telephone Directory

The local telephone directory Yellow Pages section contains a complete government/business listing. This can provide some leads to companies that interest you.

Business Organization/Trade Councils

Philippine Chamber of Commerce and
    Industry
Phone: (632) 833-8591-95
Fax: (632) 833-8895
E-mail: PCCIINTR@mozcom.com
Web site: www.philcham.com

Department of Trade and Industry
E-mail: mis@dti.gov.ph
Web site: www.dti.gov.ph

Department of Foreign Affairs
The Economic Diplomacy Unit
2330 Roxas Boulevard, Pasay City
Phone: (632) 834-4000
Fax: (632) 832-0683
E-mail: webmaster@dfa.gov.ph
Web site: www.dfa.gov.ph/

WORK PERMITS/VISAS

Visas

Consular jurisdiction applies to all visas for the Philippines. Jurisdiction is determined based on your country of residence. A business and permanent residence visa is required for most foreign visitors who intend to stay for a period of time. For more information, you should contact the nearest Philippine embassy or consulate.

Residence and Work Permits

Residence and work permits are required for all foreign citizens who want to work in the Philippines. Proof of employment/contract have to be presented along with the application. Usually, assistance pertaining to applications for residence and work permits is provided by the hiring party. For other necessary documents, see the web site www.info@traveldocs.com.

INTERVIEW ADVICE

▶ If you are responding to a newspaper advertisement, strictly adhere to the job specification in your correspondence and discussions.
▶ The interviewer is to be addressed as Mister or Miss unless specified otherwise.
▶ Dress in business attire for the interview.
▶ Be prompt.
▶ Answer questions as succinctly as possible to avoid straying to unnecessary points.
▶ Ask questions that demonstrate the sophistication of your thinking and your ability to grasp the problems and issues of the job.
▶ Avoid asking questions about salary, benefits, and other perquisites in the first and second interviews. Those will come later, at the time of negotiation.
▶ It is common practice for interviewers to ask personal questions about religion, civil status, age, compensation information, and so on.
▶ Most Filipinos are reserved and nonconfrontational in formal settings. Being too talkative or assertive can be misinterpreted as overconfidence or overselling yourself.

Poland

Dr. Rafal Dutkiewicz and Moritz Herfert, Signium International

COUNTRY OVERVIEW

Poland is the largest country in Central Europe, with an area of 312,683 square kilometers and 38 million inhabitants. Poland borders Germany, the Czech Republic, Slovakia, Ukraine, Belorussia, Lithuania, and Russia (Kaliningrad). In the northern part of the country, there are more than 500 kilometers of coast on the Baltic Sea. The capital, located in central Poland, is Warsaw with 1.7 million inhabitants. Other major cities include Lódz, Kraków, Katowice, Wrocław, Poznan, and Gdansk.

Poland is a democracy. The president, who is directly elected by the people, serves for five years as head of state. The representative body of the people is the Sejm, which elects the prime minister as head of government. Poland is a young and constantly growing market economy. The economic conditions differ significantly between the economic center of the big cities and the poorer countryside. Poland has applied for European Union membership and is expected to enter the EU in the near future.

The official language is Polish. Today, English is the primary foreign language, followed by German, Russian, and French. The vast majority of Poles are Catholic (90 percent), many of whom actively practice their religion.

The upturn in the Polish economy, after its transformation to a free market economy, has led to a successful restructuring of many Polish companies, as well as to an increase in foreign investments.

The largest and most successful Polish companies are:

▶ Telekomunikacja Polska S.A. (telecommunications).
▶ Kombinat Gorniczo-Hutniczy Miedzi (KGHM) S.A. (copper).
▶ Elektrim S.A. (production, trade, services).
▶ Agora S.A. (publishing).
▶ ÿywiec S.A. (brewery)
▶ Procom S.A. (software).

The most important foreign investors are:

▶ Fiat (Italy).
▶ Daewoo (Korea).
▶ Gazprom (Russia).

- ▶ Uni-Credito Italiano (Italy).
- ▶ Hypo-Vereinsbank (Germany).
- ▶ Allied Irish Bank (Ireland).
- ▶ European Bank of Reconstruction & Development (EBRD) (UK).
- ▶ Metro (Germany).
- ▶ Polish-American Enterprise Fund.

RESUME SPECIFICS

Education

State the name of the high school you attended and your graduation year. If there has been any specialization, note that information. More important are the details of your university graduation. List the year of graduation, honors, major, and degree title. If your diploma work is related to your potential employer's focus area, provide the details.

Extracurricular Activities

Any extracurricular activities that show your interest and commitment to the employer's line of work will be of interest to a potential employer.

Awards/Honors

Explain scholarships, student awards, and so on, if relevant.

Additional Education/Specialized Training

Any additional university courses, further education, stays abroad, and so forth, should be mentioned.

Work Experience

University graduates should begin by listing their internships and professional experience as students. With regard to work experience after graduation, list job title, name of employer, and employment dates. Summarize your responsibilities.

Achievements/Accomplishments

Any awards, special recognition, training, or promotion received during employment should be highlighted.

Special Skills

Language, computer, and any other relevant skills should be mentioned.

Professional Affiliations

These should be mentioned, if relevant to your job purpose.

Military Experience

Military service should be briefly noted, along with any special achievements.

Volunteer Experience

Volunteer service may be mentioned.

Personal Information

Briefly summarize your personal interests.

References

It is common to write: "References upon request." If you list them on your CV, make sure that your references have been informed in advance.

RESUME PRESENTATION

Format and Layout

The standard format of a CV:

1. Personal data (name, date of birth, address, marital status, etc.).
2. Educational background.
3. Internships/training.
4. Work experience (positions held, responsibilities).
5. Additional information (e.g., personal interests).

Note: The European chronological description (oldest experience listed first) is more common than the American style (most recent experience listed first). However, either method may be used.

Length

Usually one to two pages, depending on the extent of your professional experience.

Attachments

Passport photos may be attached. If you decide to attach a photo, make sure that it is a recent and representative picture, not a holiday snapshot. Grades, certificates, and letters of reference do not necessarily have to be included with your application, unless requested in the job advertisement.

E-mail Applications

It is more common to send applications by post than by e-mail. However, some employers also accept e-mail applications.

COVER LETTERS

A cover letter should not exceed one page. The perfect motivation letter contains three or four short paragraphs addressing the following questions:

▶ Who am I?
▶ Why should I be of interest to you?
▶ What can I offer my (potential) future employer?
▶ Why am I interested in this particular job?

Do not repeat in detail what you have already written in your CV. Make use of the additional space to present yourself, your skills, and your experience. CVs and motivation letters should be written to be complementary documents.

JOB INFORMATION SOURCES

Newspapers

Both national and local daily papers contain employment ads. The largest selection of job advertisements can be found in *Gazeta Wyborcza* on Monday, in the section entitled "Gazeta o Pracÿ" (regional and national ads). Some ads appear on Wednesday in *Rzeczpospolita*. Also consult specialist publications according to your interests and experience (e.g., Media & Marketing).

Gazeta Wyborcza   www.gazeta.pl-link: praca (jobs)
Rzeczpospolita   www. rzeczpospolita.pl-link: praca (jobs)

Note: Most recruitment ads are in Polish. Bilingual ads or ads in English, German, or French can also be found.

Business Organizations

Izba Przemysÿowo-Handlowa Inwestorów Zagranicznych (Foreign Investors
  Chamber of Commerce)
ul. Krakowskie Przedmieÿcie 47/51
00-071 Warszawa
Phone: (+48 22) 827 22 34

Ogólnopolska Izba Gospodarcza (National Chamber of Commerce)
ul.Trÿbacka 4
00-074 Warszawa
Phone: (+48 22) 630 96 66

Note: There are also Polish-foreign chambers of commerce (e.g., Polish-German, Polish-French, etc.) that can be found in the Yellow Pages (Panorama Firm and Polskie Ksiÿÿki Telefoniczne).

Internet Sites

Some companies advertise through the Internet. It is worthwhile to look for companies in your interest area. Two of the employment sites in Poland are www.topjobs.pl and www.jobaid.pl.

Country Employment Offices

The Polish employment bureau, Urzÿd Pracy, prints lists of jobs that can be found at local employment bureaus (Rejonowy Urzÿd Pracy) whose addresses and telephone numbers are in the local telephone directories.

Telephone Directory

In the Polish telephone directories (Panorama Firm and Polskie Ksiÿÿki Telefoniczne), organizations involved in business and commerce can be found. Panorama Firm has headings indexed in English and German. All companies are listed in alphabetical order at the ends of the directories.

Contact with Personnel Consulting Companies

Almost all of the big international executive search companies are active in the Polish market. Most of them are located in Warsaw. If you send your CV to these firms, they will save your data in their databases and contact you if they have a project that suits your profile.

WORK PERMITS/VISAS

Almost all foreigners staying longer than three months in Poland require a visa.

Work Permit

You may apply for a work permit only after you have signed an employment contract. A written offer of employment must be attached to the work permit application.

Visa

You may apply for a visa at the Polish embassy (consulate) in your country or in a country that adjoins Poland (e.g., Czech Republic, Germany).

INTERVIEW AND CULTURAL ADVICE

▶ You can contact the prospective employer's human resources department in advance for further information about the job. You should be as well prepared for these preliminary talks as you are for the actual qualification discussions.

▶ Dress in business attire for the qualification talks.

▶ Do not exaggerate; be yourself!

▶ Be punctual! However, do not worry if the interviewer makes you wait.

▶ Compensation is usually discussed at the end of the first or second meeting with your possible employer. Upon request, state your current compensation or expectations.

▶ During annual vacations (July and August) and Christmas holidays, it is difficult to make contacts with the business community.

▶ Be punctual professionally and socially.

▶ In social circumstances (private visits), arrive with a small gift, usually flowers.

Russia

Igor Chugay, Amrop International

COUNTRY OVERVIEW

Russia has the largest population in Europe, with 145.7 million inhabitants (as of October 1999). It is a vast country (17.1 million square kilometers) with a wealth of natural resources, a well-educated population, and a diverse industrial base. More than 45 percent of the territory is covered by forests. The average winter temperature in the European part of Russia varies from 0°C to –30°C, and in eastern parts of Russia and Siberia from –10°C to –50°C. Average summer temperatures vary from +10°C to +40°C. Approximately 73 percent of Russians live in cities and towns. Moscow is the capital of Russia with 8.63 million inhabitants. Other major cities include St. Petersburg (4.8 million inhabitants), Nizhnij Novgorod (1.4 million), Novosibirsk (1.4 million), and Ekaterinburg (1.3 million). Russia is a multinational country comprised of more than 100 nationalities.

Russia is a parliamentary republic with a president as head of state. The country is led by a parliament, democratically elected every four years, and an executive government, with a prime minister as head of the government. The prime minister is appointed by the president and approved by the parliament.

The official language of the country is Russian. However, the overwhelming majority of Russians occupied in international business speak English. Most Russians are members of the Orthodox faith, though many are nonpracticing, as religious activity was prohibited during the Communist period.

Russia continues to experience formidable difficulties in moving from the old centrally planned economy to a modern market economy. Former President Boris Yeltsin's government made substantial strides in converting to a market economy after launching its economic reform in 1992. The government has succeeded in freeing nearly all prices, slashing defense spending, eliminating the old centralized distribution system, completing an ambitious voucher-privatization program, establishing private financial institutions, and decentralizing foreign trade. Russia has also made significant headway in privatizing state assets. Foreign investments in the Russian economy in 1997 equaled 10.5 billion U.S. dollars. Many multinational companies have established representative offices and built production facilities in Russia, especially in the consumer goods sector (Coca-Cola, Gillette, Nestlé, Philip Morris, Japan Tobacco, Rothmans, and Monsanto Searl).

Foreign sales in Russia consist largely of oil, natural gas, and other raw materials. However, after a devaluation of the Russian currency, the ruble, in August

1997, the price of many consumer products (e.g., vodka, beer, and chocolate) and technological products (e.g., gas and steam turbines, power stations, and automobiles) became rather competitive and showed significant growth. The largest Russian companies are connected with gas, oil, and energy (Gazprom, United Electrical Systems [RAO UES], Lukoil).

Most of the international companies in Russia are headed by expatriates who play a significant role in the business community. Russia is a very good place for career development and a great challenge for those who would like to test and develop their business skills. (See the section on expatriate leadership in Russia at www.amrop.com/moscow/news.)

RESUME SPECIFICS

Education

Describe your college/university education. State your graduation year, if you have studied abroad, your major, and the title of your degree. Briefly describe any international experience as a student and any thesis work.

Extracurricular Activities

Describe your extracurricular activities, such as participation in the organization of different student affairs. Highlight your participation in any international student projects.

Awards/Honors

List any awards/honors received for scholastic achievement or outstanding performance in other areas.

Additional Education/Specialized Training

List any additional courses, seminars, training in specialized areas (such as sales, language, computers, etc.). Participation in specialized educational programs should be mentioned in this context.

Work Experience

Begin by listing your job title and the name of your employer in reverse chronological order, starting from your current job. Describe the company (employer) if its business activities are not generally well known throughout the world. Specify the employment dates and whether it was a full-time or a part-time job. Give the details of your work, and list your responsibilities, using a bullet-point format. Emphasize information that is relevant to the position for which you are applying. Summer jobs and shorter periods of employment prior to your professional career should be briefly summarized.

Note: If there are any gaps in employment history, it is important that you explain the reason for each gap in reasonable detail. Also, for part-time employment, explain the reason why you chose not to work full-time.

Achievements/Accomplishments

Any awards, special recognition, or promotions received during employment should be highlighted.

Special Skills

Define your knowledge of foreign languages, specific computer skills, and any other special knowledge or skills.

Professional Affiliations

List any professional affiliations relevant to your focus area. Include information regarding your involvement with special activities or any leadership roles.

Military Experience

Include information in your resume/CV about your military service. State the focus of your training, your field of responsibility, and any managerial positions. Include the dates and location of your service.

Note: Military managerial experience is very much appreciated in Russia.

Volunteer Experience

Any previous or current commissions of trust should be described. These may include activities with associations, clubs, or areas of personal interest (connected to your children's school, sports, charity, etc.). Any volunteer experience that you have initiated or participated in should be briefly described.

Personal Information

Describe your personal interests such as sports activities, gardening, reading, rebuilding old cars, and so on. It is better to be brief in this section. Do not list too many hobbies; just mention those that are the most important.

References

The references you select should be connected to your professional experience, such as previous managers. These people should be well acquainted with your work performance, and be rather recent in time. List their names and contact information.

RESUME PRESENTATION

Format and Layout

A reverse chronological order, where the most recent experience is listed first, is preferable. Your resume/CV should represent a clear picture of your education, internships, and employment, as well as other important experiences that might interest an employer, such as professional memberships.

Always begin your resume/CV by describing your educational background, including additional education and training programs, followed by the details of your professional experience.

Length

Your resume/CV should be no longer than three pages.

Attachments

Grades, certificates, and letters of reference do not necessarily have to be included with your application, as you can present them at the interview. No thesis papers or diploma work should be sent initially.

If you prefer to attach such documents, choose your most recent grades and a letter of reference from your current employer.

Note: Any documents attached to your resume should be the original documents, not copies, as these will be returned to you.

To personalize an application with a small photo is becoming more acceptable. Including a photo gives the reader a more vivid picture of the person and allows the reader to put a face with a name for future reference.

E-mail Applications

It is becoming more common that employers in Russia accept, appreciate, and prioritize applications sent via e-mail. In this case, always attach your resume to the letter/e-mail. Video recordings are not recommended.

COVER LETTERS

An application should always include a personalized cover letter and a complete resume. Furthermore, you may attach grades, certificates, and letters of reference or recommendations.

A personal cover letter of one page is usually sufficient. The application should be typed in A4 format.

Note: It is better not to use regular (state-owned) post services for delivery of your documents to Russia. If you prefer to send your information by post, use courier services (DHL International, TNT, Federal Express, UPS, etc.).

Content/Detail

Your cover letter should start with a phrase stating the position for which you are applying. Remember that the purpose of the letter is to raise the reader's interest, so try to let your personality influence the content. Everything you say in the letter should also be found in your resume/CV. Start by describing your current position: work content, field of responsibility, organizational level/reporting structure, and the name of the employer.

Explain why you are applying for this job.

Note: If you are a foreigner and applying for a job in Russia, the reader will appreciate knowing the reason(s) why you would like to work here. Any experience connected with Russia or the former Soviet Union, from either an educational or a professional standpoint, is very important to emphasize.

Analyze your experiences and emphasize those which are connected to the position for which you are applying. Continue with a concentrated description of your previous professional experiences. Include details concerning your current personal situation: marital status, ability to relocate, availability to travel on business trips, and so on. If you are unemployed at present, you should state that in the letter.

JOB INFORMATION SOURCES

Newspapers

Daily business newspapers, business journals, and special employment editions contain employment ads. The most common ones with employment ads in English are *Moscow Times*, *St. Petersburg Times*, *Carrier Capital*, *Career Forum*, *Delovoj Peterburg*, and *Exclusive Personnel*. Most of these editions are distributed free of charge in the larger hotels, restaurants, supermarkets, and other places aimed at an English-speaking audience. Most of the employment ads aimed at experienced personnel (including the openings for international companies) are in English.

An excellent new publication, (*Vedomosti*), is a joint venture of *The Wall Street Journal* and the *Financial Times*. Although the paper is in Russian, the job ads are in English.

Note: No newspaper covers the entire country. The majority of job opportunities are concentrated in Moscow and St. Petersburg.

Moscow Times (Moscow)
Phone: +7-095-200 0650
E-mail: info@mn.ru
Web site: www.mn.ru

St. Petersburg Times (northwest region of Russia)
Phone: +7-812-325 6080
E-mail: postmaster@sptimes.ru
Web site: www.sptimes.ru

Kariera Kapital (*Carrier Capital*) (northwest region of Russia)
Phone: +7-812-325 6080
E-mail: kariera@sptimes.ru

Career Forum (Moscow)
Phone: +7-095-209 0115/17
E-mail: rc-it@ruscon.ru

Career Forum (St. Petersburg)
Phone: +7-812-118 1915
E-mail: ruscon@sovintel.ru

Delovoj Peterburg (business St. Petersburg)
Phone: +7-812-326 9710/20
E-mail: contact@delo.spb.ru
Web site: www.dp.ru/english

Exclusive Personnel (all Russia)
Phone: +7-095-911 1294
E-mail: exclusiv@rdw.msk.ru
Web site: www.rdw.ru
www.cv.ru
www.narod.ru

Vedomosti
Phone: +7-095-232 1750
Fax: +7-095-232 1761
E-mail: info@vedomosti.ru

Internet Sites

The Internet is quite a new tool for job-searching in Russia. Nevertheless, the Internet is booming in Russia, and web sites about job information can be found at www.BIZ.ru, www.job.ru, and www.career.ru. Use Russian search engines at www.yandex.ru or www.rambler.ru.

Note: It would be helpful if your software supports the Cyrillic alphabet.

Telephone Directory

It could be useful to look for job search assistance through the Yellow Pages, which are published in every large Russian city. There you can find a list of recruitment companies and international companies in that particular region. In the White Pages, all companies are listed in alphabetical order. All information is bilingual (Russian and English).

Local Employment Offices

State employment agencies exist in every district in every city. They provide services for unemployed people and usually fill blue-collar and low-profile office vacancies for state enterprises inside the city. Some of them hire people for seasonal work abroad.

WORK PERMITS/VISAS

Visas

A business or permanent multientry visa is required for most foreign visitors, except for persons entering from the countries that have special agreements with the government. Russian labor codes require work permits for foreign employees.

Residence and Work Permits

Residence and work permits are required for all foreign citizens who want to work in Russia. A written offer of employment must accompany the work permit application. For further information contact the Russian embassy or consulate closest to your place of residence.

INTERVIEW AND CULTURAL ADVICE

▶ Russians, as employers, are rather subjective in their choice of employees. In a recruiting situation, do everything to reveal (open) your personality.

▶ During face-to-face interviews, try to avoid selling yourself as a "product" with a set of specific skills and experiences. Show your personal characteristics: Give examples of your behavior in different situations, try to add emotional substance, make jokes.

▶ Because of the unpredictable nature of the current business environment, Russians are quite short-term oriented. They appreciate employees who are dynamic and flexible.

▶ Russian businesspeople work quite hard, sometimes putting aside their private lives. They expect their subordinates to share the same attitude toward work.

▶ It is very important that you show your interest in Russia. Explain why you would like to work in Russia and for this particular company. Do not exaggerate your motivation; avoid giving a false impression.

▶ Show your ability to establish personal contacts, which is very important in the Russian business environment. Give some examples from your previous experience when your contacts were beneficial to your company.

▶ Feel free to telephone the contact person listed in the employment advertisement for further details or just to introduce yourself, before sending in your application. However, do not persistently telephone for the status of the recruitment process.

▶ It is wise to avoid discussing salary and other parts of the compensation package early in the process. However, if requested, you should state your salary preference. Keep in mind that there are distinct salary differences between Russia and other western countries. Gather information from other sources on what is an appropriate salary range for the position you are applying for.

▶ In social circumstances, always arrive at someone's home with host and hostess gifts. Present a bottle of any strong alcohol or wine to men and a box of chocolates to women. Do not touch your drink until your host has said *"Za zdorovje,"* ("For health").

Saudi Arabia

Nada M. Rizkallah, Rasd Limited—Amrop International

COUNTRY OVERVIEW

Saudi Arabia has a population of some 18 million people, of whom more than 4.6 million are foreign nationals. Its area encompasses approximately 2,240,000 square kilometers. Saudi Arabian society has deep historical roots; the land has been inhabited for over four millennia. The country is ruled by "The Custodian of the Two Holy Mosques," King Fahd bin Abdul-Aziz, who also serves as the prime minister of the Council of Ministers, some of whom are members of the royal family. For administrative purposes, the country is divided into provinces (or governorates), each governed by an emir.

Until the 1940s, the Saudis lived in a relatively simple society. However, the income derived from oil and natural gas has since enabled the country to move very quickly toward a modern society with a maturing market economy, modern highway and transportation systems, and telecommunications facilities and infrastructure, all of which use state-of-the-art computer facilities and systems. The Saudis generally appreciate the longer-term benefits of this modern transformation, provided it takes place within the Islamic framework. There are conservative and traditional elements in this large society.

Saudi Arabia is a predominantly desert country with a great deal of variety in its topography. There are vast areas of true desert, but considerable areas bear vegetation. In the west and southwest, the Hejaz and Asir mountain ranges rise in places to almost 10,000 feet. Most of the country consists of a plateau that slopes very gradually from the western mountains to sea level on the Persian Gulf in the east. The inland climate is dry, but the coastal regions and cities are humid. Bordering the length of the Red Sea in the west is the coastal plain of the Hejaz.

The southern part of the country includes the Rub al-Khali (the Empty Quarter). It is the largest area of sand in the world and contains dunes that can rise to a height of 500 feet. The Nefud desert in the north of the kingdom is much smaller and is distinguished by the reddish color of its sand.

The temperatures tend to be high in the summer months—50°C is not unknown. However, it does cool considerably in the winter—in Riyadh, it has been known to go below freezing at night. The climate during the months of October to May is temperate and pleasant. The time difference is three hours ahead of Greenwich mean time (GMT) all year round.

The native tongue is Arabic. English is widely spoken, especially among the business community. Saudi Arabia is an exclusively Islamic (Muslim) kingdom. You should note that Christmas Day is a normal working day.

RESUME SPECIFICS

Begin your CV with a clear heading containing your name, address, and all contact numbers. Your e-mail address should also be noted.

Education

Your college/university education should be noted along with qualifications gained and the attendance dates. Include the name and address of each institution.

Note: You will be asked to produce the original certificates following an offer of employment. Check with the visa section at the Saudi embassy in your country regarding the proper authorities to certify educational degrees.

Awards/Honors

Any awards and honors received for scholastic achievement or outstanding performance should be noted in the relevant section (i.e., education work or other areas).

Work Experience

Start with your most recent or current employer. Give a brief description of the company, including your start date (and finish date if currently unemployed), followed by the dates of each position held. Describe how your skills have developed through your tasks and achievements. Note any key achievements and special recognition or awards received.

Note: Do not leave out any positions held during your career, even if you do not think they are relevant.

Specialized Training

List any training courses you have attended, including the dates and locations. List any special skills, including languages you speak. Knowledge of specific computer programs should also be noted.

Personal Information

This section should be used to provide your date of birth, marital status, number of children, nationality, and citizenship(s).

Note: You are also expected to list your religion in this section.

References

References may be listed; however, it is acceptable to state that references will be supplied upon request.

Residency Permit/Letter of Release

If you are already working in Saudi Arabia, it is important to note on your CV whether you have a transferable *igama*, or can obtain a letter of release from your present employer. For those wishing to work in Saudi Arabia, an *igama* is your residency permit. It lists the sponsor you work for and is issued shortly after you commence employment. A letter of release enables you to leave one employer and work for another in Saudi Arabia.

RESUME PRESENTATION

Format and Layout

The headings described in the previous section should be used to give a clear and concise format and layout. Your name and contact details should be followed by your education, professional experience, and personal details.

Note: Remember not to leave any gaps in dates.

Length

Your CV is your first point of contact; therefore, as much relevant information as possible is required. A CV of three to four pages is acceptable.

Attachments

Unless specifically asked for in the job application, do not send any certificates or letters of reference at this stage.

Note: After an offer of employment, you will be asked for the originals. Remember to bring them with you to Saudi Arabia.

E-mail Applications

It is acceptable to apply for positions via e-mail, provided the advertisement offers that as a choice. Most recruiting is done via agencies in your country of origin. The advertisement will typically state the employer's preference.

COVER LETTERS

Each application should include a cover letter introducing yourself, your current working status, and your interest in this particular position.

Content/Detail

Give a brief outline of why you think you have the most relevant experience for this position. Give details of any commitments preventing you from traveling for an interview on particular dates.

JOB INFORMATION SOURCES

Newspapers

Your local newspaper may carry advertisements placed by agencies in your area offering work in Saudi Arabia.

Chambers of Commerce

Council of Saudi Chambers of Commerce and Industry
P.O. Box 16683, Riyadh 11474
Kingdom of Saudi Arabia
Phone: (+966 1) 405 3200
Fax: (+966 1) 402 4747

Riyadh Chamber of Commerce and Industry
P.O. Box 596, Riyadh 11421
Kingdom of Saudi Arabia
Phone: (+966 1) 404 0044, Exts. 265, 280, & 272
Fax: (+966 1) 402 1103.

Note: Major companies in Saudi Arabia, both native and international, often use the services of executive search firms to hire expatriates for senior positions.

WORK PERMITS/VISAS

Note: It is *absolutely essential* that you have a valid and appropriate visa for Saudi Arabia in your passport *before* you travel. This necessary visa can be obtained at the nearest Saudi Arabian embassy by submitting your passport, a signed copy of your contract, and a letter from your sponsor in the country, along with an application form. The procedure can take some time. A couple of weeks before your departure date is usually sufficient. However, allow additional time for processing applications submitted prior to the major holidays.

Note: To work in Saudi Arabia, an expatriate must be invited by a sponsor. Approval from the sponsor is needed to travel within the country and outside the country.

INTERVIEW ADVICE

▶ The Saudis are a hospitable and dignified people. They are, on the whole, a tolerant people, and will not generally be offended by social mistakes stemming from ignorance.

▶ Most Saudi businessmen are involved in several, often diverse, business activities and may work out of more than one office. Delays, although unintended, are sometimes unavoidable. However, you will be expected to arrive punctually. Allow extra time for canceled, unexpected, or postponed meetings.

▶ The meeting, when it does take place, may take place with the assistance of several conference calls with other participants. However, the serious stages of negotiations are discussed in private. The Saudis have a strong inclination toward privacy in their approach to business, and foreigners are advised to be discerning in the disclosure of information about themselves and their business partners. Saudis shy away from people who lack discretion.

▶ Saudis find it offensive to sit opposite a foreign businessperson who has a superior attitude or exhibits traces of arrogance. Foreigners who exhibit understanding, courtesy, and open-mindedness not only win respect, but often have the greatest business success.

CULTURAL ADVICE

▶ While in Saudi Arabia, you are subject to the laws and moral standards of the authorities and people of the country. You will find that they are considerably stricter than those of other countries. In certain cases, notably involving dress, drink, and moral behavior, what is not a crime elsewhere is treated as one in Saudi Arabia. All visitors are advised to get to know the cultural values of the society, and are strongly urged to abide by the laws of Saudi Arabia while they are there.

▶ Before you leave your home country, make sure you have a confirmation from someone in Saudi Arabia about your arrival plans.

▶ Your sponsor will usually have arranged for someone to meet you at the airport. If for any reason your travel plan or flight changes, be very careful to have the name and telephone numbers of your sponsor, so that you will not be stranded at the airport on arrival.

▶ Customs restrictions strictly prohibit bringing in alcoholic beverages, pork products, pornography, firearms, and drugs. Fashion magazines may be confiscated or have offending pages that show models with bare arms or legs torn out. Videos and computer diskettes are liable to be checked for inappropriate content.

▶ Baggage searches are thorough. Businesspeople bringing in special equipment or presentation materials may choose to have a representative of their Saudi sponsor help them clear customs. All newcomers are advised to check with a Saudi embassy or consulate, or with other expatriates who are familiar with the system, to avoid the distress of having seemingly innocent belongings confiscated.

▶ Women must remain covered at all times when out in public—this includes foreign women. Black *abayas* are worn and the hair is covered. Men may wear short-sleeved shirts; however, they must wear long trousers when in public. Suits are the usual business attire.

▶ Many expatriates live on compounds where Western ways can be followed. However, it is illegal for women to drive, and this law can apply on compound roads as well.

▶ Ramadan, which typically falls between December and January, *must* be observed. This is the month of fasting, and it is forbidden to eat, drink, or smoke during the daylight hours when in public. All restaurants and coffee shops will be closed, although other shops will be open between the usual hours. During Ramadan, office hours are usually abbreviated during the day and extended to evening hours—sometimes well into the evening. The end of Ramadan is celebrated by the 'Eid. This holiday usually lasts four or five days. Approximately two months later, the 'Eid Al Adha holiday ends the Hajj pilgrimage season. Once again there is a customary four-to-ten-day holiday.

▶ The Muslim Holy Day of the week is Friday, making the weekend Thursday and Friday (though some businesses do open on Thursday morning). There are generally five prayer times throughout each day: sunrise, midday, afternoon, evening, night.

▶ During these times all shops close and some companies will not answer their telephones. The shopping hours are usually from 9:00 A.M. to midday prayer and then 4:00 P.M. until 10:00 or 11:00 P.M. You will find that all shop assistants are male.

▶ Business hours tend to vary depending on the company, but 8:00 A.M. to 1:00 P.M. and then 4:00 P.M. to 8:00 P.M. is usual.

▶ If invited to a social occasion, it is normal to take a gift for the hostess, such as flowers. However, a male who is not related to the family is not allowed to present the gift in person. Unrelated males are not allowed to see the females in the house, as women do not completely cover themselves in their own homes. The men sit in one room, talking, eating, and sometimes playing board games, and the women sit in a separate room socializing.

Note: Saudi Arabia is a dry country; therefore, in all social and business occasions there are only soft drinks available.

▶ The segregation rule (segregating men and unrelated women) applies to other areas as well. There are separate waiting rooms in various establishments—for example, banks tend to have ladies' sections. There are also "family sections" in restaurants and coffee shops where single men cannot enter. Because of this rule you will not find any forms of entertainment where single men and women can mix (e.g., theaters or cinemas).

▶ Photography remains a sensitive subject in Saudi Arabia. Discretion and approval are advised at all times. Do not photograph local people, particularly women, without asking permission first. Photographers who ignore such courtesies risk an encounter with local authorities. Exercise caution when photographing certain scenery or architecture. Your motives may be misinterpreted. Never photograph military installations or government structures without prior approval—this includes the airport!

Note: Visitors should carry their identity papers with them at all times.

Singapore

Tan Soo Jin, Amrop International

COUNTRY OVERVIEW

Singapore is an exciting, young city-state, with a multiracial population of nearly four million people. Cosmopolitan in nature, the island is populated by Chinese (about 75 percent), Malay (15 percent), Indian (7 percent), Sikh, Eurasian nationals, plus a varied business population from almost every corner of the globe. The island-state is about 240 square miles (or 622 square kilometers) in size, comprising Singapore Island, which is low and flat, and some 57 other small islands. In spite of its relatively small size, the island has large areas covered by forests.

Founded in 1819 by Sir Stamford Raffles, Singapore was originally leased as a trading post from the Sultan of Johore by the British East India Company. It became part of the British Straits Settlement from 1867 to 1942, when it was invaded by the Japanese. After World War II, Singapore became a separate British Crown Colony until 1965 when it became a republic. It has a democratically elected government, which is headed by a prime minister. Every five years, there is also an election for a president as head of state.

Since its independence, Singapore has grown from its once traditional trading status to a busy financial center with a developing high-tech research and development (R&D) added-value manufacturing and logistics emphasis. With a pro-business government leading in the development of a world-class infrastructure, Singapore boasts of an outstanding port and a first-rate airport and support system. Its 1999 per capita GDP income was US$28,565, which is second only to the U.S. (US$31,469). Singapore is viewed by many to be a model of a successful economy. It has enjoyed an unprecedented continuous rate of growth with the exception of 1997–1998 when the Asian economic crisis hit the region. Its people enjoy a high standard of living and quality of life. The country is generally very safe, and has an outstanding record for public health, communications, and public transport.

There are four official languages—English, Mandarin, Malay, and Tamil. However, most visitors find that English is widely spoken and used in business and social contact. The main religions are Buddhism, Taoism, Islam, Hinduism, and Christianity.

Singapore is generally considered to be one of two regional centers, the other being Hong Kong. Today, it has major banks (Citibank, ABN-Amro, Deutsche, BNP, Nomura, etc.), oil companies (Shell, Esso, Caltex, etc.), insurance companies (CIGNA, Allianz, AIG, AIA, etc.), manufacturing companies (Hewlett Packard, Compaq, Siemens, Seagate, etc.), and a host of other international names. Companies like Caltex have made Singapore their global headquarters.

Because land is scarce, property prices are extremely high when compared to those in the United States, Canada, Australia, or even Europe. More than 80 percent of the population lives in government-built Housing Development Board (HDB) flats. The Scheme for Housing of Foreign Talents (SHiFT) was launched in 1997 to enable foreigners to rent HDB flats at a lower cost. The cost of owning a car can also be prohibitive. However, public transportion is excellent in Singapore, with the Mass Rapid Transport (MRT), a developing Light Rail Transport (LRT), and extensive bus services.

RESUME SPECIFICS

Education

Start with your college/university education. List details about your degree and any postgraduate qualifications, the year of graduation, and any major area of focus. This should be followed by information about your secondary education, the years of study, school or institution, and any student internships.

Extracurricular Activities

The extracurricular activities that you participated in during your education help to give your prospective employer an idea of your interests and involvement outside your studies. They also provide some indication of your leadership and social skills.

Awards/Honors

List any awards or honors received for scholastic or athletic excellence or outstanding achievements in other areas.

Additional Education/Specialized Training

Provide a list of any additional academic or work-related training you might have received. In this computer age, computer literacy is highly advantageous.

Work Experience

It is usually preferred that you list your work experience beginning with your most recent position. You should state the dates of employment, the positions held, and the names of your employers. Describe your roles and responsibilities. Equally important is the need to state your achievements. What you have done especially well and how you have contributed to the performance of your unit or department and to the company as a whole are important details. You should also include reasons that led you to change jobs. If there are gaps in your employment history, provide an explanation. Do not leave the reason to the imagination of your prospective employer, who will always think the worst!

Special Skills

Note: Multilinguistic skills are highly advantageous. In Singapore and the Asian region, an ability to speak Mandarin is a great asset. Japanese, Bahasa Indonesia/Malaysia, or Thai are useful depending on the countries your new job will cover. Chinese dialects that are helpful are Cantonese in Hong Kong and Kwangchou, and Hokkien in Taiwan and some parts of China. Knowledge of GAAP (generally accepted accounting principles) is helpful if you are working in an accounting or a finance function for an American company, while Commonwealth GAP (general accounting principles) is useful for British companies.

Professional Affiliations

List any professional affiliations that are relevant to your area of training or expertise (e.g., CPA, CA, ACA, CFA, MIS, etc.) If you have held committee roles, include them. This helps to show your willingness to participate in a professional role or activity.

Military Experience

Since its independence, Singaporean males are eligible for national service. It is useful to include any military service you have undertaken and state your rank, achievements, and areas of training and responsibility.

Volunteer Experience

Service in volunteer organizations speaks well of a person's values, concerns, and interests. If you have been active in any volunteer organizations, list them, with a brief statement of your involvement and contributions.

Personal Information

Describe your personal interests in sporting activities, reading, and any hobbies you may have. Participation in religious activities may also be included.

References

Your references should include at least one person who has worked with you in recent times. If you do not have anyone in this category, then include the names, addresses, and contact telephone numbers or e-mail addresses of people who might know you well—for example, your university professors, your church pastor, or someone in a professional role.

RESUME PRESENTATION

In Singapore, there is no law against mentioning your age, race, nationality, sex, and so on, in your resume. In fact, this is generally expected. Most people, in writing about their work histories, tend to produce job descriptions about the roles they have played. You should highlight your achievements and contributions in each role. Describe your experience in a way that makes you stand out and be easily differentiated from others who are also applying for the job.

Format and Layout

Your curriculum vitae or resume should clearly state personal details, such as your name, date of birth, address, telephone number, e-mail address, nationality, and language(s) spoken. It should also clearly set out your employment history arranged either in a chronological or in a reverse chronological order.

Length

While a one-page CV is commonly received, a CV can be two or three pages long. This gives you sufficient space to spell out your experience and achievements.

Attachments

In your application letter, it is useful to attach copies of your degree, diplomas, certificates, grades, and letters of reference. You should not forward your originals at this stage. A photograph of yourself, while not compulsory, is helpful— but make sure it is a good photograph!

Note: When the time comes for an application to the immigration authorities, it will be necessary to present original documents together with photocopies. Please refer to the requirements set out in the immigration documents.

E-mail Applications

E-mail applications are becoming increasingly commonplace. However, it is still recommended that a formal letter also be sent.

COVER LETTERS

Content/Detail

Your application should always be presented in a proper format and not appear as if you have written the same letter to a thousand other companies! The name and address of the person to whom you are writing should be correct. You should also ensure that all your letters are personally signed.

Note: In Singapore, the Chinese surname always appears first—for instance, if someone's full name is Tan Eng Hock, you should address the person as Mr. Tan in a formal context, or Eng Hock if you know the person well. But it is definitely not Tan Eng.

Note: You should attach copies of your diplomas, certificates, grades, and any reference or recommendation letters. While you do not need to have these certified as true copies at this stage, when you do eventually arrive in Singapore you will need to present the original copies, especially to the immigration authorities. This includes marriage certificates.

The cover letter should be like a bikini—sufficiently revealing to make the reader want to read more, and yet covering up enough to make the reader want to read more anyway! It should also include a paragraph about your personal strengths and achievements.

JOB INFORMATION SOURCES

Newspapers

The main English paper is *The Straits Times*, which carries employment advertisements on Wednesdays and Saturdays. The others are the *Business Times* and *The New Paper*, but neither of these features recruitment ads.

The Straits Times
Phone: 65-7378700
Web site: straitstimes.asia.com.sg

Chambers of Commerce

There are several chambers of commerce or business associations:

Singapore International Chamber of
  Commerce
6 Raffles Quay #10-01, John Hancock
  Tower
Singapore 048580
Phone: 65-2241255
Fax: 65-2242785
E-mail: singicc@asian connect.com
Web site: www.sicc.com.sg

The American Chamber of Commerce
  in Singapore
1 Scotts Road #16-07
Shaw Centre
Singapore 228208
Phone: 65-2350077
Fax: 65-7325917
Web site: www.amcham.org.sg

British Chamber of Commerce
10 Collyer Quay #03-04
Ocean Building
Singapore 049315
Phone: 65-2277861
Fax: 65-2277021
E-mail: asstdir@britcham.org.sg

French Business Association
89 Neil Road
Singapore 088849
Phone: 65-2266101
Fax: 65-2266378
Web site: www.fbasingapore.com

Singapore Australian Business Council
25 Napier Road (Level 3)
Australian High Commission
Singapore 258507
Phone: 65-7387917
Fax: 65-7387916
E-mail: thesabc@singnet.com.sg
Web site: www.sabc.org.sg

Swiss Business Association
C/o UBS AG
5 Temasek Boulevard
#18-00 Suntec City Tower
Singapore 038985
Phone: 65-431 8025
Fax: 65-431 8029
E-mail: Singapore.SBA@ubs.com

Telephone Directory

Each year, the Singapore phone book produces the following listings: business, residential, commercial/industrial, and buying guide. These are useful guides for looking at companies that may interest you.

Country Employment Office

Inquiries about work opportunities and how to apply for work permits, and so on, can be made at the Singapore High Commission in your country. At the same time, the international branches of the Economic Development Bureau are useful contact points. The EDB maintains offices in Boston, Chicago, Los Angeles, New York, San Francisco, Washington, Frankfurt, London, Milan, Paris, Stockholm, Hong Kong, Jakarta, Osaka, Tokyo, and Suchou.

WORK PERMITS/VISAS

The Singapore government recognizes the importance of foreign talent in its quest to develop a world-class economy with the highest standards of global practices. To this end, it adopts an open immigration policy to attract foreign professionals, entrepreneurs, graduates, and skilled workers who can contribute to this objective.

Visas

A visa is not required for those coming from North America, Western Europe, Australia, New Zealand, Japan, Hong Kong, or the ASEAN countries (i.e., Malaysia, Indonesia, Philippines, Thailand, Brunei, and Vietnam).

Residence and Work Permits

There are several categories in this section:

Employment Passes

All foreigners who are not Singaporean permanent residents are required to apply for an employment pass to be employed or do business in Singapore if their basic salary exceeds S$2,000 per month. Foreigners who hold an acceptable university degree or diploma from a local polytechnic or recognized educational institution in Singapore may also apply for an employment pass even if their basic monthly salary is S$2,000 or below. A local sponsor, normally the applicant's employer, is required for the employment pass application. The normal processing time is about six to eight weeks.

Work Permits

Foreigners who earn a basic salary of S$2,000 or below are required to apply for a work permit with the Ministry of Labor. A non-Malaysian worker is not allowed to be in Singapore prior to the granting of an In-Principle Approval. A security bond of S$5,000 per worker is also required.

Application forms can be obtained from:

Singapore Immigration
SIR Building
10 Kallang Road
Singapore 208718
IMMI-Link: 1800-3916400
General phone enquiries: 65-3916100
Immigration Postline: 65-7383352
Fax: 65-2980837

Permanent Residence

Professionals and skilled workers who are below 50 years of age and are in Singapore on employment passes are eligible to apply for permanent residence. Approval and acceptance will be made on a case-by-case basis depending on the applicant's academic qualification, employment history, and expertise.

CULTURAL ADVICE

Singapore has a multiracial, multinational populace. Some cultural advice:

- ▶ Be sensitive to the religious backgrounds of all the races represented in the country. It is important to respect the religious beliefs of others even if you do not agree with them. Never belittle someone else's religious beliefs.
- ▶ Always observe punctuality in keeping business appointments.
- ▶ Socially, especially during Chinese wedding dinners, be prepared to be flexible with your time.
- ▶ When visiting someone's home, you are expected to take off your shoes at the door.
- ▶ Because of the humid weather, it is perfectly correct to attend meetings not dressed in a suit. A shirt and tie is a generally accepted standard for business attire for a man. Women should wear attire that is suitable for a business environment. Increasingly, many U.S. companies observe Friday as "dress-down" day.

South Africa

Woodburn Mann (Pty) Limited, Whitehead Mann PLC Group

COUNTRY OVERVIEW

South Africa is the southernmost country on the continent of Africa, bordered on the east and south by the Indian Ocean and on the west by the Atlantic Ocean. The climate is temperate and subtropical. It has a multiracial and multiethnic population of 40 million people from vastly different cultural backgrounds. To accommodate this diversity, the country has 11 official languages, although English is the main language of business. Nonwhite (non-European) people make up 76 percent of the population and white (European) people make up the remainder. The administrative capital of South Africa is Pretoria, and the legislative capital is Cape Town.

The president is the head of state in South Africa and has the ultimate authority in governing the country. Racial segregation, known as apartheid, and the white monopoly of power characterized South Africa from 1940 to 1990, during which period nonwhite people were disenfranchised. Apartheid was dismantled in 1990. The first multiracial democratic elections in South Africa's history were held in April 1994, and Nelson Mandela became the first democratically elected president of the country. He retired in April 1999 when Thabo Mbeki was elected president.

South Africa remains a society where approximately 14 percent of the population has a standard of living equal to that of Western Europe. However, the remainder of the population suffers from the poverty patterns of the Third World as a result of unemployment, lack of education, and limited job skills.

In 1998, the Employment Equity Bill was passed to ensure that qualified people from previously disadvantaged groups, namely nonwhite people, women, and the disabled, have equal employment opportunities and that they are represented according to the demographics of the country at all levels of the workforce. These legislative measures are interpreted as affirmative action, which is required to ensure greater levels of equality in employment in organizations in South Africa. These measures may have an impact on the availability of jobs for foreigners.

Until 1914, the South African economy was based principally on mining (especially of diamonds and gold) and agriculture. Since then manufacturing has developed rapidly and is now the leading sector of the economy. The country also has the most developed financial services sector in sub-Saharan Africa. The top industrial companies in South Africa, based on turnover, are South African

Breweries PLC, CG Smith Limited, Sappi Limited, Pepkor Limited, and Barlows Limited. The top mining houses are Anglo American PLC and Gold Fields Limited.

RESUME SPECIFICS

Education

List the level of education achieved in your final high school year and the year in which the studies were completed. It is also useful to indicate any distinctions obtained or significant leadership roles.

Continue with a description of college/university education. State your degree or diploma, graduation year, as well as the institution attended.

Extracurricular Activities

Describe achievements in extracurricular activities or any significant leadership roles.

Awards/Honors

List any awards and honors received during school or university years.

Additional Education/Specialized Training

Any relevant extra courses should be mentioned as well as training or experience in specialized areas such as language, public speaking, computers, or international conferences.

Work Experience

List a brief career synopsis with job titles, names of employers, and specific employment dates for each position. Continue with a more detailed description of key performance areas, with emphasis on specific achievements, reporting lines, staff responsibility, budget/financial responsibility, and reasons for leaving each position. It is also helpful to give a short description of the nature and size of business at each position. Explain any gaps in employment history.

Professional Affiliations

List any relevant professional affiliations.

Military Experience

Details about military experience (which was mandatory before 1990 in South Africa) do not have to be listed, except if there were any outstanding achievements or where experience was gained in areas relevant to career history, such as logistics, accounting, or medicine.

Volunteer Experience

Any relevant voluntary or charity experience may be mentioned.

Personal Information

It is useful to include your full name, date of birth, marital status, current contact details (postal address, telephone number, and e-mail address), nationality, and languages spoken (with level of proficiency).

Note: According to labor legislation in South Africa, no individual may be discriminated against in terms of age, race, gender, and so on.

References

List a number of work references with names, designations, and contact telephone numbers.

Note: The obligation of employment consultants or potential employers is to contact references only with your permission. This should happen only when an offer is about to be made by the potential employer.

Other

List your personal attributes—that is, your own perceived strengths, character, and interpersonal skills.

RESUME PRESENTATION

Format

In general, there are two types of resumes that can be used according to personal preference or depending on the circumstances: a brief profile or a comprehensive CV.

Brief Profile

This is a summarized version of the comprehensive resume. The brief profile should include your personal information and educational background. In this format, you do not need to elaborate on each of the positions in your career history, as a chronological list of the positions you have held will be sufficient. Provide more details about your current or most relevant position, such as duties and responsibilities, reporting lines, and financial and staff responsibility. When applying for a position, it is acceptable to submit a brief profile initially. Should you then be notified that you are a potential candidate for the position, you may furnish your full CV.

Note: In your profile, mention that you also have a comprehensive CV should it be required.

Comprehensive Curriculum Vitae

Incorporate all the categories of information mentioned in the previous section and, in particular, include specifics on each position in your work history.

Layout

Your resume should start with your personal information, followed by your educational background. The next section should cover your work experience. In terms of work experience, it is acceptable to lay this out chronologically, reverse chronologically, or functionally.

Length

There is no prescribed length for either a brief profile or a comprehensive CV. However, the information contained in a brief profile should be kept to a minimum.

Attachments

Recent College Graduate

Grades, certificates, diplomas, and letters of reference/recommendation should be attached to your application.

Note: In South Africa, the letter of reference given to graduates is generally referred to as a testimonial.

Professional

Grades, certificates, and letters of reference need not necessarily accompany your profile/CV. If the position for which you applied is at a relatively senior level, and should you be the preferred candidate, the company or recruitment consultancy will corroborate your qualifications and conduct reference checks with those individuals supplied as references by you with your permission.

Photos

If you wish, you may personalize your application by including a photograph of yourself, but this is not necessary.

E-mail Applications

E-mail is increasingly being utilized by employers as a means of receiving job applications. When word-processing your e-mail, pay attention to the normal standards and protocols of handwritten/word-processed correspondence, such as spelling and grammar and using upper- and lowercase type correctly. Lack of due care in editing can destroy the image of a professional individual.

COVER LETTERS

When applying for any position, your curriculum vitae should be accompanied by a brief and to-the-point cover letter. Your letter should be no more than one page in length.

Content/Detail

Begin by introducing yourself in terms of your qualifications and current area of expertise. State the name of your current company and briefly describe your current position and responsibilities as well as reporting structures. Give a brief synopsis of your particular strengths and your reasons for considering a career change. When applying to an executive search consultancy or recruitment agency, set out your requirements regarding industry sector and function as well as at least two geographical preferences.

If replying to an advertisement, quote the reference and job title at the top of the page and then clearly set out how your abilities and experience are relevant to the requirements of the position. If you are not a South African citizen, a work permit is required.

If you are presently unemployed, briefly state the reason.

Finally, set out clearly your availability to attend interviews. Ensure that your name, address, and contact details are clearly legible, as fax machines and e-mails can distort the typeface.

JOB INFORMATION SOURCES

Newspapers

Daily newspapers and the Sunday newspaper, *The Sunday Times*, are the principal sources of information for employment advertisements.

The Business Times, a supplement of *The Sunday Times*, is the publication of choice to attract candidates from around South Africa. The paper also publishes a web site as a supplement to the weekly printed newspaper. This has a searchable function as well as an e-mail alert to jobs that match a particular interest area. The appointments web site and job advertisements can be found at www.bigbreak.co.za.

The Independent Newspaper Group owns 14 daily local newspapers. They have combined all these publications into a searchable web site with a large career section. This site gives advice on various topical issues with regard to the South African work scene and can be found at www.careers.iol.co.za.

Internet Sites

Many of the country's largest employment agencies and search consultants have their own web sites (for example, www.woodburnmann.co.za). However, if they have advertised the position, the ads can be found on the newspaper web sites just mentioned. Web sites and companies continue to go through major changes in the South African environment, so to give more detailed job source information is difficult in a printed publication. For more specific web sites relating to specific industry sectors, see the South African search engine www.max.co.za.

Note: This site will also be useful in terms of finding out any other information required on South Africa.

WORK PERMITS/VISAS

If you intend to seek work actively in South Africa, a work seeker's permit is required. This must be obtained from outside South Africa. Once a firm job offer is obtained, application for a work permit must be made, again from outside South Africa. Application can be made with the South African diplomatic mission nearest to the applicant's residence. The work permit application must be accompanied by:

▶ A firm offer of employment from the prospective employer. This must include a job description and the details of a service contract.

▶ A letter of motivation by the prospective employer is very important and must explain why a South African citizen could not have filled the vacancy. Proof must also be provided regarding the advertising process that was followed to fill the post, the outcome of the responses, and why the South Africans who responded were not considered suitable.

▶ The applicant's detailed curriculum vitae with full details of academic or technical qualifications and practical experience.

▶ Certified copies of the applicant's passport.

It takes approximately eight weeks for a work permit application to be processed. The applicant may not commence work with an employer until the application has been approved. The initial application will be approved for a period of six months. After that period, the applicant will have to apply for an extension and provide a letter from the employer to state that the applicant is still in the employ of the company.

INTERVIEW ADVICE

▶ Prepare yourself thoroughly on the background of your potential employer company. The Internet is especially useful. This will also enable you to ask searching questions of the interviewer.

- ► Listen to the questions and answer them with insight and confidence. Be incisive and speak clearly.
- ► Dress appropriately for the interview and for the industry in which you wish to further your career. Your choice of attire emphasizes your professionalism.
- ► Arrive at the interview punctually; if running late for the interview, it is appropriate to advise the person who is awaiting your arrival. Ensure that you know exactly where the discussion will take place. Allow sufficient time for the interview. Turn off your cell phone during the interview.
- ► In order to sell yourself, be prepared to discuss your strengths, weaknesses, and career achievements. Have a clear idea of your goals and your planned career path. Know how you rate in terms of the requirements for the position.
- ► Do not adopt an arrogant or flippant approach. Even if the interviewer is able to put you at ease, never become familiar.
- ► Avoid smoking during the interview.

CULTURAL ADVICE

- ► South Africa has a long history that encompasses many people, both native and European. This heterogeneous nature of South Africa's population has given rise to a cross-pollination of cultures, manifesting itself in a range of languages, arts, and religions.
- ► Although English is the most widely recognized business language in South Africa, official status has been given to the prominent 11 languages at national level. Each culture includes its own customs, assumptions, beliefs, values, rules, norms, practices, and arts. Therefore, it is important that the variations in culture be effectively managed, understood, and incorporated within a corporate culture.
- ► It is helpful to understand that the Western view of time is diametrically opposed to the African view. Although there has been a move among locals toward a more Westernized approach to time, the traditional African view is based on a circular concept. This concept is an acceptance of an external locus of control, as opposed to the lineal concept where a person has the ability to determine his or her own destiny.
- ► There is an impact on business due to these fundamentally differing views. However, the variety and intricacies of the 11 cultures are difficult to condense. You are advised to read *The African Way*, by Mike Boon (Zebra Press, 1996) when contemplating a leadership role in South Africa.

Spain and Portugal

Alberto Fuentes and Helena Silva, Mercuri Urval

COUNTRY OVERVIEW

Spain

Spain is made up of the Iberian Peninsula, which borders with France to the north and is separated from Africa by the Strait of Gibraltar, and also includes two island chains, the Balearic Islands and the Canaries, and town cities in the northern tip of Africa, Ceuta and Melilla. Spain is located in the southwestern-most part of Europe and is bordered on the east by the Mediterranean Sea and on the west by the Atlantic Ocean.

Spain is well known for its warm, Mediterranean climate, especially in the eastern and southern parts of Spain. Yet there are major differences in temperatures in the Meseta or central part of Spain, where winters are very cold and summers extremely hot. Overall, this weather is favorable to the habitat of numerous species and the creation of the large natural parks located throughout the country.

Spain is a parliamentary monarchy with the king as head of state. The country is led by a parliament democratically elected every four years and an executive government, with a president and cabinet ministers. Spain is basically a middle-class society active in a variety of enterprises including agriculture, fishing, and industrial manufacturing, and specialty services of all types highlighting the importance of tourism in the country.

Spain's constitution is relatively new, having been put into place only in 1978. This document recognizes and guarantees the right of the country to divide its 50 provinces into 17 autonomous communities, which gives them freedom to establish laws and govern themselves in certain areas. These communities are: Galicia, Principado de Asturias, Cantabria, País Vasco, Comunidad Foral de Navarra, Castilla-León, La Rioja, Aragón, Cataluña, Comunidad de Madrid, Comunidad Valenciana, Castilla La Mancha, Extremadura, Andalucía, Región de Murcia, Baleares, and Canarias.

Spain has a population of approximately 50 million inhabitants. The capital of Madrid is home to six million people. The official language is Castellano, although there are other recognized languages in the different communities.

Portugal

Portugal is a country in southwestern Europe. The mainland is located at the extreme southwest of the Iberian Peninsula and has an area of 91,985 square kilometers. It is bounded north and east by Spain and west and south by the Atlantic

Ocean. The Portuguese territory also includes the archipelagos of the Azores and Madeira in the Atlantic Ocean.

Portugal has a population of 9.9 million inhabitants. Portugal has one of the youngest populations in the European Union: about 25 percent are under the age of 15 years.

The foundation of Portugal dates back to the year 1143. The stability of its continental borders, which have remained virtually unchanged since the thirteenth century, make Portugal one of the oldest nations in the world, reflecting its distinctive and internal unity. Under the terms of the present constitution, the Portuguese Republic (founded in 1910) operates under a democratic rule of law based on popular sovereignty, pluralism of expression, and democratic political organization.

The constitution establishes a semipresidential system based on the rules of representative democracy. Sovereignty is exercised by four entities in accordance with the principles of the division of powers: president of the Republic, Assembly of the Republic, government, and courts.

Portugal's accession to the European Union was a historic landmark in the development of the Portuguese economy. There has been a progressive opening of the Portuguese economy to the outside world since 1988. This has led to an increase in the average growth rate of GDP due to increases in consumption, investment, public expenditure, and exports.

The business world is comprised primarily of small and medium-sized family-run companies. Traditionally, and in view of favorable natural conditions, economic activities focus on textiles, shoe manufacturing, tourism, cork, and paper pulp. Reflecting a recent trend, new sectors have evolved in the car industry and electronics.

The official language of the country is Portuguese. However, the Portuguese are comfortable engaging in a business or social conversation in English. Other Latin languages are also commonly known (e.g., French, Spanish, and Italian). For historical reasons, dating back to the foundation of the Portuguese nation, the Catholic Church still plays a dominant role in everyday life.

RESUME SPECIFICS

Education

Include in this section specifics about your junior/high school education, including the name of school, location, and year graduated. Any studies taken abroad are highly valued and should be included.

Note: Technical training or *formación profesional* in specific courses should be included if applicable toward the position of interest.

Secondly, include your college/university education. Identify the name of the institution, location, degree, and graduation year (or years attended). Include your major and describe any courses of special interest. Highlight any honors attained.

Note: Most Spanish and Portuguese university programs are lengthier than those of many other countries. In addition, foreign studies are viewed as quite practical. Unless they have to be accredited or certified by local professional organizations (doctors, lawyers, engineers, etc.), there is no problem in such foreign studies being considered.

Extracurricular Activities

Such activities are seldom discussed. Because of the intense study program, most students only focus on passing their courses, and spend what little time they have left pursuing leisure activities with friends.

Awards/Honors

List awards or honors of importance attained for scholastic achievement. It is preferable to use the Latin term *cum laude* rather than grade point average. The GPA evaluation of academic achievement is not used and is seldom understood in Spain.

Additional Education/Specialized Training

Any postgraduate or specialized courses should be listed in this section, including where and when they were taken. Highlight the training that is relevant to the type of job you are applying for. Avoid listing courses that are not remotely applicable or that were taken just to satisfy a hobby. Language and computer courses are highly valued and should be included. Highlight any diplomas or titles attained, as well.

Work Experience

List the companies that you have worked for, your job title, and employment dates. It will be assumed that the position was full-time unless you specify otherwise (e.g., internship). Give a brief description of the company and your main responsibilities. Note any major accomplishments achieved during these periods. Do not omit any functions performed that are applicable to the type of job you are applying for.

Achievements/Accomplishments

Promotions, awards, and special accomplishments obtained on the job should be highlighted. For managerial and sales positions, identify figures and percentages over established objectives, contributions to the companies' profit, or any special distinction within a team.

Note: It is very uncommon for companies to recognize their employees with awards. Spaniards and Portuguese are quite practical, and generally give importance only to monetary bonuses earned.

Special Skills

Foreign language proficiency is exceedingly important in the global market. English is requested for most positions with multinational companies. Identify other languages you can speak, read, and write. Describe language levels as basic, middle, high, or fluent. Include certificates or test grades from commonly recognized institutions.

It is a must to include your knowledge of specific computer programs, regardless of the position you are applying for. Of course, if you are applying for a job in the computer/telecommunications sector, then you need to be quite detailed in your description.

Professional Affiliations

List any professional affiliations relevant to your focus area. Include information about your involvement with activities within the organization or any leadership role.

Military Experience

Military service is still mandatory in Spain and Portugal. However, for foreigners it is not necessary to make reference to this experience unless your home country has similar requirements. For ex-military professionals, it is important that the positions and responsibilities performed be translated into civilian terms so that they can be better understood by local companies.

Note: Until the Spanish and Portuguese armed forces become totally volunteer/professional organizations, society will continue to consider its members as poorly trained, laid-back public workers. It is difficult for many companies to understand and value military experience, unless the employers themselves come from countries where the military is appreciated.

Volunteer Experience

Any previous or current volunteer work (*voluntariado*) should be described. Although this activity is not often found in resumes, it can be an indicator to potential employers of the person's interest and commitment to helping others. Identify if any managerial or responsible positions were held.

Personal Information

This is the first information found on a resume after the person's name. Employers expect to see the individual's address, date and place of birth, marital status, telephone number, and e-mail address, if available. Not providing this information can lead to your resume not being considered for the selection process.

At the end of the resume, you may include your personal interests such as sports, hobbies, and so forth, but keep the list short and credible.

References

It is becoming less common to see a list of references written at the end of a resume. More often "References available upon request" is written at the end. If they are listed, they should be current and include the name, title, company, and telephone number of each person (preferably managers). In any case, this topic will come up at a later stage of the selection process with the employer.

RESUME PRESENTATION

Format and Layout

Your resume should be written in a way that is easy to read. The majority of resumes are done in reverse chronological order (beginning with your current job). Functional resumes (grouping work performance by type of activity instead of by date) give the impression that there are gaps in the employment history and are much harder to follow.

Make frequent use of headings, indentation, underlining, bold letters, and so on to highlight the most important points. Since this first impression is critical, make sure there is not too much information on one page. Use an easy-to-read font and select a clean, quality A4-size sheet.

After the personal information section, begin with your educational background.

Length

Ideally, only two pages should be used, but there are still individuals from the old school who use additional sheets. For certain managerial and technical positions, a third page is acceptable.

Attachments

Other than a cover letter, there is no need to send any attachments with your resume. Grades, certificates, and letters of reference, if needed, will be asked for later on in the selection process. Do not send any original documents, since these will most likely not be returned to you.

It is quite common to send a photo with your resume. If this is done, ensure it does you justice. Too often, poorly taken photos are sent that could significantly reduce your chances to be called for an interview.

E-mail Applications

It is increasingly common for employers to list their e-mail address to receive resumes.

Note: Because the practice of sending resumes via e-mail is still fairly new, many individuals who are skeptical of the capability of the employer to receive and download the thousands of applications prefer to be safe and send a paper copy as well. If the position applied for is important enough, it is better to be safe than sorry and also mail a hard copy.

COVER LETTERS

A cover letter should always accompany a resume. It should be one page and typed on A4 paper. If you prefer to handwrite it, your letter must be clear and legible. This letter should be personalized and adapted for each position. Using a standardized or canned letter can actually have a negative effect on your application. Although it is not uncommon to send a resume by itself, a cover letter can sometimes make the difference and permit you to explain why you are the right person for the job. When sending a resume to a company that has not advertised a specific position, it is essential that a cover letter be included.

Content/Detail

Your cover letter should start by making reference to the position you are applying for. The main objective is to catch the reader's attention so that he or she will be interested in scheduling you for an interview. Be sure that the letter expresses your feelings about the job and why you feel that you can be an asset to the company. Avoid listing too many details that are also found in the resume. Highlight key studies and experiences applicable to the position. Interpret this information as added value to the firm, and let the reader know why you are interested in joining the team. This letter also provides you the opportunity to address specific requirements stated in the advertisement. If you fall short of certain demands, be proactive and identify them, explaining how you can compensate or can overcome these shortfalls. It is best to address these issues, since an employer will spot your limitations when reading your resume.

Note: It is very common that resumes arrive without a cover letter or with brief notes that basically state "Here is my resume." For this reason, a well-developed cover letter can make the difference. It can be especially useful for a foreigner as a way of explaining one's particular situation and reasons for applying for a job in Spain or Portugal.

JOB INFORMATION SOURCES

Newspapers

Spain

The majority of employment ads are found in the Sunday edition of daily periodicals, the most important being *El País*, *ABC*, and *El Mundo* with national coverage and the *Vanguardia* for the Barcelona/Cataluña region. There are also specific weekly employment periodicals such as *Mercado Laboral* and *Mercado de Trabajo*, which usually list lower- to mid-level positions. If you are interested in a job in a specific city other than Madrid or Barcelona (or Lisbon or Porto in Portugal) then you can supplement the national-coverage newspapers by buying the local periodical. Generally, the ads are published in the local language. However, it is becoming increasingly common to see these in English, if the company is advertising for an international position.

El País (Madrid, national)
Phone: 34 91 337 82 00

ABC (Madrid, Sevilla, national)
Phone: 34 91 339 90 00

El Mundo (Madrid, national)
Phone: 34 91 586 4800

Vanguardia (Barcelona)
Phone: 34 93 301 54 54

Las Provincias (Valencia)
Phone: 34 96 350 22 11

El Correo (Bilbao)
Phone: 34 94 487 01 00

La Voz de Galicia (Galicia)
Phone: 34 981 18 01 80

Mercado Laboral
Phone: 34 91 575 00 39

Mercado de Trabajo
Phone: 34 91 517 17 98

Portugal

In Portugal, the majority of employment ads are found in a weekly newspaper called *Expresso*, which has national coverage. For positions in the north only (Porto), then the Sunday edition of *Journal de Noticias* will be useful. All types of positions are listed in these papers, but they generally include only supervisory and managerial openings for larger companies.

Expresso (national)
Phone: 351 1 311 40 00

Journal de Noticias (north—Porto; use the Sunday edition)
Phone: 351 2 209 61 00

Diario do Noticias (national; use the weekend editions)
Phone: 351 1 318 75 00

Semana Informatica (for the computer market)
Phone: 351 21 356 70 00

Business Organizations

Camara de Comercio de Madrid
Plaza de la Independencia, 1
28001 Madrid
Phone: 34 91 538 35 00

Camara do Comercio American
Pza. D. Estefania, 155—5° E
1000 Lisbon
Phone: 351 1 357 25 61

Internet Sites

Although It is not yet very common for national companies, larger multinationals often advertise open positions on their web sites. It may be useful to direct your job-hunting efforts by contacting the web sites of companies in your field of interest. Employment web sites in Spain are:

www.teleline.es
www.todotrabajo.com
www.jobline.com
www.itjobworld.com
www.infojob.com

Currently, there are no specific web sites for jobs in Portugal.

Telephone Directory

The telephone directory and Yellow Pages are not very useful tools in finding companies you may be interested in working for. In many cases, companies are listed under other names, making it difficult to identify them. It is much more useful to get the latest Dun & Bradstreet or Dicodi Company reference works, in either book or CD-ROM format. Another effective source is to contact the commercial office of foreign embassies and get their company directories, though there is typically a fee involved (which ranges from US$20 to US$150). Most directories are organized in alphabetical order or by sector.

Country Employment Office

The Spanish employment entity called "INEM" and the Portuguese counterpart, Instituto do Emprego e Formaçao Professional, are mostly used by local nationals. These organizations assist the unemployed to find jobs, normally in technical, sales, and lower-level supervisory positions.

WORK PERMITS/VISAS

Visas

The need for a visa depends on your country of birth or your current residence. For details, contact the Spanish or Portuguese consulate or embassy in your home country. Members of the European Economic Community do not require visas.

Residence and Work Permits

Residence and work permits are required for all foreign citizens other than EEC members who want to work in Spain. Work permits can be applied for only if you have a letter of intent signed by a potential employer. This of course must be accompanied by a work permit application. Processing permits and residence applications can take between four to eight months. For more information contact:

Spain
Ministerio del Interior
C/ Bretón de los Herreros, 41
28003 Madrid
Phone: 34-91-441 15 00

Portugal
Ministerio da Administraçao Interna
Serviço de Estrangeiros e Fronteiras
Rua Conselheiro José Silvestre Ribeiro, 4
1649-007 Lisboa (Portugal)
Phone: 351-1-715 52 68, 351-1-711 50 00

INTERVIEW ADVICE

▶ There is nothing like good preparation prior to attending a job interview. Use the company's web site or reference books to get the basic information. Review the job ad and its requirements to ensure that you address these issues in the interview.

▶ It is important to show interest and enthusiasm for the job you are applying for, but be careful not to exaggerate this point. Extreme self-confidence can be viewed as naïveté or arrogance by locals.

▶ Do not be surprised if the first interview lasts only 20 to 30 minutes. It is intended merely to give you an overall picture of the company and position, and give your prospective employer a first impression of you. Do this part well, and you will have a chance to get into more details in the next meeting.

▶ Dress appropriately for the interview. Spaniards and Portuguese are quite conscious of their appearance and keep abreast of fashion. For almost any position, men wear a suit and tie and women wear a conservative outfit (suit with either skirt or pants).

▶ Although there are equal opportunity laws, it is quite common to be asked to disclose personal information such as age, marital status, and family details. Of course you are not obligated to answer, but not doing so could hinder your chances of continuing in the selection process.

CULTURAL ADVICE

▶ Business traits such as can-do attitudes, resourcefulness, and being results oriented are characteristics highly sought after in the labor market. Take advantage of this, but don't go overboard.

▶ Socializing with colleagues and clients is quite common in the Spanish and Portuguese cultures. Although lunch meetings tend to be shorter, do not be surprised to spend up to two hours at these events. You can try to cut them short, but be tactful. After a full meal, the challenge is to stay awake and be productive in the afternoon.

▶ Other than in a few multinational companies, there are seldom opportunities for family events. Spaniards and Portuguese tend to separate their family lives from their work environments.

▶ Do not expect to do any job-hunting during the month of August. Spain shuts down and goes on summer vacation (recruitment is virtually nonexistent). The situation is similar in Portugal, though you may be able to contact companies that are working during this period.

Sweden

Hans Rosengren, Mercuri Urval

COUNTRY OVERVIEW

Sweden is one of the northernmost countries in Europe with 15 percent of its surface north of the polar circle. One-tenth of the country is covered by lakes, and there are extensive forests and wildlife. Swedes thrive on being outdoors, no matter the season. Over 85 percent of the 8.8 million inhabitants live in cities and towns. Stockholm, located in central Sweden, is the capital, with 1.5 million inhabitants. Other major cities include Göteborg, Malmö, Orebro, Norrköping, and Uppsala. Approximately 20 percent of Sweden's inhabitants have a foreign background.

Sweden is a monarchy, with the king as head of state. The country is also a democracy, led by a parliament elected every four years, and an executive government, with a prime minister and advisory ministers. The prime minister is the head of Sweden's government. Sweden is a market economy, with an extensive social welfare system. State benefits, supported by hefty personal taxes, include child care, health care, and generous pension plans. Sweden is a member of the EU and has 22 representatives in the EU parliament.

The official language of the country is Swedish. However, most Swedes are very comfortable engaging in a business or social conversation in English. German and French are also commonly known. The majority of Swedes are Lutheran (though most are nonpracticing), with other Christian denominations also represented.

Sweden is basically a middle-class society. There is a strong feeling of security among the population, in large part due to the strong welfare system. Swedes pay great attention to equality between men and women, both at home and at work. Many companies of global importance are based in Sweden, including Ericsson, Saab, Volvo, ABB, and Electrolux. Because of its geographic location, Sweden is typically dark by 3:00 P.M. in the winter and still light at midnight in the summer.

RESUME SPECIFICS

Education

Explain your focus areas during upper secondary school/high school, with reference to specific courses and programs. Also, state your graduation year and if you have studied abroad.

Note: In Sweden, students select focus areas in their high school studies, such as engineering or biology, similar to having a major in college.

Devote the most attention in this section to details about your college/university education. State your graduation year, major, and education title. Briefly describe any student internship or diploma work: length of time and number of credits.

Extracurricular Activities

Describe any extracurricular activities in which you participated, such as arranging different types of student projects, working within the student administration, and so on.

Awards/Honors

List any awards and honors received for scholastic achievement or outstanding performance in other areas.

Additional Education/Specialized Training

Any additional college/university courses should be mentioned in this context. Also, include courses or training in specialized areas, such as language, computers, or sales. Mention in-house company training programs, as well.

Work Experience

Start with listing your job title and name of the employer. Specify the employment dates and whether it was a full-time or a part-time job. Give the details of your work and your field of responsibility. Emphasize information that is relevant to the position for which you are applying. Describe how your skills have developed through your tasks and achievements. Summer jobs and shorter periods of employment, performed prior to your professional career, should be summarized. If there are any gaps in employment history, it is important that you explain the reason for each gap in reasonable detail. Also, for part-time employment, explain the reason why you chose not to work full-time.

Achievements/Accomplishments

Any awards, special recognition, or promotions received during employment should be highlighted.

Special Skills

Proficiency in foreign languages and knowledge of specific computer programs should be noted.

Professional Affiliations

List any professional affiliations relevant to your focus area. Include information about your involvement with activities within the organization or any leadership roles.

Military Experience

Include information in your resume/CV about your military service (which is mandatory in Sweden). State the focus of your training, your field of responsibility, and any managerial position. Include the dates and location of your service.

Volunteer Experience

Describe any previous or current volunteer activities or *commissions of trust*. These may include activities with associations, clubs, or areas of personal interest (connected to your children's school, sports, charity, etc.). Any volunteer experience that you have initiated or participated in should be described.

Personal Information

Describe your personal interests such as sports activities, gardening, reading, rebuilding old cars, politics, and so on. Do not exaggerate, as it is important to appear believable. Family activities and hobbies may be mixed in with this section.

Note: In Sweden, "civil" status refers to your marital status.

References

The references you select should be connected to your professional experience, such as previous managers. These people should be well acquainted with your work performance and be rather recent in time.

RESUME PRESENTATION

Format and Layout

Your resume/CV should represent a clear picture of your education, internships, and employment, as well as other important experiences that might interest an employer, such as professional association memberships. A chronologically arranged list with the aforementioned headings is best. (List your oldest experience first and end with your most recent.)

Always begin your resume/CV by describing your educational background, followed by the details of your professional experience.

Length

Your resume/CV should be no longer than two pages.

Attachments

Grades, certificates, and letters of reference do not necessarily have to be included with your application, as you can present them at the interview. If you prefer to attach such documents, choose your most recent grades and a letter of reference from your current employer. Any thesis papers or diploma work should not be sent initially.

Note: Any documents attached to your resume should be the original documents, not copies, as these will be returned to you.

To personalize an application with a small photo is becoming more and more accepted. Including a photo gives the reader a more vivid picture of the person and allows the reader to put a face with a name for future reference.

E-mail Applications

It is increasingly common that employers in Sweden accept, appreciate, and prioritize applications via e-mail. In this case, always attach your resume to the letter/e-mail. Video recordings are usually not recommended.

Other

Note: It is recommended that you have your resume/CV "attested" or "verified." This means asking someone who can verify the validity of the information contained in your resume/CV (such as a parent, teacher, or good acquaintance) to sign it on the final page. This also applies to any copies of grades, certificates, or letters of reference.

COVER LETTERS

An application should always include a personalized cover letter and complete resume. Furthermore, you may attach grades, certificates, and letters of reference or recommendations. A personal cover letter of one page is usually sufficient. Although a typed application in A4 format is preferred, a handwritten letter is acceptable provided that the writing is legible.

Note: A postcard can be mailed in advance to tell the employer that you are interested in the announced position but unable to send in a set of documents before the deadline. However, this must be followed promptly by a complete set of application documents.

Content/Detail

Your cover letter should start with a phrase stating the position for which you are applying. Remember that the letter aims to raise the reader's interest, so try to let your personality influence the content. In other words—be yourself. Everything you say in the letter should be found in more detail in your resume/CV. Start by describing your current position, the work content, field of responsibility, organizational level/reporting structure, and the name of the employer. Also, state the date when you entered your current position and your personal and professional development within the company.

Explain why you are applying for this job. Analyze your experiences and emphasize those which are connected to the position for which you are applying. Continue with a concentrated description of your previous professional experiences. Include details concerning your current personal situation: marital status, ability to relocate, availability to travel on business trips, and so on. Also, include relevant volunteer experience, longer periods of foreign travel, and your future professional goals. Describe your personal interests in a reasonable manner (do not list so many personal interests that you could not possibly have done them all!)

Note: If you are unemployed at present, you should state that in the letter.

JOB INFORMATION SOURCES

Newspapers

Daily papers, trade journals, and the like all contain employment ads. The most common daily papers are *Dagens Nyheter, Dagens Industri, Svenska Dagbladet, Göteborgsposten,* and *Sydsvenska Dagbladet.*

Note: No newspaper covers the entire country. Also, no Swedish newspaper has a complete supplement of recruitment ads in any language but Swedish. However, you do find that these publications contain individual company advertisements in different languages, primarily in English.

Dagens Nyheter (News of Today, Stockholm area)
Phone: +46-8-738 10 00
E-mail: prenservice@dn.se

Dagens Industri (News of Industry, entire Sweden)
Phone: +46-8-736 50 00
E-mail: pren@di.se

Svenska Dagbladet (Daily News of Sweden, Stockholm area)
Phone: +46-8-13 50 00
E-mail: kundservice@svd.se

Göteborgsposten (Göteborg, west coast area)
Phone: +46-31-62 40 00
E-mail: prenservice@gp.se

Sydsvenska Dagbladet (Daily News of southern Sweden)
Phone: +46-40-28 12 00
E-mail: sydsvenskan@sydsvenskan.se

Chamber of Commerce

Stockholm Chamber of Commerce
Vastra Tradgardsgatan 9
Box 16050
S.103 22 Stockholm
Phone: +46-8-23 12 00
Fax: +46-8-11 24 32

Internet Sites

Through the Internet, companies usually advertise open positions on their own web sites. It may be worthwhile to look for companies in your field of interest. The most popular employment web sites in Sweden are:

www.jobline.se
www.stepstone.se
www.jobfinder.se

www.mercuri-urval.com.
www.topjobs.se
www.smartjobb.nu

The largest daily papers also place their employment ads on the Internet.

Dagens Nyheter   www.dn.se
Dagens Industri   www.di.se
Svenska Dagbladet   www.svd.se
Göteborgsposten   www.gp.se
Sydsvenska Dagbladet   www.sydsvenskan.se

Telephone Directory

In the Swedish telephone directory Yellow Pages, you will find companies listed under the relevant trade heading. This can be a fruitful way to start looking for companies that interest you. In the Pink Pages, all companies are listed in alphabetical order.

Country Employment Office

The Swedish employment bureau, Arbetsförmedlingen, issues weekly papers. One of them, *Platsjournalen*, is geographically divided, whereas *Nytt Jobb* is divided into different employment sectors. Local addresses and telephone numbers can be found at the web site for the national employment bureau at www.ams.se.

WORK PERMITS/VISAS

Visas

A business or permanent residence visa is required for most foreign visitors staying more than three months.

Residence and Work Permits

Residence and work permits are required for all foreign citizens who want to work in Sweden (only citizens from the other Nordic countries are excluded from this requirement). Work permits can be applied for only after you have signed an employment contract. A written offer of employment must accompany the work permit application. Work permits are processed and approved by:

Statens Invandrarverk
Phone: +46-11-15 60 00
Fax: +46-11-15 66 70
E-mail: invandrarverket@siv.se

INTERVIEW ADVICE

▶ Feel free to telephone the contact person listed in the employment advertisement before sending in your application, for further details, or just to introduce yourself. However, do not persistently telephone for the status of the recruitment process.

▶ It is wise to avoid discussing salary and other parts of the compensation package early in the process. However, if requested, you should state your salary preference.

▶ Environmental awareness issues are being more and more highlighted in Swedish society. An individual's environmental beliefs and practices can be brought up in the interview.

▶ Swedes expect and want independence in their work. Office hierarchies are flat (horizontal) and lack the constant hands-on management style of the more vertical structure.

▶ Sweden has strong trade unions, which means that the employee's rights are carefully regulated within the field of labor laws and collective agreements. For example, the minimum union-regulated vacation is five weeks per year.

CULTURAL ADVICE

▶ It is wise to show a humble spirit and style. Bragging or appearing aggressive or overly ambitious is considered to be in poor taste.

▶ Swedes are always punctual, both professionally and socially, and expect punctuality from others.

▶ Swedes are very consensus-oriented and avoid confrontation. Just because someone does not openly disagree with you does not necessarily mean that the person agrees!

▶ Since most Swedes take their five-week annual vacation after June 21st (Swedish midsummer), the period immediately prior to, during, and after is a difficult time for conducting new business. Christmas holidays are also lengthy and extend to January 6th.

▶ In social circumstances, always arrive at someone's home with a hostess gift (typically flowers). Do not touch your drink until your host has said, "Skoal!" ("Cheers!") Even at restaurants, when the first drink is served, everyone "skoals" everyone else while looking them directly in the eye.

▶ There are severe penalties in Sweden for driving with any amount of liquor in your system.

Switzerland _____

Petra Augustin, Amrop International

COUNTRY OVERVIEW

Switzerland is situated in the center of Western Europe. Approximately 60 percent of the total surface area (41,285 square kilometers) is covered by mountains and foothills. The country has seven million inhabitants of whom 19 percent are foreigners. The majority of the population live between Lake Constance and Lake Geneva in a high-density crescent about 300 kilometers long.

Structurally, Switzerland has evolved as a federal republic, a confederation with 26 member states known as cantons and half-cantons, which have retained a high degree of autonomy. The legislature (Bundesversammlung) consists of two chambers: the National Council (Nationalrat), which represents the population as a whole, and the Council of States (Ständerat), which represents the cantons. The senior executive body is the Federal Council (Bundesrat), consisting of seven ministers, who are elected individually for a four-year term by the parliament. The group is headed by the Bundespräsident.

The federal capital is Berne. The largest cities are Zurich, Basle, Geneva, and Berne. The economic and employment centers of Switzerland are Zurich and Basle in the east and Geneva and Lausanne in the western region. Switzerland is not a member of the European Union, which failed to pass in a countrywide vote.

The country is characterized by its linguistic and cultural diversity. According to the Federal Constitution, Switzerland has four official languages: German (spoken by about 65 percent of the population), French (18.4 percent), Italian (9.8 percent), and Raeteromansch (0.8 percent). Most businesspeople in eastern Switzerland are English-speaking; however, in the west, especially in the Italian regions, they prefer to speak their own country language. Christianity is the dominant religion; 48 percent of the population are Roman Catholic and 44 percent are Protestant.

Despite a lack of raw materials, Switzerland is an important player in world trade and one of the world´s wealthiest industrial nations. It has a highly developed economy with trading and financial relations with countries all over the world. The economic importance of this small country is reflected in the gross national product, which is higher than that of any other European state.

Switzerland has a working population of over three million. Foreigners make up almost a quarter of the workforce. The most important industrial sectors are engineering, machine industry and electronics, chemicals and pharmaceuticals, the manufacture of precision instruments, watchmaking, textiles, and food industries. Insurance companies and tourism comprise the service sector, which is dominated by the exceptionally strong banking industry.

Foreign trade is the country's lifeblood. Switzerland's main export market is the European Union. Many companies of global importance are based in Switzerland, and a great number of foreign companies have their European headquarters, offices, and/or factories in Switzerland. This is especially true in the financial services sector (UBS, Credit Suisse Group, Zurich Group, Swiss Re Group), in the machine/engineering industry (ABB, Sulzer), food (Nestlé, Kraft Jacobs Suchard), and the chemical/pharmaceutical industry (Novartis, F. Hoffmann-La Roche).

RESUME SPECIFICS

Note: Because of the variety of languages and the international character of business in Switzerland, you will find two forms of CVs: German resumes and English CVs. The English version is the one that should be sent to international companies, if not specified otherwise, or both can be sent.

Older applicants are in the habit of sending a complete set of documents with detailed attachments, such as diplomas, testimonials, and so forth. Younger applicants typically send shorter international CVs.

German Resume

The German resume has a detailed chronological format, including:

► Education.

► Awards/honors.

► Additional education/specialized training.

► Work experience describing all steps of your professional career, including the name of your employer, job title, and areas of responsibility. You should also mention any gaps in your employment history.

► Special skills, especially language skills.

► Testimonials (including diplomas).

► References (for higher-management levels).

► Military experience/career (this area is not as important today as it was in the past).

► Personal information: personal interests such as family activities and hobbies.

► Details about your age, salary requirements, and period of notice.

English Resume

The English CV has a detailed reverse chronological format, including:

► Education.

► Awards/honors.

► Additional education/specialized training.

► Detailed work experience descriptions (beginning with the most recent).

▶ Achievements/accomplishments.

▶ Special skills (especially languages).

▶ Outside interests/hobbies.

▶ Personal information.

Information on military experience is not required. Do not include testimonials.

RESUME PRESENTATION

German Resume

Format: Cover letter plus chronological CV typed on A4-size paper.
Length: Very detailed; usually two to three pages in length.
Attachments: References, recommendations, testimonials, and photograph.

English Resume

Format: Cover letter plus reverse chronological CV, typed on A4 paper.
Length: Concise, not so detailed; one to two pages in length.
Attachments: None (unless requested).

E-mail Applications

These are becoming more common for management positions, especially for international applicants.

COVER LETTERS

An application should always include a personalized, typed cover letter that is approximately one page in length. Handwritten cover letters are not acceptable.

State your current position. Provide detailed information about: your interest in the position for which you are applying; career goals; your relevant skills and work experience; geographical preferences; flexibility to relocate; salary range. The tone of the letter should be low-key. Honesty is a key factor; if you are unemployed, you should mention that fact. Everything you say in the letter should also be found in your resume. Address your resume to a specific person.

Note: Switzerland is a small country and developing and nurturing personal contacts is key to success.

JOB INFORMATION SOURCES

Newspapers

Large daily papers, specialist/technical journals, and commercial newspapers all contain weekly employment ads. The *NZZ* (*Neue Zürcher Zeitung*) is the most popular and widely read paper in Switzerland. Job market advertisements are limited to the four language regions (with the exception of international positions).

Note: No newspaper covers the entire country because of the language variations.

Main Newspapers

German-Speaking Regions (Ostschweiz)
NZZ—*Neue Zürcher Zeitung* (news of today)
Phone: +41 1-258 11 11
E-mail: zeitung@nzz.ch
Web site: www.nzz.ch

Tages-Anzeiger (news of today)
SonnlagsZeitung (publication on Sunday)
Phone: + 41 1-248 41 11
E-mail: inserat@tamedia.ch
Web site: www.tagesanzeiger.ch

Alpha (employment ads for management [*Kaderstellenmarkt*]; supplement of the *Tages-Anzeiger* and *SonntagsZeitung*)

Basler Zeitung (news of today; Basle area)
Phone: +41 61-639 11 11
E-mail: baz@publicitas.ch
Web site: www.baz.ch

Der Bund (news of today; Berne area)
Phone: +41 31-385 11 11
E-mail: derbund@derbund.ch
Web site: www.ebund.ch

Berner Zeitung (news of today; Berne area, main job ads)
Phone: +41 31-330 31 11
E-mail: bzonline@btm.ch
Web site: www.bzonline.ch

Neue Luzerner Zeitung (news of today; Lucerne area)
Phone: +41 41-429 51 51
E-mail: verlag@neue-lz.ch
Web site: www.neue-lz.ch

St. Galler Tagblatt (news of today; St. Gallen area)
Phone: +41 71-272 78 88
Web site: www.tagblatt.ch

Aargauer Zeitung (news of today)
Phone: +41 62-836 61 61
E-mail: inserate@azag.ch
Web site: www.azag.ch

Western Region (Westschweiz)
Le Temps (news of today)
Phone: +41 22-799 58 58
E-mail: info@letemps.ch
Web site: www.letemps.ch

Le Matin (news of today)
Phone: +41 21-349 49 49
E-mail: matin-redaction@edicom.ch
Web site: www.lematin.ch

Italian Region (Ticino)
Corriere del Ticino (news of today)
Phone: +41 91-960 31 31
E-mail: cdt@cdt.ch
Web site: www.cdt.ch

Commercial Journals/Trade Newspapers

Finanz und Wirtschaft
Phone: +41 1-298 35 35
E-mail: redaktion@fuw.ch
Web site: www.finanzinfo.ch

Die Weltwoche
Phone: +41 1-448 73 11
E-mail: redaktion@weltwoche.ch
Web site: www.weltwoche.ch

Cash
Phone: +41 1-298 28 11
E-mail: cash@ringier.ch
Web site: www.cash.ch

Chambers of Commerce/Trade Organizations

Swiss chambers of commerce and industry for each canton can be located by visiting the web site: www.cci.ch/adrcci.html.

Vorort (Swiss Trade and Industry Association)
Hegibachstrasse 47
Box 1072
CH-8032 Zurich
Phone: +41 1-389 93 00
Fax: +41 1-389 93 87
E-mail: vorort@vorort.ch
Web site: www.vorort.ch

Internet Sites

Through the Internet, companies are more and more advertising open positions on their own web sites. All the large newspapers publish their ads on the www.swissclick\jobclick.ch web site in addition to publishing ads on their own web sites. The most popular employment web sites in Switzerland are:

www.jobboerse.ch	www.job.inserat.ch
www.jobindex.ch	www.jobcenter.ch
www.swisswebjobs.ch	www.arbeitsboerse.ch
www.topjobs.ch	www.edv-jobs.ch
www.jobnet.ch	www.jobmail.ch
www.stellen.ch	www.firststudy.ch
www.job-box.ch	www.web-pool.ch

Telephone Directory/Trade Publications

In the Swiss telephone directory on the Internet (www.pearsoft.ch) you will find companies listed alphabetically. Also, in the Swiss Wirtschafts CD-ROM (based on the official Swiss register of companies) and the TOP2000 published by the newspaper *Handelszeitung*, you can find companies listed by industry and region.

Country Employment Office

The employment office on the federal level is the SECO Staatssekretariat für Wirtschaft und Arbeit (formerly BIGA—Bundesamt für Industrie Gewerbe und Arbeit) in Berne. Foreigners who are looking for work in Switzerland should address their correspondence to the Bundesamt für Ausländerfragen, Berne. The regional organization on the cantonal level is the KIGA (Kantonales Amt für Industrie Gewerbe und Arbeit), located in the capital of each canton.

WORK PERMITS/VISAS

Visas

For specific information, please refer to the Internet site www.seco.admin.ch.

Residence and Work Permits

Residence and work permits are required for all foreign citizens who want to work in Switzerland. This also applies to European citizens. Work permits can be applied for only after signing an employment contract. A written offer of employment must be submitted by the employer and accompany the work permit application. Work permits are processed and approved by the Bundesamt für Ausländerfragen, Bern, and the KIGA in combination with the police department dealing with aliens (*Fremdenpolizei*).

For all employment questions (employment conditions, employment policy, guidelines, permits) refer to the Internet site www.seco.admin.ch.

Seasonal Permit

Primarily for blue-collar workers, the seasonal permit is valid for nine months (maximum). You must exit the country for three months before the company can apply for a renewal.

B-Permit

For professional people on a management level or highly skilled/qualified specialists, the B-permit is valid for one year and can be automatically renewed if the work contract has not been canceled. You must reapply if you change employers.

C-Permit

For professional people on a management level or highly skilled/qualified specialists, the C-permit gives open-ended permission as long as there is a valid work contract (no matter the employer). You will receive this permit officially after 5 to 10 years (depending on the country of origin) of work and residence in Switzerland.

Grenzgängerbewilligung

A special agreement for inhabitants of the border zones of the neighboring countries of Switzerland, (Austria, France, Germany, and Italy), this is a work permit only and does not include permission for residence. It is processed and approved by the KIGA of the canton in combination with the police department dealing with aliens (*Fremdenpolizei*).

Note: Switzerland is not a member of the European Union.

INTERVIEW AND CULTURAL ADVICE

- ▶ Switzerland is a very small, close-knit society. To be successful, it is crucial both to develop and to nurture key contacts who can be beneficial to you throughout your career.
- ▶ It is best to have a humble style and spirit. Aggressive or overly ambitious behavior is considered inappropriate. The best approach both in business and in private life is to be understated.
- ▶ It is wise to phone the contact person mentioned in the employment ad for further details before mailing your application.
- ▶ The Switzerland of today is in transition in terms of company organization. Vertical, top-down office hierarchies are still prevalent. However, Anglo-Saxon–dominated work cultures are more horizontal in structure. This is also the trend for newer companies.
- ▶ Direct democracy, federalism, and neutrality are deeply rooted in Swiss political tradition and culture. Personal autonomy and individual responsibility dominate. This is reflected in the country's free market economy and philosophy of private enterprise. Freedom of trade is the cornerstone of the Swiss economy.
- ▶ Instead of an extensive social welfare system, the government policy is to keep restrictions to a minimum. The state grants a basic social system only for health care and pensions. This philosophy extends to a mini-

mum of state regulations in the employment sector: The official work week is 42 hours; official regulated vacations are 20 days; there is no maternity leave; very brief periods of notice are required to dismiss an employee—one to three months for middle management, six months to one year for top management. Trade unions do not play an important role.

▶ One of the consequences of the Swiss system is very low interest rates, low tax rates for companies and individuals, and low rates of unemployment in comparison to other European countries. Switzerland has a highly developed social standard where salaries and cost of living (rent, food) are concerned.

▶ Swiss are always punctual, both professionally and socially, and expect punctuality from others.

▶ In social circumstances, you always arrive at someone's home with a little gift, typically flowers or sweets.

Thailand

Prapapan Bualek, Amrop International

COUNTRY OVERVIEW

Thailand, or Muang Thai to local residents, is located in Southeast Asia. It was formerly known as Siam. Thailand has a population of approximately 60 million with over 5 million inhabitants living in the capital city, Bangkok. The country has an area of 513,115 square kilometers and is divided into 76 provinces or *changwats*. Major cities include Chiangmai, Nakorn Ratchasima (also known as Korat), Khonkaen, Nakorn Sri Thammarat, and Songkhla. Thailand's immediate neighbors are Myanmar, Laos, Cambodia, and Malaysia.

Thailand is a monarchy with the king as head of state, advised by a 12-member Privy Council. The country is governed by a prime minister, a cabinet, and a bicameral National Assembly consisting of a 347-member House of Representatives and a 216-member Senate.

Agriculture is the most important economic activity. The main exports include rice, manioc, maize, banana, pineapple, sugar cane, rubber, teak, textiles, electronics, cement, chemicals, food processing, tin, tungsten, manganese, antimony, lead, zinc, copper, and natural gas. Ethnic groups include Thais (75 percent) and Chinese (14 percent). The official language is Thai, spoken by approximately 40 million people, with many dialectal variations. English is also widely spoken in the business community. The primary religion is Buddhism. Thailand enjoys an equatorial climate in the south and a tropical monsoon climate in the north and central regions.

RESUME SPECIFICS

Education

Academic achievements should be recorded in reverse chronological order, starting from the highest (most recent) degrees or diplomas. Describe your university education together with graduation year, major subjects, and education title. Information about student training work/thesis projects should also be included, stating the length of time and references.

State the major subjects studied during upper secondary school, providing details of specific courses and programs. Indicate year of graduation and if you have studied abroad.

Note: Students in Thailand decide on their focus areas at the beginning of their third year of secondary school studies. There are basically two branches of studies, arts and sciences.

Extracurricular Activities

Include any extracurricular activities, such as student activities, voluntary work, and so on. Involvement in these activities can help to demonstrate your social skills and awareness.

Awards/Honors

List any awards and honors received (e.g., scholastic achievements or outstanding performances in other areas).

Additional Education/Specialized Training

Any additional courses should be added in this context, especially courses completed in computer studies and languages.

Work Experience

Describe work experience in reverse chronological order. List your job title, name of the employer, employment period, and description of work. Emphasize information that is relevant to the open position, and provide examples that demonstrate development of skills through the tasks handled. Give an explanation for any gaps in your employment. For part-time employment, give the reason why you chose not to work full-time.

Achievements/Accomplishments

Any awards received during employment should be mentioned.

Special Skills

Foreign language knowledge and computer literacy should be highlighted.

Professional Affiliations

Include information about your involvement with activities within professionally related organizations and any leadership roles.

Military Experience

Military service is compulsory for selected Thai males. Physically and mentally fit Thai males must either enroll at their own will or be enlisted by drawing cards (red or black). Volunteer enlistees serve in the forces for only one year, while those drawing red cards serve for a period of two years. Those who draw black cards can consider themselves free of any military service obligations.

Note: Employers in Thailand are eager to learn the military service status of prospective Thai employees, as relief of military service responsibilities implies a noninterruption of employment.

Volunteer Experience

Include your participation with associations, clubs, or areas of personal interest (youth activities, sports events, charities).

Personal Information

Describe your personal interests including recreational activities and hobbies.

Note: Some Thai employers use this section to evaluate your personality.

References

The individuals selected should be connected to your professional experience or be well acquainted with your academic performance, if you have no career-related references. Two or three names are sufficient.

RESUME PRESENTATION

Format and Layout

Your CV should be laid out for easy reading, and be presented in an informative manner without being long-winded. Fancy fonts, as well as scented and/or colored paper, are considered in poor taste.

Begin your CV with personal information, then list academic achievements, additional information (training, professional associations, hobbies), employment record (in reverse chronological order), and references. Remember, your work experience and education history should be listed in reverse chronological order beginning with your most recent experience.

Length

Your CV should not be longer than two A4 pages. Three pages are the absolute maximum.

Attachments

No attachments (copies of transcripts, passport, etc.) should be included unless requested. A passport-size photograph, neatly affixed to the top right-hand corner of the CV, would be appreciated.

E-mail Applications

Applications sent via e-mail are accepted by most employers. However, it is a good idea to confirm that your application has been received by the employer.

COVER LETTERS

Content/Detail

The cover letter should be viewed as a tool for introducing yourself and your background. Your cover letter should have a concise introduction stating the position you are applying for and, if relevant, where you obtained the information about that particular opening. The content should highlight your skill set, personal qualities, and/or background relevant to the job in question. All information should be clear, concise, and in accordance with international standards. Long-windedness will not be considered favorably.

It is always wise to find out the correct name and title of the person in charge of recruitment. Take the time to create a tailor-made cover letter.

Note: A legible handwritten letter is fine, though one that is typed will likely be more impressive.

Length

The cover letter should be no longer than one A4 page.

JOB INFORMATION SOURCES

Newspapers

English-language daily newspapers classified sections in *The Bangkok Post* and *The Nation* are especially useful in locating multinational organizations that are looking for English-speaking personnel. Employment opportunities in *The Bangkok Post* can be found in the career section of its web site, www.bkkpost.co.th.

Trade Publications

Trade publications are usually in Thai, not English, and cover a more limited part of the job market.

Business Organizations

Chambers of commerce can be a good starting point, as most have a "Job Wanted" section. Major chambers of commerce are:

American Chamber of Commerce in Thailand
Web site: www.amcham-th.org

Australian-Thai Chamber of Commerce
Web site: www.atcc.or.th

British Chamber of Commerce Thailand
Web site: www.bccthai.com

Franco-Thai Chamber of Commerce
E-mail: ftcc@ksc.th.com

German-Thai Chamber of Commerce
E-mail: ahkbkk@box1.a-net.net.th

Thai Chamber of Commerce
150 Ratchabophit Road
Bangkok 10220
Phone: (66-2) 622-1860
Fax: (66-2) 225-3372

Internet Sites

Internet sites are very effective job-hunting tools. There are several sites worth visiting:

Asian Career Web	www.intercareer.com
Career Mosaic	www.careermosaic.com
Catapult	www.wm.edu/csrv/career
Career Profile	www.careerprofile.com
Loxinfo	www.job.loxinfo.co.th
JobsDB	www.jobsdb.com
Topjobs	www.topjobs.net
Cyber Job Space	www.systop.com/job/jobspace
Siam Job Search	www.job.siam.th.edu
PR Recruitment	www.prtr.com
Job & Adverts	www.jobsadverts.co.th

Recent additions include www.searchdragon.com/thai/employ.shtml,www.jobpilot.co.th, and www.asiadragons.com/thailand/employ.

Country Employment Offices

The Department of Employment has a web site worth visiting: www.doe.go.th.

WORK PERMITS/VISAS

An alien wishing to work in Thailand must first obtain a work permit by submitting an application to the Labor Department of the Ministry of the Interior. The

Labor Department will consider the size and type of business that wants to hire an expatriate before granting the work permit.

Ministry of Labor and Social Welfare
Alien Occupation Division
Mitr-Maitri Road
Dindaeng, Bangkok 10400
Phone: (66-2) 245-6763
Fax: (66-2) 246-1795

INTERVIEW AND CULTURAL ADVICE

▶ Thais are fun-loving people. Thais smile even though they may be feeling disappointed, embarrassed, or discontented. It is considered improper to show one's emotions in public. However, this value is slowly fading as more and more Thais are exposed to westernization in one form or the other.

▶ When a Thai replies "yes" to a question in English such as "Aren't you going tonight?" it in no way means that he or she is actually going. It simply indicates confirmation of your assumption (i.e., that he or she is *not* going). There are many instances where yes might mean no and no may mean yes. Similarly, if a person acknowledges what is being said with a nod, it does not necessarily mean that he or she agrees with you. It just means, "Yes, I'm following what you're saying."

▶ Thais do not appreciate being patted on the head unless the person doing so is more senior to the individual and the patting is done with an element of affection. Thais believe the head is the locus of the soul or *winyarn* that should be treated with the greatest respect.

▶ By nature, Thai people are modest, and presenting oneself modestly will be considered favorably. Showing aggressive or excessive behavior, boasting, or appearing too relaxed or casual will most definitely be viewed in poor taste. Do not discuss financial issues during the first interview unless asked, as doing so will most likely be taken negatively.

▶ Thailand has 13 annual holidays. The vacation period for each organization varies from 7 days to 15 or more.

▶ When going for an interview, a business suit in earthen tones is always appropriate. It is wise to find out exactly which route you must take to the venue of the interview—Bangkok streets can be rather confusing even for the locals.

United Kingdom

Mercuri Urval

COUNTRY OVERVIEW

The United Kingdom forms the greater part of the British Isles, which lie off the northwest coast of mainland Europe. The full name is the United Kingdom of Great Britain and Northern Ireland. Great Britain comprises England, Wales, and Scotland.

The area totals some 242,500 square kilometers. Britain is just under 1,000 kilometers long from the southern coast of England to the extreme north of Scotland, and just under 500 kilometers across in the widest part. The climate is generally mild and temperate. It is subject to frequent changes, but few extremes, of temperature. The temperatures rarely exceed 32°C or fall below –10°C. Rainfall is fairly well distributed throughout the year.

With some 59 million people, of which 80 percent are English, 9 percent Scottish, 5 percent Welsh, and 3 percent Northern Irish, Britain ranks 16th in the world in terms of population. The population has remained relatively stable over the past decade, but has aged. Britain is relatively densely populated. England has the highest population density of the four lands and Scotland the lowest. Britain's languages are English, Welsh, Irish Gaelic, and Scottish Gaelic.

For centuries people from overseas have settled in Britain, either to escape political or religious persecution or in search of economic opportunities. The Irish have long formed a large section of the population. Jewish and other European refugees came to Britain, particularly from the late nineteenth century to the immediate post-1945 period. Immigration from the Caribbean and the south Asian subcontinent dates mainly from the 1950s and 1960s. There are also other sizable ethnic communities, among them Chinese, Greek and Turkish Cypriots, Italians, and Spaniards.

The United Kingdom has a constitutional monarchy which is the oldest institution of government. Queen Elizabeth II is not only head of state but a symbol of national unity. The government comprises the monarchy (head of state), prime minister (head of government), cabinet with a bureaucratic parliament, House of Commons (electoral), and House of Lords (partly elected).

The main political parties are Conservative, Labour, and Liberal Democrats. There are various smaller parties throughout the country. A major program of constitutional reform is in progress. Its aim is to decentralize power, open up government, reform parliament, and increase devolving individual rights. Legislation was passed in 1998 devolving power from the parliament in London to set up a Scottish parliament and a nationalist assembly for Wales.

Britain's democratic system of government is long established and has provided considerable political stability. Britain is one of the 12 member-states of the European Community. Close links are maintained with many other countries, notably within the Commonwealth, which links 50 independent nations. Ties to the Continent of Europe were strengthened by the opening of the Channel Tunnel in late 1993. London's Heathrow Airport is the busiest international airport in the world.

The economic and industrial pattern has altered considerably in the past few years. As in other industrialized nations, service industries have become much more important and now account for 71 percent of employees. Financial and other business services have grown in significance. The City of London has the greatest concentration of banks in the world and one of the largest stock exchanges. Manufacturing still plays a significant role, and many high-technology industries have been developed. Offshore oil and gas drilling have had a major impact on the economy. Britain is the fifth largest trading nation in the world and, as a member of the European Community, is part of the world's largest trading bloc.

RESUME SPECIFICS

Secondary Education Up to Age 18

Cover this area in broad terms—that is, dates and names and locations of educational institutions, plus qualifications obtained.

Postsecondary/College Education

List the name of your college/university and details about your course work. Highlight specific qualifications gained. Include dates, thesis topic, and internship experience, where applicable.

Awards/Honors and Professional Affiliations

List any special prizes and honors received and professional affiliations.

Other Training

List any other training courses attended and the subject matter of the training.

Work Experience

Start with your current employment, and work backward. List dates, name of employer, location, and job. Include your responsibilities, achievements, and reason for leaving.

Volunteer Experience

Include any voluntary service. Keep listing brief and use bullet-points where appropriate.

Special Skills

Proficiency in foreign languages and knowledge of specific computer programs should be noted.

Other Skills/Hobbies

Give a brief list of any other skills. Describe how you spend your time outside of work.

References

References should be from professional individuals who have knowledge of your work or academic performance. If references are not included on the CV, state that you will provide them upon request.

RESUME PRESENTATION

Format and Layout

Your CV should be a brief but accurate picture of your education and career to date. Make it clear and concise. The reader needs only enough information to decide if he or she wants to find out more about you. A CV should ideally be no longer than two pages.

Start the first page with your personal details (i.e., name, address, and contact numbers). Move to education, then career, in reverse chronological order, with your current experience listed first. The reverse chronological format is considered to be generally the preferable CV style.

Note: You do not need to put date of birth or marital status on your CV.

Attachments

Certificates, letters of reference, and so on, can be brought to the inverview unless otherwise requested.

Note: Attaching a photograph is not normal practice in the United Kingdom, but, if of good quality, it would not have an adverse effect on your application.

E-mail Applications

It is more and more common for applications to be sent via e-mail. Other methods such as CD-ROMs or videos are more time-consuming for the recipient, not common, and not particularly appreciated.

COVER LETTERS

Length

Every application, should have a customized cover letter, preferably typed and drafted for that particular company and position. It should be no more than one page.

Content

You should state the position you are applying for and why you are interested in working for that company. You should describe your experiences in line with the requirements of the position. You may state your salary expectations and how flexible you are to relocate, if this is appropriate.

JOB INFORMATION SOURCES

Newspapers

There are several national and regional newspapers. Different days of the week cover different interest areas for job seekers (e.g., law on one day, business on another). The most popular national papers that contain recruitment advertisements are:

The Daily Telegraph
Phone: 44 171 538 5000

Financial Times
Phone: 44 171 873 3000

The Times
Phone: 44 171 782 5000

The Guardian
Phone: 44 171 278 2332

Internet Sites

Through the Internet, companies usually advertise open positions on their web sites. It may be worthwhile to look for companies in your field of interest. One of the most popular employment web sites in the United Kingdom is www.mercuri-urval.com. The largest daily papers also place their employment ads on the Internet.

Daily Telegraph	www.DT.com
The Times	www.The-times.co.uk
Sunday Times	www.Sunday-Times.c.uk
The Guardian	www.Guardian.co.uk
The Observer	www.Observer.co.uk
Financial Times	www.FT.com

Telephone Directory

In the British telephone directory Yellow Pages, you will find companies listed under the relevant trade heading. This can be a fruitful way to start looking for companies that interest you.

Country Employment Office

The regional offices of the Department of Employment and their addresses can be found in the telephone directory.

Trade Publications

There are magazines and journals for most trades and professions. Inquiries may be made from most libraries, professional/business organizations, chambers of commerce, and trade journals.

Business Organizations/Trade Councils

The majority of professional bodies have their own organizations, which may be found in the telephone directory. In addition, the larger countries have their own chambers of commerce affiliated with their embassies or consulates.

Department of Trade and Industry
Victoria Street
London
SW1H OET
Phone: 44 207 215 5000

Foreign and Commonwealth Office
King Charles Street
London
SW1A 2AH
Phone: 44 207 270 1500

London Chamber of Commerce
33 Queen Street
London
EC4R 1AP
Phone: 44 171 248 4444
Fax: 44 171 489 0391

British Chamber of Commerce
Manning House
Carlisle Place
London
SW1P 1JA
Phone: 44 171 565 2000

WORK PERMITS/VISAS

When planning to work in the United Kingdom, you are advised to check with the nearest British mission offering an entry clearance service for work permits and/or entry clearances. Alternatively, you should consult the Immigration Advisory Service. Anyone who is a resident of a country within the EEC can work without a visa.

Immigration Advisory Service
County House
190 Great Dover Street
London
SE1 4YB
Phone: 44 171 357 7511
Fax: 44 171 403 5875
E-mail: lasuk@gn.apc.org.

INTERVIEW AND CULTURAL ADVICE

▶ It is important to be punctual. Interviews are generally formal, and suitable business attire is expected.
▶ It is acceptable to contact the person listed in the advertisement. However, do not ask for information that may be obtained easily from the Internet or library.
▶ Britons generally have a good work ethic, are comfortable working in a hierarchical bureaucratic organization, and pride themselves on their loyalty and integrity.
▶ Until certain of the corporate culture of one's company, it is judicious not to be drawn into debates regarding religion, cultural matters, or any other sensitive issues.
▶ Britons are generally modest people with a generous spirit and style. They like open and direct people. Loyalty and integrity are important. They are not averse to debate, but do not like arrogance.

United States

J. Lee Perrett, The Coca-Cola Company

COUNTRY OVERVIEW

The United States (U.S.) remains one of the world's most powerful nations, as the economy over the past 10 years has been marked by steady growth, the lowest inflation in decades, and rapid advances in technology. The United States is the third largest country in landmass (behind Canada and Russia) and covers 9,629,091 square kilometers. It is approximately two and one-half times the size of Western Europe and about half the size of Russia. It is bordered on the north by Canada, on the east by the Atlantic Ocean, on the south by Mexico, and on the west by the Pacific Ocean.

The United States is made up of 50 separate states plus the District of Columbia, where the capital, Washington, is located. The governmental system is a federal republic, with a very strong democratic tradition. There are two primary political parties, commonly called the Democratic Party and the Republican Party. There is a president and a vice president with a bicameral legislature of 100 elected senators (two from each state) and 435 elected representatives (based on the population of each state). The legal system is based on English common law, with judicial review of legislative acts.

The total population of the United States is 272 million. The nation is made up of people whose ancestors have come from virtually every country in the world. For centuries, it has been known as a melting pot of peoples from around the world—thus the rich assortment of blended cultures throughout the country. Practically every religion in the world is represented, and there is a strong historical tradition of religious freedom. English is the spoken language, but a sizable minority of the population speaks Spanish. People of Hispanic descent make up the fastest-growing section of the population.

There are over 40 U.S. cities whose metropolitan areas have populations over 1 million people. The largest 10 cities (measured by metropolitan area), all with populations in excess of 4 million, are: New York–northern New Jersey; Los Angeles metropolitan area; Chicago; Washington, D.C.–Baltimore metropolitan area; San Francisco metropolitan area; Philadelphia; Boston; Detroit; Dallas–Fort Worth; and Houston–Galveston.

The United States has the most powerful, diverse, and technologically advanced economy in the world with the largest per capita domestic product of all the industrial nations. U.S. business firms enjoy considerably greater flexibility than their counterparts in Western Europe and Asia in decisions to expand capital and plants, lay off surplus workers, and develop new products. At the same time, they face higher barriers to entering foreign markets than foreign firms encounter entering the U.S. market. The past 10 years have shown solid growth, low inflation rates, and a drop in unemployment to below 5 percent. As a result, many companies have had a difficult time quickly finding qualified applicants for open positions. This has created the most competitive U.S. job market for talent in many years.

RESUME SPECIFICS

Education

List your highest level of education first. If you have completed college or university (undergraduate degree level), list the name and location of the university granting the degree, the name or title of the degree (for example: "The University of Michigan, Ann Arbor, Michigan, bachelor of science degree in chemistry"). Describe any specific internships or special programs that you might have been involved in, especially in the field or area where you are now looking to find employment. If you specialized in a specific area in high school (such as business, engineering, etc.), note your high school degree and area of study after listing your university studies.

Note: If you have studied in a country outside the United States, use terms or phrases that will explain what your particular degree means in comparison to U.S. degrees. Many U.S. employers and interviewers are unfamiliar with the educational systems or university degree programs in other countries and the terminology used. For example, a four-year university-level program undertaken after high school would typically be equivalent to a bachelor's degree in the United States.

Extracurricular Activities

If you participated in any extracurricular activities, such as individual or team sports, clubs, organizations, or student projects, describe them along with any leadership positions or outstanding achievements.

Note: Many U.S. employers place a high degree of importance on extracurricular activities, especially if the candidate has little or no previous work experience. Leadership abilities, teamwork, time management, and communication skills are a few of the skill areas that such activities tend to enhance, and which are attractive to companies.

Awards/Honors

Describe any awards, honors, or achievements attained while attending school. Any activities or performance awards that were competitively won, especially those that show a strong work ethic or high degree of determination (example: "Achieved highest grade point average and finished first in graduating class of 125"), are particularly important to list.

Additional Education/Specialized Training

If you have taken any additional courses at the college/university level, these should be listed as additions to your education credentials. If you have taken computer courses, language classes, sales seminars, and so on, list these along with any certification level that you have attained (example: "Certified COBOL and C++ programmer, January 1999").

Work Experience

It is customary in the United States to have a reverse chronological resume starting with your current position and working backward. Begin with your job title and the name and location of the employer, and then list the dates you worked with each employer. If it was a part-time job, list it as such. Give a brief description of your job duties and areas of responsibility. Highlight any specific accomplishments or achievements you attained while in this position. Focus on the areas that are similar to the position you are seeking.

Note: It is very important that you be specific and accurate in listing the dates and titles of your previous positions. Many U.S. employers do background checks on potential new employees, using the data that the prospective employee has provided. If this information is inaccurate, it can cause a negative report from the background check. This could lead to an offer being delayed or not being extended, or, in the worst case, to an offer being rescinded or the employee terminated. In addition, it is important to highlight any gaps in employment and explain the reason (example: "July 1997 to June 1998, spent one year fulfilling military obligation").

Achievements/Accomplishments

List any special recognition, promotions, or advancements received during each of your assignments. Focus on achievements or job-related accomplishments that show that you are a person with a proven record of getting things done, a person that a company would want to hire. Emphasize accomplishments that are a close fit to the job duties of the position in which you are interested.

Special Skills

Language

List any proficiency in foreign languages. If you have been certified or tested, give the range or score of your proficiency. Even if you are not fluent in a language, but can speak it well enough to conduct a conversation, list that language on your resume, but include the word "conversational" as your level of competency in that language.

Note: Many U.S. companies actively seek multilingual candidates. If you have language skills in several languages, it is a positive feature to include on your resume.

Computer

If you have any specific skills or knowledge of computer languages or certifications, list them, along with how often you use those skills. Computer skills are important for any job. Be sure to list them, even if they are not spelled out in the job description.

Professional Affiliations

If you are involved in any professional organizations in your occupation or profession, be sure to list them. List any leadership positions or involvement with any of the organization's events or activities.

Military Experience

Since military service is not compulsory in the United States, many people do not have military backgrounds, and thus may not be familiar with military terms, ranks, and service requirements. If you have military service, list your highest rank, the branch of service (Army, Navy, etc.), dates of service, and your field of responsibility or expertise. Make sure to list any special commendations, awards, or other achievements that were earned.

If you were in a position of leadership or managed, trained, or supervised people, list the number of people who reported to you and your areas of responsibility. Leadership ability is a sought-after skill that many employers desire, so if you have successfully supervised people during your military service, this is a positive experience to include in your resume.

Volunteer Experience

List any current or previous experience you have in unpaid or volunteer positions, especially if you have limited or no full-time work experience.

Note: Volunteer experience is more common in the United States than in other countries. Many people develop professional experience working with volunteer organizations such as the Red Cross, Scouts, and so on. Volunteer projects often require skills similar to those utilized in paid positions. Many U.S. employers fill entry-level or trainee-type positions with people whose talents and skills have been attained or developed from a volunteer or nonpaying position.

Describe the volunteer experience that you participated in and give the length of time or dates. These may include associations, clubs, and civic or government organizations linked to schools, churches, charities, sports organizations, or other groups (example: "Served as finance chairman of Community Civic Club from 1996 to 1997. Responsible for all budgeting, fund-raising, and financial decisions for 100-person organization with an annual budget of $25,000.").

Personal Information

Note: Although it is a common and accepted practice in other countries, in the United States it is *not* customary to list personal information such as age, marital status, family information, and so forth. In fact, it is illegal for employers to ask applicants for this information. Therefore, you should not include references to age, marital status, gender, or ethnic background on your resume.

If you have personal interests such as sports activities that might also show skills that could be job-related or of interest to a company (such as teamwork, organization, etc.), it is permissible to include them on your resume.

Note: Unless a candidate has reached a competitive level in an outside activity or participated in something unusual, such information is not included at all in a U.S. resume. Most U.S. employers are of the opinion that outside interests are of no relevance to a person's work potential and thus are not a relevant topic for a resume. However, your personal interests and how you spend your free time will likely be discussed in the interview.

References

Many companies do not check personal references that are listed on a resume. Instead, an employer may contact former employers or supervisors to obtain information about the candidate's work history. It is appropriate to make a statement at the bottom of the resume indicating that references will be provided upon request. If the employer requests personal or business references, prepare a separate list.

It is important to remember that any people you list as references should be familiar with your background, skills, and experience. They should be prepared to speak on your behalf as to your level of proficiency relating to the requirements of the position for which you are applying. Ideally, your references should be managers or others who have worked directly with you, but they may also be individuals such as college professors or others who know you.

It is prudent to ask permission of your references in advance and inform them that you may be giving out their names as references. It is generally not advisable to list close family members as references.

RESUME PRESENTATION

Whereas in some countries a CV may be four to six pages in length with complete descriptions of job responsibilities and duties, in the United States it is customary to have a more abbreviated resume with very brief, though detailed, descriptions of job duties. In general, most U.S. employers prefer a resume of two pages in length, accompanied by a cover letter. Many recent college graduates have only a one-page resume because they lack extensive work experience.

Your resume should describe in a concise manner who you are, what you've done, and what you want to do. It should contain facts about your educational background, employment experience, internships, and other information such as association memberships, achievements, honors and awards, and extracurricular activities.

Your resume should be viewed as your ticket to get the reader's attention. It should entice the reader to want to know more about you and to schedule an interview. There is no one correct or right way to prepare a resume—there are a variety of styles, formats, and opinions about preparing effective resumes. Length is less important than content and how it is packaged.

Due to the high volume of resumes that large employers receive, many resumes may be initially reviewed for only 60 seconds. Therefore, a resume needs to be easy to comprehend and absorb in a short time frame.

Format Options

Reverse Chronological (Most Recent Experience Listed First)

The reverse chronological style is the style most often used in the United States. This format starts with the current or most recent experience and traces the work history backward, from most recent to first experience. The same format is used for describing education (college or universities and then high school).

Functional (Grouped by Experience)

The functional format is not used very often, as it can be difficult to interpret and is disliked by many employers and recruiters. The format allows the writer to emphasize skills and accomplishments instead of work history. It enables you to group skills together regardless of where they were attained—most likely in different jobs. This style of resume is used primarily by those who are seeking a career change or by people who have been away from the job market for a long time and want to emphasize their skills rather than their work history.

Layout

The layout of the resume should be in the following order:

- ▶ Name, address, and contact information at the top of the resume.
- ▶ Work experience.
- ▶ Accomplishments/achievements.
- ▶ Military experience.
- ▶ Education.
- ▶ Awards and honors.
- ▶ Extracurricular activities.
- ▶ Special skills (e.g., language/computer).
- ▶ Additional education/specialized training.
- ▶ Professional affiliations.
- ▶ Volunteer experience.
- ▶ References.

Note: For recent graduates, the education section moves up to the top of the resume, just under the name and contact information. The general rule is that education is listed after work experience on the resume once the candidate has more than five years' professional experience.

Spelling and Grammar

When preparing your cover letter and resume, use U.S. standard English. You can usually find this in your computer by going to the "set language" feature and selecting U.S. English. If using U.K. or other British English terms, these may be interpreted as typos or mistakes by an interviewer in the United States who is unaware of the difference. For example, many words spelled with an *s* (organisation) in Britain are spelled with a *z* (organization) in the United States.

Length

Ideally, your resume should be no longer than two pages. If you are a recent graduate or have limited or no experience, one page is adequate. Do not drag out your descriptions just to fill two pages, but do not sell yourself short, either.

Attachments

References

Do not attach personal or business references, but have them available on a separate page. List the name, title, address, and telephone number of each reference. Explain the basis of the relationship (professor, former supervisor, etc.) and how long this person has known you.

School Transcripts

School transcripts are generally not included with a resume, unless specifically requested. If you have photocopies of your transcripts, university diploma, or other information, it is advisable to have this information available. If you need it, you can volunteer that you have copies of your transcripts if the company would like to have them. Never provide original documents to a company, as copies are generally acceptable.

Photographs

Do not include photographs with your resume.

Note: In many countries, it is appropriate and common to personalize the resume by attaching a photo. However, due to strict employment laws in the United States that prohibit discrimination based on age, race, gender, and so on, it is not legal to keep a photograph attached to the resume. Therefore, if you attach a photo, it will usually be separated from the resume and discarded.

E-mail Applications

For a variety of reasons, e-mail applications are becoming the preferred way of receiving resumes at many companies. It is becoming increasingly common for companies to specifically request that resumes be sent as e-mail attachments.

E-mail resumes may go directly into a company's applicant-tracking system, an electronic database that converts resumes into text. It stores them electronically and retrieves them based on the skills and experience that match the requirements of an open position. Therefore, it is critical to follow the directions outlined in the job advertisement to make sure your resume is properly evaluated and stored. These instructions may include information on how to attach your resume and the preferred format for word processing (RTF, etc.). It is important to note that if you fail to follow the instructions, it might result in your resume being lost, discarded, or unable to be read. Simple formats work best and have less of a chance of becoming jumbled up in the transmission. Be sure to send your resume as an attachment, especially if it is highly formatted. Always send your resume to yourself first to test the transmittal before sending it to an employer.

COVER LETTERS

Content/Detail

A resume should include a cover letter that explains why you are sending your information to the company and what type of position you are interested in. The cover letter, as well as the resume, should be typed on professional quality paper and mailed in a business envelope with the typed address.

Note: Handwritten cover letters are not considered appropriate in the United States.

If you have been referred to that company by a specific person, mention that individual by name in your letter. As is true around the world, if you are already known to someone in the company, or by a customer or client, your CV will receive a little more attention from the reader than if your resume arrived in the unsolicited mail.

If you have a specific position that you are seeking or know that the company has a certain position open, state that you would like to be considered for that position. Tell the reader that the attached resume highlights some of your qualifications, background, and experience that qualify you for consideration. If you are replying to an advertisement for a specific position, make sure you reference that position and the place where you saw the advertisement. Proofread the cover letter several times and make sure that there are no errors. A poorly written cover letter can destroy all of the effort you put into perfecting your resume!

Length

The cover letter should be brief, generally half to three-quarters of a page, easy to read, and customized to the company and position you are seeking. It should raise the reader's interest in reviewing your resume further and giving it further consideration. Start your letter by saying why you are writing. Include a general statement about your background, years of experience, and education. Concentrate on the areas of your background that would be a match for a position at that particular company.

Note: Most U.S. companies will send an acknowledgment of some type (letter or e-mail) that your resume has been received. If you have not heard anything from a company in a reasonable time frame, follow up with a letter, e-mail, or phone call to determine if your resume has been received. It is also appropriate to ask about the current status of the position.

JOB INFORMATION SOURCES

Newspapers

Most major cities in the United States have at least one large daily newspaper that contains daily classified advertisements that include a section entitled "Help Wanted." The classifieds list the position, location, and contact information for open positions. Many of these advertisements are large display ads and may list more than one position that the company has open. Make sure in your cover letter that you state the name of the position for which you are applying and the newspaper and date where you saw the ad.

In addition to the local city newspapers, there are some national publications such as *The Wall Street Journal* and the *National Business Employment Weekly* that advertise positions in locations all across the United States. It is advisable to determine what city or cities you would like to live in, and then narrow your employment search using newspapers from those locations. Most companies advertise for local positions in the local papers or their online equivalent.

Many newspapers now have online editions on the Internet that allow you to see the classified ads on a daily basis, as well as search ads from past issues. This is a great time and cost saver, particularly if you are not located in that city. Use a search engine, such as Yahoo!, to search for specific newspapers by name or for newspapers by city or state. CareerPath.com provides numerous newspaper links, too.

Large newsstands around the world can order the Sunday edition of the larger papers no matter where you are based. Some universities stock major U.S. newspapers like *The Washington Post*, *The New York Times*, and *The Wall Street Journal*. The business section of *USA Today* keeps track of employment trends, although it does not contain job listings. A few of the leading newspaper/publication web sites:

National Business Employment Weekly	www.nbew.com
Wall Street Journal Interactive	www.careers.wsj.com
CareerMagazine	www.careermag.com
CareerPath.com	www.careerpath.com (great site for linking to all major U.S. newspapers)

Industry and Trade Publications

Many industries and professions have trade publications that also carry employment ads. These can be a good resource if you are seeking a position in a specific trade or technical field. These publications also often have web sites containing the same information.

Chambers of Commerce/Better Business Bureau

In many cities, the local chamber of commerce can furnish information on local companies and hiring organizations. These can be located through the telephone directory for the local city of interest. In addition, many of the chambers also have web sites containing similar information on the area. You can locate them through the web site www.uschamber.org, which has access to programs and services including links to the chamber branch in specific cities. The Better Business Bureau is a consumer watchdog group whose mission is to maintain an ethical marketplace. Link to its web site to find information on any company operating in the United States, including the company's history, commerce record, and reputation in the community (www.newyork.bbb.org).

Internet Sites

The Internet provides access to thousands of positions and companies worldwide. Candidates now have at their fingertips a trove of information that they can use in their job searches, in addition to the traditional sources.

The Internet is also becoming the fastest growing tool for companies to utilize for recruiting purposes. It is currently estimated that there are over 30,000 employment web sites containing over one million jobs—with more than 20,000 new positions posted each week. Many companies have full-time recruiters whose jobs are to "mine" web sites on the Internet for qualified candidates. Many companies are also installing online applications on their web sites to allow candidates to enter their information and attach a resume.

Yahoo! is one of the most comprehensive job-search engines. It provides a choose-your-own-adventure selection of links to job listings, job services, career advice, and job fair calendars. It narrows itself down by professional category and job location. Going a different route, Yahoo! can take you to a city and give access to business services, travel information, and local newspapers. When Yahoo! takes you to a city's page, it offers the option of a career search within that city. That search comes complete with cost-of-living information, median salaries, traffic conditions, and real estate classifieds.

Monster.com is another major web site offering job listings and career services. It discusses trends in employment and provides links to job banks. Again, the searches can be narrowed by career or by location or by both. In addition, Monster.com offers information about what to expect from a winning job in the form of benefits, salary, and retirement options.

Other helpful U.S. sites include:

America's Job Bank	www.ajb.org
CareerBuilder	www.careerbuilder.com
CareerCity	www.careercity.com
Classifieds 2000	www.classifieds2000.com
CareerMosaic	www.careermosaic.com
CareerPath.com	www.careerpath.com

CareerXroads	www.careerxroads.com
Headhunter.net	www.headhunter.net
Hot Jobs	www.hotjobs.com
Job Trak	www.jobtrak.com
Online Career Center	www.occ.com
Top Jobs USA	www.topjobusa.com
Wall Street Journal Careers	www.wsj.com

At the Riley Guide site (www.dbm.com/jobguide), Margaret Riley Dikel, the well-respected author of *The Guide to Internet Job Searching 2000* (NTC/Contemporary Publishing, Chicago, 2000), provides excellent, up-to-date reviews of all the leading employment sites and then some! Helpful reviews can also be found in *CareerXroads 2000* (MMC Group, Kendall Park, NJ, 2000). Mark Mehler and Gerry Crispin, the authors, are former HR professionals who give detailed reviews for more than 500 job, resume, and career management web sites.

WORK PERMITS/VISAS

The United States issues a confusing range of visas, which are broadly divided into immigrant (permanent resident) and nonimmigrant (temporary resident) visas. An immigrant visa gives you the right to live and work in the United States on a permanent basis and to qualify for U.S. citizenship after five years' residence. A nonimmigrant visa (of which there are 18 categories) allows you to enter and remain in the United States on a temporary basis (e.g., from six months to five years), and in certain cases to accept employment.

Permission to work in the United States must be obtained through the Immigration and Naturalization Service (INS), a division of the United States Department of Justice. U.S. embassies or consulates abroad do not have the authority to grant work permits. In all cases, permission to work must be obtained in the United States by an employer who wishes to hire you. Briefly, you must:

- ▶ Find an employer in the United States who wants to hire you.
- ▶ Have the employer file a petition with the appropriate authorities in the United States to get permission for you to work. Once approved, the employer or agent is sent a notice of approval. This process can be a long and protracted procedure, requiring the employer to prove that there are no qualified American workers available to take the job (e.g., by advertising the job vacancy in newspapers, etc.).
- ▶ After your employment sponsor has been granted approval for you from the INS, it is up to you to apply for a nonimmigrant visa at the nearest American embassy by completing a Nonimmigrant Visa Application (Form OF-156). Be careful to answer honestly, as the INS maintains meticulous records and can easily check whether you have previously had a visa refused or canceled.

Diversity Visa Lottery Program

The U.S. Diversity Visa Lottery program makes available approximately 55,000 permanent residence visas each year to persons meeting the eligibility requirements. Applicants for diversity visas are chosen through a random computer-generated lottery drawing. Visas are apportioned among six geographic regions, with a greater number of visas going to areas of the world with lower rates of immigration, and no visas going to countries sending more than 50,000 immigrants to the United States in the prior five years. No one country can receive more than 7 percent of the available diversity visas in any one year.

To enter, an applicant must be able to claim "nativity" in an eligible country, and must meet either the education or training requirement of the DV program. Nativity in most cases is determined by the applicant's place of birth. To enter, an applicant must have either (1) a high school education or its equivalent, defined in the United States as successful completion of a 12-year course of elementary and secondary education; or (2) two years of work experience within the past five years in an occupation requiring at least two years of training or experience to perform.

Since many of the U.S. regulations for work permits and visas depend on your country of birth/residence, it is best to access the U.S. embassy web site at www.usembassy.state.gov, which will provide you with a direct link to the embassy or consulate in your country.

INTERVIEW ADVICE

▶ Have a positive attitude—most employers seek people who are positive, upbeat, and energetic. Be genuine, but show enthusiasm when talking with a prospective employer.

▶ Be patient—even though you may arrive early, sometimes the company reps may not be on time due to meetings and so forth. While you are waiting, make good use of your time by reviewing your notes and preparing for the interview.

▶ Have a native English-speaker review your resume to see if everything in it is stated clearly and to give suggestions on how to reword something to make it clearer.

▶ In the United States, panel interviews are becoming more common. These are interviews that have two to four interviewers and may be several hours in length. Rather than three one-hour interviews with different managers, many companies have found that it maximizes the interviewers' and candidate's time by having one session. This allows all the interviewers to have the opportunity to see and hear the same things at the same time. Make sure you maintain confidence and eye contact during the interview. This is not meant to be an interrogation or to be intimidating.

▶ Videoconferencing interviews are also occasionally conducted, particularly if all of the interviewers cannot be in the same location as the candidate. The videoconference interview is the same as the face-to-face interview, but you will be speaking to someone on a TV monitor rather than to a live person. Be sure that you speak slowly, as there is sometimes a slight delay in the sound transmission. Look at the camera, not at the monitor, so that your face will show up fully on the TV monitor on the other end. There is usually a technician present who will be able to help you with the logistics of where to sit, where to look, and so forth.

▶ It is common to conduct interviews over meals—primarily lunch. But it could also be breakfast or dinner. If you are in an interview situation over a meal, be careful what you choose to eat—select something that you can manage to eat while still being able to talk.

▶ Some companies may arrange for colleagues who are your age or in similar positions to take you to lunch or dinner. This is so that they can get to know you and you to know them, and is designed to be a little more casual than a formal interview. However, be aware that you are still being evaluated—even though it may not be an official interview. Be careful what you say and how you say it. Use this situation as an opportunity to ask questions about the company culture, working conditions, and so on, that you may not have asked in the interview.

▶ Address interviewers by their titles (Mister, Ms., Doctor, etc.) unless they ask you to call them by their first names. Let them invite you to do this rather than taking the lead in doing so.

▶ It is not advisable to discuss politics, religion, ethnic backgrounds, and so forth. Do not make prejudicial or judgmental remarks or off-color jokes.

▶ Proofread—typos are deadly. In a competitive world, a typo or error may be the reason your resume gets passed over in favor of someone else's.

▶ During the interview be prepared to give real-life examples of your accomplishments and achievements. Many companies are now using behavioral-based interview techniques, which call for the candidate to give real examples of skills that they have.

▶ Be sure you answer the questions directly, clearly, and concisely.

▶ It is customary to break the ice or make small talk during the first 5 to 10 minutes of an interview before the interviewer begins to ask serious questions about your background. Try to be conversational and give more than "yes" or "no" responses.

▶ Save your questions for the end of the interview. If not enough time remains to obtain answers to all your questions, it is appropriate to ask if you can follow up by telephone at a later time.

▶ When you arrive for an interview, it is extremely important that you be friendly and courteous to everyone you meet from the receptionist on up. Your actions and behaviors may be observed to see how you interact with a wide variety of people at different levels in the organization and what kind of team member you might be. The interviewer may ask the receptionist and secretary what they thought of you and how you interacted with them. Someone who can get along well with a variety of people in all types of positions is generally more favorably thought of than someone who cannot.

▶ Do your homework and know the company, its products, history, and other pertinent information. You do not want to be embarrassed by an interviewer asking you what you know about the company when you do not have an answer.

▶ Many companies give written and verbal tests to evaluate your personality or suitability for the position. There is no way to prepare for them, so just be yourself and answer the questions honestly.

▶ Be honest and open. Don't try to hide anything or be less than honest. However, there is no need to point out negative aspects of your background unless you are specifically asked about those areas.

▶ Be ready to explain things that the interviewer might not understand about your background, your country, and your experiences. It is appropriate to ask if you were clear in your description, or if the interviewer has any additional questions.

▶ It is important that the contact information you list be current and up-to-date (telephone, fax, e-mail, address, etc.). If possible, have a message machine or voice mail take calls when you are unavailable. Speed is of the essence, and if a company wants to reach you quickly, you need to give it a way to do so.

▶ You should always be prompt and on time for appointments. Show up approximately 10 minutes prior to your appointment. Make sure you know where the interview will take place. Confirm the appointment, location, and directions the day before the interview. If you are unfamiliar with the location, make a trip in advance to time how long it will take for you to make it to the appointment. Being late for an interview is a sure way to get off on the wrong foot with a prospective employer.

▶ When introducing oneself or being introduced, it is appropriate to look the other person in the eye and offer a firm handshake. Most employers expect personal confidence and a positive demeanor from both men and women. In the United States, the appropriate space between two people standing and talking is about one foot.

▶ During an interview, it is appropriate to give yourself credit for your accomplishments and achievements. Do not be shy about truthfully communicating your ambitions and your successes. While you may think of this as boastful or bragging, you are really showing self-confidence in why this employer should hire you.

▶ After an interview, the courteous and polite thing to do is to send short, personal thank-you notes to the persons who interviewed you. Thank them for their time and consideration, and reiterate your interest in the company or position. While this is certainly not the norm in today's business environment, the recipients usually appreciate it, and it will make you stand out from others who also may have been interviewed.

▶ Some corporate cultures are more formal than others. Before going in for an interview, try to determine what the dress code is for that location. You want to reflect a professional image, so if possible go by the office at some point before the interview and observe what people are wearing. Is everyone in a dark suit, or is the dress code more casual with slacks and sweaters? You may wish to ask the person arranging the interview about the appropriate attire for the interview. When in doubt, it is better to be overdressed than vice versa, so a business suit would be the wise choice if the dress code is unknown.

▶ Confirming that a company received your resume/CV is acceptable, but it is not wise to persistently follow up regarding the status of the recruitment process (unless you are instructed to do so by the interviewer once you have met with him or her). Most companies have specific processes and procedures that they follow in the recruiting and hiring process. Don't become known to the staffing department for the wrong reasons—as someone who is bothersome or unprofessional.

▶ It is not unusual for the employment process to take a long time. Don't take it personally! Most people working in a staffing organization have multiple open positions that they are responsible for filling at any one time, and as a result have hundreds of potential candidates to consider. However, it is appropriate to ask when a decision about the position will be made.

▶ Once you have established contact with someone at the company, keep your contact person apprised of any changes in your job status, interest, address, or other pertinent information so that your file will be updated. If you have another job offer, but are still interested in a particular company, call and let the contact know. If the company is interested in you as a candidate, the fact that you were professional enough to call is usually appreciated—and it just might speed up the decision process on that end if you are a viable candidate for a position.

▶ Ask enough questions during the interviews to be able to make a decision as to whether you would like to work for that company. It is just as important that the job be the right choice for you as it is for you to be the right person for the job.

▶ *Living and Working in America* by David Hampshire (Survival Books UK, 1999) contains great detail about everything you need to know about "surviving" in the United States.

Interviewing across Cultures

Pamela Leri, UNIFI/PricewaterhouseCoopers

Employment interviews are stressful whenever and wherever they occur. In one's own country or culture, it is easier to know what to expect and how to establish credibility. Interviewing in a country other than one's own can be an extremely challenging experience. Each company has its own criteria for assessing the desirability of a candidate. These criteria may reflect certain cultural preferences and expectations.

As you prepare for your interview in another culture or country, here are a number of specific questions you may want to consider:

- ► What will impress the interviewer?
- ► What are the local expectations for establishing credibility?
- ► Are these expectations different for local people than they are for foreign nationals?
- ► How do these expectations differ from what you are accustomed to?
- ► How can you adjust your behavior to be credible and effective in the interview?

The key to success is being prepared. Yet proper preparation is difficult if you are unfamiliar with a culture or country. You may want to read books on the culture of the country. Because there are relatively few books that focus specifically on interviewing techniques and situations, you may want to interview local nationals about the way interviews are conducted in their country. Be aware that it may be hard for local nationals to explain their own culture or something as seemingly commonplace as an interview to an outsider.

Points to consider in your preparations include understanding expectations regarding:

- ► **Dress and appearance.** Is there a standard interview uniform or outfit that interviewees typically wear? Are the standards of dress different according to the industry? For example, if you are interviewing for an advertising or marketing position, is the expectation that you will look "creative" or "flashy"? Is there such a thing as overdressing for an interview? In some cultures, the quality and sophistication of your dress is assumed to reflect your quality and sophistication as a person. In other cultures, being too well dressed can send an inappropriate message of elitism or arrogance to the interviewer.

▶ **Your role in the interview.** In some cultures, you are expected to "sell" yourself during the interview. Being proactive, expanding, and elaborating on your responses may be expected. You may be asked questions designed to test your creative problem-solving abilities. You may be expected to ask questions of the interviewer. In other cultures, your role in the interview may be more passive. You may be expected to follow the lead of the interviewer and, while being attentive, only answer the questions you are asked and not take the initiative to ask questions. With the interviewer taking the lead, you may be expected to review the information, point by point, contained in your resume or curriculum vitae. If invited to ask questions, the expectation may be that the questions are more general, open-ended, and exploratory in nature rather than detailed and direct. It may not be appropriate to ask targeted questions about job responsibilities, working conditions, and payment unless specifically invited to do so.

▶ **Formality and the appropriate etiquette.** In some cultures, you may be evaluated more on how you behave than on what you know or what your credentials are. Often, the quality of a person is judged by his or her attention to social niceties and the details of etiquette. In other cultures, formality and a perceived overattentiveness to etiquette can be negatively evaluated. The emphasis, instead, may be on experience, competence, or credentials.

▶ **The atmosphere of the interview.** In some cultures, the tone of interviews may be very serious and formal. The interview is not a venue for lightness, joking, frivolity, or informality. Instead of friendliness, a certain degree of reserve is expected and admired. Behavior construed as superficial, insincere, or exaggerated will be evaluated negatively. The interview is treated as a test. Everything the candidate says may be questioned or viewed with extreme skepticism. In other cultures, friendliness and informality are expected and seen as appropriate behaviors for the workplace. The interview may be more social and relaxed and seem more like an easygoing conversation.

▶ **The pacing of the interview.** In some cultures, the interview may be part of a multistep review process. The interview may proceed slowly, involve lengthy questioning, and end in an ambiguous fashion. In other cultures, the interview may proceed rapidly with questions asked in rapid-fire fashion and answered directly and to the point.

▶ **Relationships.** In some cultures, the most important aspect of the interview may be who introduced the candidate to the company. The status of this individual or his or her relationship to the company or the interviewer may be crucial in setting a receptive tone for the interview. The interviewer may want to explore at length the history and circumstances of the relationship the candidate has with this third party. The ability to form and maintain relationships and networks may also be a key criterion in hiring. Questions asked in the interview may focus on how the candidate has interacted with colleagues, managers, and customers in the past. In other cultures, the focus may be more on achievements, experience, competence, and credentials. The emphasis is more on what the candidate has done than on the individuals one knows or networks one is a part of, based on class, educational, and/or family background.

▶ **The value of educational credentials, certifications, and intellect versus experience.** In some cultures, experience that can be documented through diplomas, certificates, and written references is the most valued. Experience can be explained only through objective and validated facts, figures, and other data. Subjective explanations, embellishment, and exaggeration of experience and background are totally unacceptable. Displays of intellectual prowess may be expected. In other cultures, it is experience itself that counts. Often, it is the ability to articulate and position the experience that is critical rather than the supporting documentation and data. An overly intellectual approach may be perceived as too academic and not suited to the rigors of the business environment.

Finally, as you would in your own country, you should conduct research on the company you are interviewing with. Beyond basic company background, you may want to gather the following information:

Who will be interviewing you? Is the interviewer from the human resources (HR) department or a line/department manager? If the interviewer is from HR, does the company have a sophisticated HR function? Or does the company have one person who fills a wide range of HR-related functions?

Does the company have a standard protocol for conducting interviews? Does the company conduct tests of potential employees? Does the company conduct a multiphased interview process that may last a period of several months? Does the company utilize an assessment-center process?

How much exposure does the company have to foreigners? How many foreigners currently work at the company? How many foreign customers and vendors does the company have? How familiar is the company with people from your country? Does the person interviewing you have international experience? Was he or she educated, or has he or she worked, outside this country?

What is the relationship between your country and the country where you are interviewing? Is there a history of oppression, colonialism, and/or conflict that may affect your interactions with the interviewer, however indirectly? Are there any sensitive issues that may affect the interaction based on your cultural or racial background and that of the interviewer? What stereotypes do you have—positive or negative—about the country where you are seeking employment? What stereotypes might your interviewer have—positive or negative—about you? For example, when interviewing people from Latin America, U.S. Americans should be aware that Latin Americans frequently feel that U.S. Americans underestimate the sophistication and development of Latin America and are unaware of its rich history and culture.

What is the company's structure? Does it operate domestically within the country? Is it a company involved in import and/or export activities? Is it an international company with overseas offices? Is it a multinational company? Understanding the company's structure will help you assess the experience the company has with foreign employees.

INTERVIEW EXPECTATIONS ACROSS CULTURES

Asia: A Regional Analysis

The following are high-level generalizations about interview behaviors in the region as a whole. Actual interview behaviors and situations may vary country to country and individual to individual depending on the interviewer's international experience, contact with foreigners, age, and economic and educational background.

▶ The interviewer may expect the candidate to avoid direct sustained eye contact. Avoidance of consistent, direct eye contact may be perceived as demonstrating respect for the interviewer.

▶ The interviewer may expect the candidate to defer to the superior hierarchical position of the interviewer and other company representatives. Therefore, the candidate is expected to be extremely careful and/or hesitant in responding to questions and may try to give the answer he or she perceives the interviewer wants or that others have given in the past rather than answering as an individual.

▶ The interviewer may have a significant amount of personal and professional information about the candidate, beyond that contained in the curriculum vitae or resume, prior to the interview. This information is typically provided by a third party such as the individual who introduced the candidate to the company. This third party may be a former classmate or schoolmate who now works for the company, a professor or teacher who has a relationship with both the company and the candidate, or a family friend. During the interview, there may be a discussion about the well-being of this individual, an examination of the history of the relationship between the candidate and this individual, or a conversation about activities of other people the interviewer and candidate may know in common.

▶ Because the interviewer may already know a significant amount about the candidate, the candidate is not expected to promote his or her own accomplishments and abilities. Talking too much about one's own accomplishments and abilities would be uncomfortable for both the interviewer and a local candidate.

▶ The interviewer would expect the candidate to take an extended period of time to formulate answers to questions in order to answer in the most thorough and complete manner possible. The expectation may be that the candidate will give considerable background in order to contextualize the answer. Answering questions in direct, bullet-pointed fashion may be construed as superficial, thoughtless, or irresponsible. In Asia, periods of silence may be perceived as mature thoughtfulness and an ability to engage in deep reflection. Hastiness and an inclination toward taking risks may also be perceived negatively.

▶ The interviewer may assume that the candidate knows the interviewer's background and experience. Again, this information may be obtained prior to the interview through third parties such as the individual who introduced the candidate to the company. While it would not be appropriate to explicitly state that the candidate has such knowledge about the interviewer, the interviewer might assume that this knowledge would help the candidate to prepare for the interview. The candidate is expected to use such knowledge to begin to build the foundations for a good working relationship with the interviewer, which would demonstrate the candidate's ability to forge successful working relationships with colleagues in the future.

▶ When interviewing in Asia, foreign nationals should be aware that people in Asia may be sensitive to perceived negative stereotypes of their countries and cultures. There is a sensitivity to the assumption that Asian countries are "less than" other countries. Asians frequently feel that outsiders are unaware of the rapid modern development of Asia and unacquainted with its long history and rich cultural traditions.

Focus on Interviewing in Japan

As a foreigner in Japan, your experiences in a Japanese job interview may vary depending on the type of company you are interviewing with, the position you are interviewing for, and the level of international experience of the interviewer. Typically, Japanese interviews are multistaged and group-oriented. Don't be surprised to find yourself being investigated by the company between your initial contact and your final acceptance into the company. This is especially true if you are pursuing a long-term professional position with an organization, less true for those applying for short-term language teaching positions. Private investigations are the norm in Japan when considering any kind of long-term partnership, from marriage to working together.

During the interview, you will be asked an abundance of personal questions—what is your age, what is your marital and family status, why are you in Japan and how long do you plan to stay, what are your future goals and career aspirations? Questions should be answered simply and clearly, without bragging or embellishment. A job interview is a serious affair, and joking or too much reliance on humor may not be appreciated. What will be appreciated are warmth, sincerity, and demonstrations of your willingness to work hard and be a team player. How well do you get along with others? Would you be willing to work on weekends during a busy time in order to satisfy customer needs? Are you flexible and other-centered, or are you rigid, selfish, and individualistic? Remember that your character and your fit within the company are often more important than your credentials.

Be aware that your character will be judged in very subtle ways throughout the interview. Is your attire neat and understated? Do you graciously accept the refreshments provided for you? Do you exchange business cards in an appropriate fashion and show proper respect for the cards given to you by the interviewing team? Do you demonstrate good manners and have excellent posture even when you are sitting in a room alone? Do you answer questions with humility and thoughtfulness? Do you adjust to the pace set by the interviewer(s)? Do you ask general exploratory questions about the job at the appropriate times? These behaviors are indicators of your quality as a person.

Do you interrupt the interviewer(s)? Do you ask very specific questions about how long the workday is and what the precise responsibilities of the job are? Do you demonstrate impatience with personal questions or the pace of the interview? Do you fidget, doodle, or play with articles on the table? Are you outspoken with your personal opinions? Do you come across as a person who wants to change things? These behaviors could be signs of your *lack* of quality as a person.

The interviewers may go through your resume with you point by point, reconfirming information with you. This process may seem repetitive, but avoid showing your impatience. In addition, the interviewers may ask you questions they already know the answers to in order to test your consistency and grasp of detail. Just because you have been asked the same questions multiple times, resist the urge to change your answers. You may want to add new information incrementally, but make sure that the essence of your answers remains constant. Also, remember that changing jobs frequently is not looked upon positively by the Japanese. In fact, Japanese are impressed by perseverance and persistence. If you have had to leave a job, it is often better that the reasons be beyond your personal control, such as the company going bankrupt, needing to relocate, or as the outcome of a restructuring process. That you were not personally challenged in the job is not a good reason to leave it.

If you have been introduced to the company by an employee or mutual contact, be prepared to discuss your relationship to the person at length. Remember that your contact is taking a risk introducing you to the company, and you need to behave appropriately in order that your contact maintains face within the organization. Throughout the interview, try whenever possible to establish commonality with the interviewer. Do you have a school in common? Has the interviewer visited your country or hometown? Does your hometown have a sister-city relationship with a Japanese town? Have you visited or even lived in the hometown of the interviewer? In Japan, attending a prestigious university or business school may have more power in getting you a position than in other countries. However, avoid the appearance of name-dropping or bragging about your accomplishments. Let your resume and third parties speak highly of you.

Preparation is the key to successful interviewing in Japan. Learn as much as you can about the company, its culture, and its employees. Gather information about the company's affiliated businesses, banks, and suppliers and how it functions internationally. Learn about the company's historical role within Japan and about the character of its leaders and founder. In the interview, be subtle about what you have learned, and most importantly, listen well. Your receptivity to the ideas and thoughts of others may be your most important attribute in the eyes of the Japanese.

Europe: A Regional Analysis

The following are high-level generalizations about interview behaviors in the region as a whole. Actual interview behaviors and situations may vary country to country and individual to individual depending on the interviewer's international experience, contact with foreigners, age, and economic and educational background. There will be substantial variations as well as among the geographic regions of Europe.

▶ The interviewer may expect the candidate to challenge ideas and questions intellectually and engage in serious debate with the interviewer.

▶ The interviewer may expect the candidate to answer questions directly, without any extraneous personal or anecdotal information.

▶ The interviewer may expect the candidate to defer to the superior hierarchical position of the interviewer and use proper titles of respect and behave as a person possessing lower status. Such behaviors may vary according to the perceived hierarchical, social, intellectual, and organizational distance between the interviewer and the candidate. The assumption of equality between the interviewer and candidate may be very inappropriate in certain European cultures.

▶ The interviewer may expect the candidate to portray himself or herself as confident, intellectually astute, reserved, and serious. In northern Europe, displays of personal warmth or friendliness may be perceived as immature or insincere. Hastiness and the inclination toward taking risks may be perceived negatively.

▶ The interviewer might expect the candidate to take an extended period of time to formulate answers to questions in order to answer in the most thorough and complete manner possible. A local candidate may also give considerable background and/or in-depth information in order to contextualize answers instead of responding in direct, bullet-pointed fashion. Superficiality or lack of depth may be perceived negatively.

▶ A local candidate might use sophisticated wordplay (such as metaphors, punning, and analogies), humor, and historical and/or cultural references to demonstrate his or her intellectual acuity.

▶ In some cultures, such as in the United Kingdom, there may be an expectation of an understated style of communication and a tendency toward modesty. It may be considered rude to flaunt one's achievements or take credit for work performed by others.

▶ While modesty is valued, being able to hold one's own is also essential. It is important to be able to handle high-pressure situations while remaining calm, articulate, and in control of one's emotions. One will gain respect and credibility if one is not diminished or cowed by others.

Focus on Interviewing in Germany

Your experience in job interviews may differ according to the size and sophistication of the company. Small and medium-sized companies, especially those outside the major cities, may not have a developed human resources function. The interviewer may be an individual who has only partial responsibility for salaries, administration, and allocation of vacation time. Interviews in these companies may not be well structured and there may be some sense of the interviewer talking at you. In newer, larger, or more modern companies with an established human resources function, the interview process, which may be quite lengthy, is structured and systematic and conducted by highly trained individuals.

It is crucial to arrive at your interview well prepared to answer detailed questions about your career over the past 10 to 20 years. Your attire should be conservative and understated unless you are applying for a position in media, marketing, or advertising. In those fields, it is appropriate to be slightly flashy. Everything you say must be in complete agreement with what is written on your curriculum vitae and your supporting application documents, such as letters of reference and certification of skills and training. Be sure to have a precise grasp of the sequences, dates, and numbers related to your career to date. The facts related to your experience need to be solid and unchanging. The interviewer may go through your curriculum vitae methodically point by point. A German interviewer may ask questions such as:

▶ Tell me about the first job you ever had.
▶ What did you do? What were your areas of responsibility?
▶ What was your position in the organizational structure? What were your reporting relationships? What were your areas of influence?
▶ Why did you leave your position?
▶ What is your career plan?
▶ How do you see yourself as a professional?

To be considered competent in a German context, your career needs to appear to be the result of careful planning, not the result of chance or random opportunity. Job-hopping is not positively viewed. Yet young Germans often take one job after graduation from college to gain experience and then move on to another company to broaden their experience after two to three years. Appropriate reasons for leaving a job are that you were not challenged or that you reached a ceiling within the organization and there was no room for advancement. The inability to apply the knowledge you have gained is also a good reason for changing jobs. Each change in position needs to be a logical, well-considered career move. There needs to be "a red thread going through it," to quote a German saying.

You may also be asked what you consider your two most important achievements in your last position. This needs to be answered without appearing to critique your current employer or last company. Acceptable answers relate to solving management, technical, or functional problems common to many companies. For example, if you have been a manager or worked in human resources, solving a problem related to high absenteeism due to sickness would be appropriate. Or if you are in a technical field, implementing a new technology or control system would be a good answer. It is crucial when answering such questions that you not appear to be boasting or use superlatives in describing your accomplishments. Emphasize the fundamentals; be serious, committed, self-confident, and assertive but not aggressive or too outspoken.

Beyond detailed questions about your work experience, be prepared to answer personal questions related to your marital and family status, hobbies, and special interests. Women should expect questions about their plans to have children and raise a family. Questions about hobbies and special interests will be asked to gain insight about your character. Are you social or not social? Group-oriented or individualistic? Depending on the type of position you are applying for, these considerations may be relevant to determine your fit within the organization.

Finally, be prepared for multiple rounds of interviewing, and expect that your potential employer will follow up on your letters of recommendation. Your patience, consistency, and persistence during this process will also demonstrate your worthiness for the position.

Latin America: A Regional Analysis

The following are high-level generalizations about interview behaviors in the region as a whole. Actual interview behaviors and situations may vary country to country and individual to individual depending on the interviewer's international experience, contact with foreigners, age, and economic and educational background.

- ▶ The interviewer may expect the candidate to demonstrate an ability to form effective work relationships through sharing a combination of personal and professional information with the interviewer. The ability to communicate genuineness and respect is essential.
- ▶ The interviewer may expect the candidate to behave in accordance with his or her family's status in the social and economic hierarchy. Backgrounds, schools attended, and family contacts are talked about in order to establish a common social ground between the interviewer and candidate. The well-being and activities of mutual contacts may be discussed at length. Taking pride in one's family, social position, educational background, country, city or region of origin, and accomplishments is expected.
- ▶ The interviewer may have a significant amount of personal and professional information about the candidate, beyond that contained in the cur-

riculum vitae or resume, prior to the interview. This information is typically provided by a third party such as the individual who introduced the candidate to the company. This third party may be a former classmate or schoolmate who now works for the company, a professor or teacher who has a relationship with both the company and candidate, or a family friend. During the interview, there may be a discussion about the well-being of this individual, an examination of the history of the relationship between the candidate and this individual, or a conversation about activities of other people the interviewer and candidate may know in common.

▶ The interviewer may expect the candidate to use wordplay (such as metaphors and analogies), humor, or historical and/or cultural references to demonstrate his or her intellectual acuity and cultural sophistication. In Latin America, displays of eloquence, personal elegance, and style may be perceived positively. Speaking in bullet-pointed fashion may be considered rude, unsophisticated, and/or superficial.

▶ The interviewer may expect the candidate to behave graciously in interactions with the interviewer and those in assisting roles, paying close attention to etiquette, the giving of appropriate thanks and acknowledgments, as well as the use of proper titles to communicate respect. Female interviewers and assistants may be complemented on their appearance.

▶ When interviewing in Latin America, foreign nationals should be aware that people in Latin America may be sensitive to perceived negative stereotypes of their countries and cultures. There is a sensitivity to the assumption that Latin American countries are "less than" other countries. Latin Americans frequently feel that outsiders underestimate the sophistication and development of Latin America and are unaware of its rich history and culture.

Focus on Interviewing in Mexico

While credentials and expertise are critical components in being hired to work in a Mexican company, your personality and quality as a person will be carefully scrutinized as well. Warmth, genuineness, and humanity are highly valued in Mexico. In this sense, humanity refers to your approach to human relationships. The ability to form and maintain deep friendships over time, especially since childhood, is respected, and attentiveness to immediate and extended family is the norm. From the Mexican perspective, *buena gente* (which literally translated means a "good person") is one who accepts and fulfills obligations to others, including economic support, assistance in finding jobs, and involvement in the social life of family and friends. Personal pride—pride in one's family, town, country, and culture—is essential. Yet, this pride should be demonstrated with consideration for the dignity of others and in accordance with your role in the social hierarchy.

Those who appear casual or disrespectful in their approach to others or who are lacking close friendships and human relationships may be perceived as superficial and not deserving of respect or confidence. When you are with people, you should be fully present. Listen respectfully; do not be distracted by thinking of your next appointment, an impending deadline, and so on. Such immediacy says much about your humanity. Human interactions should not seem like a task or something to be checked off a to-do list.

A "good person" is courteous and displays excellent manners at all times.

In Mexico, there is a more formal approach to greetings and shaking hands, and to extending courtesies to women (such as opening doors). First impressions are based on your manners, appearance, and personal style, such as the quality of your shoes, clothing, briefcase, pens, and notebooks. Graciousness and dignity are expected; attentiveness to small details that smooth human interactions is greatly appreciated. It is critical to consider the feelings of others and avoid causing people to lose face. While it is important to be accurate when answering questions, you may want to exercise a more indirect, diplomatic, and deferential approach in interview situations. If you have been introduced to the company by an employee or other contact, remember that your behavior will reflect positively or negatively upon that person. In a sense, this person is present at the interview with you and is being judged as you are being judged. If your contact is highly respected, you may be given more latitude, but try not to take advantage of this.

Finally, a "good person" knows his or her place in the hierarchy and acts appropriately within it. Respect is shown to elders and superiors. The ability to show deference to those in authority is critical. Use cultural resource people to learn the symbols and behaviors that are appropriate for a person of your status. Your position carries with it certain expectations, and acting within these expectations will make others more comfortable with you. For example, if you have been working in a managerial or professional position, emphasizing your ability to be hands-on or do physical labor may be inappropriate. Acting out of your role may cause anxiety and confusion even though your intentions may be good.

Be aware that hierarchy is also accorded to you based on your educational affiliation. Mexicans are impressed by people who have graduated from prestigious universities. However, Mexicans may not be aware of the educational system in your country or understand the rank and status of your university or college. It may be important for you to respectfully explain, without being condescending, about your institution's place in your country's educational hierarchy and what aspects of the institution (i.e., courses of study) are famous, both nationally and internationally.

Interviewing in the United States

Job interviews in the United States pose particular challenges for foreign nationals. While job interviews in other countries may tend to be more structured and predictable in nature, the style and content of job interviews in the United States may be more random and reflect the individuality and personality of the interviewer and the corporate culture of the company. For example, a person seeking a position in a financial services firm in Boston, Massachusetts, may have a very different experience in a job interview than a person applying for work in a high-technology start-up in Northern California's Silicon Valley. Just as people seeking work in the United States may tailor their curriculum vitae or resume to emphasize certain aspects of their experience when they apply for a job, you may have to think about how to customize your style to the expectations of the company where you are interviewing. Research and preparation are essential to understand the regional, organizational, and functional differences among companies in the United States. Be aware that while you may be interviewing for a job in Georgia, the person interviewing you may originally come from a Midwestern state like Minnesota, so a basic knowledge of U.S. geography, regional communication styles, and culture will be helpful to you in presenting yourself most effectively to the interviewer or interview team.

Another challenge to the foreign national interviewing in the United States is that while the nation appears to be very multicultural and ethnically diverse, interviewers may actually have little knowledge of your country's culture and political, economic, and educational systems. It is best not to take offense at the interviewer's lack of knowledge but to develop strategies to explain quickly and concisely the relevant aspects of your background.

For example, your university may be quite prestigious in your own country, but the U.S. interviewer may not have heard of it nor recognize the difficulty of entering such a renowned institution. Do not assume knowledge on the part of the interviewer. A Japanese man interviewing for a position in a chemical company in the United States was quite astonished to find out that the interviewers he met had no idea that the university he graduated from in Japan was attended primarily by the royal family and members of Japan's aristocracy. Graduation from this university, while not the most famous in terms of academic credentials, carried with it a great deal of status and said much about his background and upbringing. Therefore, in preparing for your interview, consider what might be well known and respected about your educational institutions or the companies you have worked for in your own country that will be important to convey to your U.S. interviewer. Practice delivering this information in terms that will be relevant and understandable to the interviewer.

Job interviews in the United States are all about selling oneself. The candidate is expected to be able to articulate the benefits and skills he or she will bring to the company. The tone of the interview is expected to be upbeat, positive, optimistic, and enthusiastic. You should avoid making self-deprecating or negative comments about your background, abilities, or experience. A typical U.S. interview is no place for humility and hesitancy. You need to answer questions honestly, but avoid focusing on the negative or difficulties you have had in the past. If an interviewer specifically asks you about what has been most challenging for you in other positions, it is best to focus the answer on things you would like to learn or skills you would like to acquire so that you can resolve those challenges in the future. In fact, the interview itself might be very future oriented. An interviewer may ask questions such as, "What are your career plans and goals?" or "What do you see yourself doing in five years?" Questions from you about the direction the company is taking may be highly appreciated.

During a U.S. interview, you should be confident and assertive and exhibit a can-do approach. In fact, the interview may focus more on what you have done, as opposed to your academic credentials or certifications. While it is important to state that you enjoy working with others and are a good team player, you may need to focus on what you have done as an individual as opposed to what you have done as part of a team or group. Taking credit for making changes, solving problems, or developing new initiatives is highly valued. Be prepared to quantify your work experience. Did you manage to cut costs in your last position? How much money did you save your company? How much money did you make for your company? How many training programs or language lessons did you conduct? How many people did you train? What was the volume of sales you achieved? How many clients did you serve? Knowing the numbers attached to your experience will help you be more persuasive in selling yourself.

Another quality that U.S. interviewers look for in candidates is spontaneity. It is unlikely that a U.S. interviewer will review your curriculum vitae or resume with you point by point, step by step. In contrast, a U.S. interviewer may jump around, asking you questions out of sequence to see how quickly you respond and how flexible you are. He or she may ask you many questions about one aspect of your experience and virtually ignore the rest of your background. You may be asked questions about how you would solve or approach particular problems. U.S. interviewers are often looking for people who are "quick on their feet" and "think out of the box." Your willingness and ability to try new things may be assessed during the course of the interview, depending on the position you are applying for and the company's culture and area of business.

Speed of communication is often critical during an interview. One high-technology company in the United States has a saying that if something cannot be said in 30 seconds it is not worth being said. While this may be an extreme example, most U.S. interviewers expect quick responses to questions. U.S. Americans often communicate in a somewhat truncated bullet-pointed fashion. The expectation is that the most important information in an answer comes at the very beginning. Keeping your answers simple and to the point is a common expectation, especially when time is limited. Avoid packing your answers with too much detail or background information. If a U.S. American wants to know more about a certain topic, he or she may ask you questions rather than assuming you will give a thorough answer. Try to read your interviewer's verbal and nonverbal cues. Is he or she impatient with your answers? Does he fidget, tap his pen, or look frequently at his watch? Does she interrupt you when you are speaking? If you are being interviewed by a team, do they look at you when you are speaking or do they look at each other? These behaviors may be indicators that your answers are too lengthy and you are not focusing on what may seem to the interviewer to be the most important points. Efficiency and time management are highly valued in the United States, and you should avoid any behavior that may make the interviewers think they are wasting their time.

U.S. Americans expect initial friendliness, openness, and the appearance of equality. While it is true that the interviewer and other company representatives are in the superior position during the interview, their preferred style of interaction may be quite informal with the use of first names, humor, and an easygoing, relaxed attitude. Being too formal and reserved may be misinterpreted by U.S. Americans as arrogance or coldness. The best approach is a balanced one. Try to adjust as much as is natural for you to the style and tone that the interviewers set, but avoid becoming too relaxed and familiar, especially if that style is unnatural for you. The interviewers may try to make you comfortable throughout the interview with informal gestures and jokes. These are not meant to be disrespectful or condescending but simply are how the U.S. Americans may prefer to be treated themselves. Also, try not to take offense if the U.S. American appears unfamiliar with the details of your curriculum vitae or resume during the interview. Depending on the rigor of the screening process or how your name came to the attention of the interviewer, he or she may have spent only a few minutes reviewing the key points of your background as opposed to scrutinizing your application in great detail. The person who selected you to be interviewed may not be the same individual now tasked with interviewing you.

In a U.S. curriculum vitae or resume, people tend not to list personal interests such as hobbies and activities. However, during a job interview, you may be asked about your outside interests and memberships in professional and service organizations. In many U.S. companies, you may be asked about your volunteer, community, or service activities. There is a tradition in the United States of helping those in one's own community or those in need. From a young age, many U.S. Americans spend time on a weekly or monthly basis volunteering in hospitals, schools, antipoverty programs, or literacy programs; fund-raising to find cures for diseases such as cancer or AIDS; supporting the arts; or working to preserve the natural environment or endangered species. They may do these things individually or through a service organization, church, or community group. Many people gain excellent organizational skills through their involvement in these activities that may benefit them in school or on the job. In fact, colleges and universities often use volunteer and extracurricular activities as criteria in evaluating students for admission. A well-rounded person is thought to have interests extending beyond work and/or school. Other cultures may not place the same emphasis on these types of activities, and if you are asked about volunteering, you may want to explain how the expectation in your country differs from that in the United States.

Finally, talking about the connections and networks you have may not be as valued in the U.S. business context as in other countries and cultures. If you have been introduced to the company by an employee or third party, the interviewer may briefly ask you about your relationship to this person, but do not expect the discussion to be in detail or go on at great length. You will be judged more as an individual, although connections will definitely help you get the opportunity to be interviewed in the first place. Finding common ground with your interviewer such as attendance at the same university or involvement in a professional organization is helpful, but discussions of this nature tend to represent a small proportion of the time spent in an interview. Try to avoid the appearance of name-dropping or talking about well-known family members, friends, or connections you have in your own country or region. While some U.S. Americans may be impressed, others may judge you as arrogant or elitist, preferring to focus on what you personally have accomplished and what talents and abilities you may possibly bring to the company. Others may have no idea of what you are talking about and judge you negatively for wasting their valuable time.

Finally, make sure that you thank the interviewers for their time and the opportunity to meet with them. Reiterate your most relevant credentials by linking them with the requirements of the position. A follow-up letter containing the same points always reflects positively on your candidacy.

Resume/CV Samples from Around the World

Name: PEDRO GÓMEZ
Nationality: Argentinean
Address: Beruti 3586 (1317) Buenos Aires
Telephone: 54-11 4837-0740

Education
Systems Engineer, National Technological University (UTN), Bs. As., 1979.
Master in Business Administration (M.B.A.), IDEA, 1987–1989.

Specialized Training
- Computing Operations Management Workshop—Agroquímicos Río de la Plata 1996 (eight hours).
- End-users Tools—Microsoft Products (1995).
- Network Computing Strategies and Plans—Gainer Group (1994).
- Control Analysis Process—PricewaterhouseCoopers (1998).

Work Experience
Molinos of Brazil (Brazil, Rio de Janeiro), 5/1997–Present
(Consumer Products Company, annual sales US $180,000,000).
Project Manager
- Responsible for managing an electronic commerce project, with the goal of producing a significant change in product marketing.

Agroquímicos Río de la Plata, 1/1976–4/1997
(Agrochemical Company, Subsidiary of Agrochemical United).

Migration Project, Manager.
- Responsible for directing the Data Processing Migration Project.
Achievements: Migration project completed on time, with no issues reported.

Manager, Technology & Services Division (3/1992–12/1995).
- Responsible for providing computer and telecommunications services to 1,000 clients. Also in charge of planning and implementing the technology required for the long/short term.
Achievements: complete satisfaction of clients, with both local and international needs.

Applications Division, Manager (5/1991–2/1992)
- Responsible for the development and maintenance of information systems and sustaining the functions of the subsidiaries in Argentina, Chile, and Bolivia.

Head of the Applications Development Group (2/1989–4/1991).
Head of Engineering and Technical Support Group (6/1987–1/1989).
Head of the Technical Support Group (7/1985–5/1987).
Different Positions—Application Division (4/1976–6/1985).

Special Skills
Unix, Novell, Lan, and Wan Network. SQL. Internet. SAP.

Teaching Experience
Seminars, Instructor, Engineering University of Buenos Aires (1980–1990).

Languages
English: Upper Intermediate Level.
Portuguese: Conversational.

Personal Information
Born in Argentina, April 4, 1953.
I. D.: 15.555.555.
Married, two children (12 and 7 years old).

Name: MS LEANNE MONROE
Date of Birth: 1st February 1970
Residential Address: 12 Pennant Ave.
Concord, NSW 2137
Phone: (W) 9239 1200
(H) 9777 7777
E-mail: leemonroe@kanga.com.au
Marital Status: Married, 1 child (2 years)

EDUCATION

1996	Master of Business Administration (M.B.A.)
	Macquarie University, Ryde
1991	Bachelor of Business (Major in Economics)
	Monash University, Gippsland Campus
1988	Higher School Certificate
	Rosebank College, Concord

PROFESSIONAL AFFILIATIONS

Associate Member, The Economic Society of Australia

EMPLOYMENT

February 1992 to Present

Warn & Hamell Business Consulting
Warn & Hamell Business Consulting is an international consulting company, representing some of the largest multinational companies in the world. It provides recommendations, advice, and research to companies who wish to restructure or re-engineer their business activities.

March 1994 to Present

Economist
Report to the Chief Economist. Responsibilities include:
— Writing reports on economic trends for both internal staff and clients and presenting the information.
— Coordinating and reviewing economic research.
— Advising clients on economic outlook and its likely impact on their company.
Achievements:
— Provided accurate economic forecasting for the last three financial years.

February 1992 to March 1994

Assistant Economist
Reporting to the Senior Economist, my responsibilities included:
— Researching both domestic and international economic data.
— Modeling, analyzing, and charting data.
Achievements:
— Development of a fully automated database for use by team members.

INTERESTS: Skiing, swimming, horseriding.

REFERENCES: References will be supplied on request.

PERSONAL DETAILS
Name: MAX MUSTERMANN
Date of Birth: 29.02.75
Address: Schillerstrasse 23, A-1070 Wien
Telephone: +43-1-556 77 88
Mobile: +43-676-567 12 34
Marital status: Single

EDUCATION
1985–1989   High School in Vienna
1989–1994   Vienna Business School, graduation (in June 1994)
1994–1999   B.A. in Economics at Vienna Economic University. Specialized in marketing and sales. Diploma in June 1999
1996–1997   University of California in Santa Cruz. Exchange student program with specialization in market research

WORK HISTORY
10/1994–8/1995 **Assistant Bar Manager for the Pink Flamingo, Vienna**
Trained and supervised three members of staff; created and implemented promotional events and was instrumental in increasing profits by 25% during my period of employment.

July–Sept. 1996 **Vacation Trainee with XYZ Chartered Accountants**
Played an integral part of a team working on tax and audit projects. This position required familiarity with database and word-processing software and involved liaising with XYZ's sister company in France.

POSITIONS OF RESPONSIBILITY
9/1995–6/1996 **Entertainment Officer for University Student Social Society**
Organized and budgeted for entertainments for one of the largest university student societies, with over 1,000 members.

1994–to date **Captain of the University's Hockey Team**
In charge of training, organizing, and motivating the women's team from 1995 to present.

LANGUAGE SKILLS: English—fluent; French—good; Spanish—basic

COMPUTER SKILLS: Extensive knowledge of Microsoft Word, Excel, and Access

HOBBIES: Sailing, mountain biking

REFERENCES: On request

MARIE PONSOT
Objective
To join a strong company where I can use and improve my knowledge and experience.
Address/telephone
Avenue Maurice, 24
1050 Brussels
Belgium
Tel +32 2 654 78 52
Fax +32 2 568 85 21

Personal data
Born: 20th of January 1971 in Lokeren
Belgian citizenship
Married, no children

Education
1991–1995:   **KIH DE NAYER, Sint Katelijne Waver**
Industrial Engineer Electronics
Specialized in Electricity-Electronics

Work Experience
April 1996–   **AVIAPARTNER, Zaventem**
February 1998:   **Network & Datacommunication Engineer**

Work with the following tools:
- Token ring network, local segments with a speed of 4 Mbps with a backbone at 16 Mbps, Hub and bridges using the IBM material as bridge (IBM 8229, the hub IBM 8238).
- A remote LAN access via an IBM module (IBM 82XX).
- The 4 Brussels buildings are connected with the backbone; the sites at a greater distance (Luik, Deurne, Oostende, etc.) are connected with the Belgacom BILAN connection (frame-relay network using a Cisco router and the IP protocol).
- Started the BILAN project as well as of other networks (Airport of Lille, France) and expanded the local network at Brussels by placing extra segments (bridge + hub).
- Monitor the network using the IBM tool, enabling activation at distance for a port of a hub.
- Report to the Network Manager.

November 1995–   **CABLE PRINT, Erpe Mere**
April 1996:   **Hardware Development Engineer**
- Reported directly to the chief.
- Developed and managed PCBs.
- Responsible for the electronic assemble (cabling, EMC) of a prototype.
- Used the standard electronic tools such as digital oscilloscope, function generator, computer program to draw electronic scheme and to print the layout of the PCB and EMC measurements tools (nearby field probe, EME and EMR measurement).
- Built a small lab to perform unofficial pretesting, the official test performed at KIH DeNayer.
- Frequently used the PIC-processor, i.e. a range of processors with RAM and ROM built-in. (The processor has built-in inputs and outputs to activate and monitor.)

Foreign languages:
Dutch: Mother tongue
English: Proficiency
French: Proficiency

Computer skills:
MS Office, Word, Excel, and Internet navigator

Interests:
Basketball on regional competition level
Reading
Beach volleyball

OLAVO BIAGGI
Av. Oswaldo Cruz, 317—22250-070—Rio de Janeiro—RJ
Phone: (21) 8551.6097
Age 26, single

Education

Bachelor in Business Administration—Pontifícia Universidade Católica Rio de Janeiro—1996
M.B.A. in Finance—Fundação Getúlio Vargas—1998 to present

Languages

- English—fluent (speaking and writing)
- French—fluent (speaking and writing)
- Danish—fluent (speaking)
- German—good (speaking and writing)

Software Knowledge

Word, Excel, Lotus Notes, Access, and Quattro Pro

Professional Background

Banco Boavista S/A—January, 1996–present

International Investments Division—Client Services
- Investment of resources of private foreign investors in offshore funds, fixed income instruments (Euro-Cd's, Eurobonds, etc.), and structured operations.

Opportunity Capital Partners—May, 1994 to December, 1995

International Client Service
- Focused on investment of resources of private and institutional foreign investors in offshore funds (Opportunity Fund).
- Company Analysis—Issued company reports and information focused on the resources of foreign investors for investment in the Brazilian stock market.

Caixa Econômica Federal—January, 1993 to March, 1993

- Summer job in client service area.

Other Training

- Technical Foundations of the Capital Market—Rio Stock Exchange (1992)
- Sales Techniques—ministered by Catho Group (1994)
- Presentation and Negotiation Techniques courses (1995 and 1997)

KRISTIN SMITH GIVERNY
7 College Avenue, Apt. 11
Richmond Hill, ON
(905) 866-4085
E-mail: Kristin_Giverny@interlog.ca

Objective: Employment in the career services field.

Qualifications: —Strong written and oral communication abilities
—Excellent computer skills
—One year's experience in Career Services

Education: B.Ed., Student Development in Higher Education (expected 6/01)
York University, Toronto, Ontario
Concentration in Administration, Chinese, and Linguistics
—3.95 G.P.A.
—Full-tuition Trustee Scholarship
—Second Year—Studied abroad at the University of Edinburgh

Relevant Experience: Career Center, York University, Toronto
Graduate Career Assistant (1994–present)

Responsibilities & Accomplishments:
• Design and implement web pages for the York University Career Centre.
• Conduct resume critiques both in the Career Centre and at a weekly resume review booth operated by the Student Union.
• Assist students in accessing career-related information, via print media and the Internet.

Other Experience: The York Region District School Board, Aurora, Ontario
English as a Second Language (ESL) Instructor (1991–1994).

Responsibilities & Accomplishments:
• Provided intensive ESL instruction to students from a wide variety of language backgrounds.
• Collaborated with fellow instructors on curriculum development and program enhancement.

Additional Information:
• Experienced with both IBM PCs and Macintosh computers.
• Proficient in MS Word 6.0, QuickMail, HTML.edit, Netscape, First Class Client, and PowerPoint 4.0.
• Limited knowledge of Mandarin Chinese and Bulgarian.

Interests: Horseback riding, waterpolo, reading, and curling.

References: Available upon request.

Name: JAMES D. S. FAN
Address: Unit 26, No. 38 Yan An Road
Telephone: 86-21-65550022
Telefax: 86-21-65550021
Mobile: 86-13900886677
E-mail: jamesf@online.sh.cn
Date of birth: June 18, 1968
Marital status: Married; one child

EDUCATION: 01/1998–09/1999   Melbourne Business School, University of Melbourne—
Master of Business Administration
09/1986–07/1990   East China Institute of Politics & Law—
Bachelor's Degree in International Economic Law
1978–1986   Shanghai Foreign Language School—
Diploma in English studies from leading national school

LANGUAGE SKILLS: Fluent English, Mandarin, Cantonese, and Shanghainese.

INTERESTS: Current affairs, theater, and golf.

CAREER SUMMARY
- 1 year: operations/general management of a business division.
- 3 years: marketing/sales management of a business division.
- 1 year: sales management of non-textile chemicals.
- 1 year: interpretation/trade coordination of textile chemicals.

ACHIEVEMENTS
- Established a liaison office and ultimately a sizable affiliated company (80 people with turnover exceeding US$15 million) in China for a multinational chemical group.
- Explored markets in China for new business segments (plastics and leather) and translation into investment commitments.
- Built a new business from scratch into being the market leader (largest foreign supplier) in China with fully integrated local operations.

CAREER OVERVIEW
07/1995–12/1999
Clariant Chemicals (Shanghai) Ltd.
The Chemical Division of the Sandoz Group merged with the Specialty Chemical Division of Hoechst. Promoted from Marketing & Sales Manager of Masterbatch Division to the Manager of the expanded division.

12/1996–present
Manager—Masterbatch Division
Responsibilities:
- Develop and implement business plans and strategies for the division.
- Manage north and east China sales and marketing organizations.
- Manage Shanghai masterbatch factory.
- Established recruitment and training plans to fit the needs of business development.

Achievements:
- Built an entirely independent team covering sales, marketing, production, laboratory, and logistics areas.
- Led the team to achieving the market leader (largest foreign supplier) position for that segment of the business.
- Established production and laboratory facilities; expanded to full operation in Shanghai.

07/1995–11/1996
Marketing & Sales Manager—Masterbatch division
Responsibilities and Achievements:
- Developed and implemented marketing & sales plans and strategies for the division.
- Built up sales and marketing team in northern and eastern China.
- Managed key accounts and inventory for the relevant region.

11/1990–06/1995
Sandoz Industrial Chemicals Ltd. Shanghai Representative Office
01/1994–06/1995
Marketing & Sales Manager—Masterbatch Division
Responsibilities and Achievements:
- Start-up work of an official-affiliated company in Shanghai.
- Feasibility studies, proposal, and preparation of local production unit in Shanghai.
- Same as the period 07/1995–11/1996.

09/1992–12/1993
Sales Manager—Non textile chemicals
Responsibilities and Achievements:
- Developed and implemented sales plans and strategies for the relevant ranges of products.
- Achieved budgeted revenue and profitability with sales management (reflected within division global newsletter).
- Identified new opportunities and developed programs to achieve business objectives.

11/1990-08/1992
Interpreter &Trade Coordinator—Textile chemicals
Responsibilities and Achievements:
- Promotion, negotiation, documentation, and daily business translation and planning.
- Import and export handling, plus logistic and sales coordination.
- General administration and external communications for the representative office.

Part-Time Employment

07/1990–11/1990
- English Interpreter and Announcer—Shanghai TV Station/English News Program

06/1990–07/1990
- English Interpreter and Advisor—International Exchange Program/East China Institute of Politics & Law

08/1989–02/1990
- Practicing Lawyer—Internship/Guangzhou Lawyers Office

09/1988–07/1989
- English Teacher—Zhonghua Evening School

Personal Data
Name: PETR MALICEK
Born: 17 April 1966
Nationality: Czech
Marital status: Married
Children: Two (Tereza, six; Richard, four years old)
Residence address: Cihlarska 21, 763 00 Zlin
Contact address: Italská 9, 120 00 Praha 2
Tel.: 00420-2-55 55 55
E-mail: pmalicek@hotmail.com

Education
1981–1985 Secondary Electrotechnical School, Zlin
1985–1991 Technical University, Brno, MSc. in Civil Engineering
1992–1994 Czech Management Institute, Praha, M.B.A.
majored in Marketing and Management
1994–date Training courses: PC skills, English language.

Work Experience
07/97–07/99 **Cosmetex**, Prague (cosmetics export co.)
PR Manager
—formulation of advertising and promotion strategies and targets, deciding the target of PR including the budget and reporting to management
—contact with journalists; in charge of press conferences
—presentation of products
—preparation of advertising campaigns in cooperation with advertising agencies

11/92–07/97 **Eurotel**, Prague (telecommunication co.)
Marketing Specialist
—market research
—promotion activities

10/91–10/92 Military service

Language Skills
Czech: mother tongue
English: fluent (Toefl Test—1996)
German: intermediate

PC Skills MS Office: Word, Excel, PowerPoint
Internet, Lotus Notes

Other Membership in the Czech Marketing Association

Prague, 8 March 2000

Petr Malicek*
Signature

*Special note: CV's in Czech Republic must be signed by the applicant.

DENIS BARTON
2, rue Aristide Briand
21 000 DIJON
Tel.: 03.87.45.93.87 (answering machine)
E-mail: denisbarton@hotmail.com

Born on 24/11/75, 24 years old
Nationality: French
Single
Holder of a "B" drivers license

EDUCATION

1998–1999: **M.B.A., Human Resources Management,** Université Paris at Nanterre. Thesis: Staff Assessment as a Management Tool.

1994–1998: Masters in Private Law (options: Labor Law), with honors, Dijon Law Dept.

1992–1993: Baccalaureate "D" degree.

PROFESSIONAL EXPERIENCE

1999: Internship at **Renault Véhicules Industriels** (site: Vénissieux), Human Resources Department (six months)

—Design of a guide (presentation of Renault management tools and reminder of the principal rules of Labor Law) for supervisors and department heads.

—Participation in recruitment of "ETAMs" through permanent contracts.

—Recruitment using study/employment contracts with vocational high school engineering program (search for appropriate training, selection of resumes, interviews, and final choices with line managers).

—Involvement in the department's daily operations: preparation of audits, training, and internal and external training programs.

1998: Internship at **Crédit Agricole**, Ile de France (Paris), Human Resources Department (two months)

—Preparation of negotiations for the transition to the 35-hour workweek: legal and organizational issues.

1997: Internship at **Air France** (Roissy), Human Resources Department (one month)—Drafting of employment contracts for recently hired staff.

COMPUTER SKILLS

Very good knowledge of Word, Excel, PowerPoint, and Lotus Notes. Good knowledge of the potential of the Internet (relationships with schools, recruitment, etc.).

LANGUAGES

English: Good. Spanish: Fair. Linguistic studies abroad: England, Ireland, and Spain.

INTERESTS

Boy Scouts of France:
• Association responsibilities: supervision of a unit of 25 scouts aged 12 to 17 from 1993 to 1997 (BAFA in 1994).
• Leisure activities: Hiking (15 days hiking every summer since 1993); book collecting.

BERND SCHULZE Telephone: 053 21 / 89496
Weingartenstrabe Date of Birth: 13th July 1965
54321 Herford Marital Status: Single

EDUCATION
1977–1981 **Primary School**
1981–1987 **Ernst-Barlach-Realschule**
  (Secondary School)
  O-Levels
1987—1989 **Höhere Handelsschule**
  A-Levels

APPRENTICESHIP
1989–1992 **Hetzel GmbH & Co. KG, Herford**
  Apprenticeship as Commercial Clerk

MILITARY SERVICE
1992–1993 **Recycling Börse**
  Alternative Civil Service

STUDIES
1993–1995 **Fachhochschule Bielefeld**
  Business Studies
  Majors: Marketing, Business Organization
  Degree: Diplom-Betriebswirt

**INTERNSHIPS/
PART-TIME WORK**
04/1993– **Hetzel GmbH & Co. KG, Herford** (sales subsidiary BASF, Ludwigsburg)
09/1993 Sales clerk

1997–1998 **Econ Research, Bielefeld** (Market Research Institute)

1997 Quantitative/qualitative market research
(Ten months)

1998 Supervisor: Field studies and Interviewer coordination
(Four months)

04/1998– **S-Punkt, Bielefeld** (Marketing Consulting)
09/1998 Internship marketing strategies; Project: EXPO 2000

02/1999– **L'Oréal, Deutschland, Düsseldorf**
03/1999 Referee in Human Resources Department

LANGUAGES German mother tongue
  English fluent
  Spanish good knowledge
    (courses in Spain
    and South America)

EDP SKILLS MS Application, Word, PowerPoint, Excel, Windows

**EXTRACURRICULAR
ACTIVITIES** Member of Marketing Club Bielefed
  Member of AIESC

HOBBIES Basketball (played on college team)
  Marathon runner

DAVID T. W. WONG
12D Repulse Bay Tower
Repulse Bay Road
Hong Kong
E-mail: davidw@hongkong.com

PERSONAL
Date of Birth: 2 July 1961
Nationality: Hong Kong Chinese
Marital Status: Married with two children

EDUCATION
1984   Bachelor of Arts (Honors) in Accountancy, University of Toronto, Canada
1994   Master of Business Administration, Chinese University of Hong Kong

PROFESSIONAL QUALIFICATIONS
1987   Chartered Accountant of Canada
1993   Associate member of Hong Kong Society of Accountants (AHKSA)
1993   Member of The Association of Chartered Certified Accountants (ACCA)
1995   Associate of The Institute of Chartered Secretaries and Administrators (ACIS)

OTHER SKILLS
Fluent written and spoken English, Cantonese, and Mandarin.
Familiar with Windows 95, Microsoft Excel, Microsoft Word, and Internet operations.

CAREER OBJECTIVE
To join the financial control function of a listed group; to apply my knowledge and abilities on financial planning, internal control, and risk management gained from my past five years auditing experience and nine years of commercial accounting experience.

WORK EXPERIENCE
6/1984–9/1989 **PricewaterhouseCoopers, Toronto, Canada**
A "Big 5" international public accounting firm providing a range of professional auditing, taxation, and management consulting services.

6/85–12/87   **Taxation Assistant**
I worked on a large number of small assignments. My responsibilities covered handling tax assessment appeals, preparation and submission of taxation computations, and dealing with routine compliance.

1/88–9/89   **Audit Senior**
I was transferred to the Audit Department in January 1988 and worked as an audit senior on a large number of assignments. Major clients included:

• ABC Banks Plc: the largest bank in England in terms of net operating assets. I was principally involved in the merchant banking operations and in particular ABC Investment Managers Limited which was established in 1988.

- XYZ Industry Limited: a subsidiary of the XYZ group engaged in the manufacture of electrical transformers. In addition to performing the audit, I was seconded for a month to assist in the development of their standard costing systems.

1989–present	**Hankal Adhesives (HK) Ltd., Hong Kong**
	Shatin Hankal Adhesives & Building Chemicals Co. Ltd.

A Fortune 500 company engaged in producing chemical products. Headquartered in Germany, the group has over 200 affiliates around the world, and 18 Joint Ventures in the PRC. Hankal Adhesives (HK) Ltd. and Shatin Hankal Adhesives & Building Chemicals Co. Ltd. are involved in manufacturing and trading adhesives products in Hong Kong and the PRC.

1989–92	**Accounting Manager**
1992–95	**Finance Manager**
1995–present	**Senior Finance Manager**

Responsibilities:
- Reported to the Managing Director; developed, set up, and monitored the accounting system of the newly established joint venture to achieve high efficiency in producing timely and accurate accounting information.
- Supervised staff of 16 in Hong Kong and the PRC.
- Prepared financial budgets and controlled costs and cash flows.
- Set up and monitored internal control procedures to avoid serious fraud or irregularity.
- Coordinated the Y2K project and managed the network system maintenance.

REMUNERATION
Latest Package: $85,000 (USD) (annual salary plus bonus and benefits)
Expected Package: $95,000 (USD) (expected salary and benefits)

AVAILABILITY: One month notice

REFERENCES: Provided upon request

MR. ATTILA GYÖKÉR
1042 Budapest, Albatrosz u. 12/a.
06-245-9871 (home) mobile: 06-30-965-7411
agyoker@datanet.hu
21/4/1959 (date of birth)

EDUCATION

1983   Master in Finance and Accounting from Paris IX Dauphine University (F).
(Maîtrise des Sciences & Techniques Comptables & Financières—MSTCF)

1981   Budapest University of Economic Sciences
Majored in Finance and Accounting

1978   József Attila High School
Majored in Mathematics

WORK EXPERIENCE

Feb. 1993   **Philip Morris Hungary Ltd.—Headquarters in Lausanne-CH**
To date   Based in Budapest, as Financial Controller of a dual company organization responsible for a comprehensive scope of business activities from manufacturing, to sales, marketing, import and export of cigarettes. Current job responsibilities encompass, but are not limited to, accounting (statutory and US GAAP), financial reporting, budgeting, capital expenditure, purchasing, and costing.

Quantitative Data:
- Total consolidated gross revenue: 330 million USD
- Consolidated headcount: 800 people
- Average annual investment: 10 million USD

Oct.1990–   **Philip Morris Europe SA**
Jan. 1993   Based in Zagreb (Croatia) then Ljubljana (Slovenia), expatriate assignment as Finance & Administration Manager Central Europe (Ex-Yugoslavia) supporting, from a finance and administration point of view, a consignment-based cigarette business. Due to the political situation, this assignment has required high flexibility with several closings and openings of offices in Zagreb, Ljubljana, Belgrade, and Skopje.

1987–1990   **Philip Morris Europe SA**
Internal Controls analyst, based at headquarters. Conducted office reviews in Africa, Sweden, Turkey, and Switzerland.

1983–1987   **CEREC (French affiliate of, at that time, Coopers & Lybrand) Paris**
From Junior to Senior auditor conducted various auditing and finance support activities including a special assignment for the Swiss Auditing Company (Societé Fiduciaire Suisse), Geneva, to conduct audits of the European steel industry on behalf of the European Commission.

LANGUAGES

Hungarian (Mother tongue)
English (Fluent speaking, reading, writing)
French (Fluent speaking, reading, writing)
German (Medium Level Certificate)
Italian (Conversant)

COMPUTER SKILLS

PC based software (MS Office, Outlook, etc.).
PC Network based Financial System (SUN).

INTERESTS & ACTIVITIES

Sailing (own 18 foot catamaran on Lake Balaton-H), including regatta.
Biking, travelling.

SABRINA WIBOWO
Jl. Darmawangsa 2 no. 27 E, Jakarta Selatan 12988
(21) 721 2222 (Res) or 0816 7722 (mobile); e-mail: brina@ibm.net

OBJECTIVE:	**Marketing Management**
SUMMARY:	Extensive background in marketing and general management; experience in strategic planning, advertising, promotion, new products, competitive intelligence, acquisitions, and business turn-around situations.
EDUCATION:	M.B.A., University of Sydney, Australia 1985 *Major:* Marketing and Finance B.A., Atmajaya University, Indonesia 1982 *Major:* Psychology
PROFESSIONAL EXPERIENCE:	**PT. INDOFOOD SUKSES MAKMMUR**, Jakarta 1996–present **Director of Marketing, Instant Noodles** Manage Crispy Noodles and Vegetarian brands and new technologies/products. Sales increased from US$120 million to US$400 million with a marketing budget of US$14 million

Selected Accomplishments:
- Achieved record volume and market share despite increased competition
- Turned-around Crispy Noodles (+7%) after two years decline, by new positioning/advertising and strengthening promotion
- Implemented revised product manufacturing strategy to improve margins over ten points
- Introduced Animated Cartoon Advertising that won First Prize in the 1998 Indonesian Advertising Awards
- Developed and successfully test-marketed microwavable shelf-stable noodles

PT. SARA LEE INDONESIA, Jakarta 1992–1996

Group Marketing Manager, Frozen Cakes (1994–1996)
Responsible for Frozen Cakes Sara Lee Brand, Shakey's Pizza Rolls and new product development. Group sales of US$30 million with a marketing budget of US$6 million.

Selected Accomplishments:
- Increased unit volumes by 30% while more than doubling profits
- Assisted in the acquisition of Shakey's Corp. (December, 1995) including responsibility of brand transition and integration. Also shared development of the combined strategies
- Established asset redeployment strategy that eliminated two marginal brands, which improved margins and increased capacity of new products
- Introduced two new microwave pizza products for retail and convenience store outlets that exceeded all objectives.

Marketing Manager, Deluxe and New Pizza Products (1992–1994)
Initial assignment in New Products division, later gaining two established brands. Initiated successful re-stage of Deluxe Brand and developed two new products through testing stage.

PT. ABC INDONESIA, Jakarta (1988–1992)
Product Manager, Soy Sauce Brands
Managed four brands with US$19 million in sales and $500,000 advertising and promotion budget. Previously, the business had been declining at an 8% average annual rate. From 1981–1983, unit sales increased 5% as well as dollar sales (+31%) and direct profit (+67%). This was accomplished through a 100% natural re-stage of the base tenderizer business, new advertising, and positioning and the national introduction of a salt-free line extension.

Marketing Trainee/Retail Sales Representative (1987)
Responsibilities included retail merchandising at five major chain accounts, presentations at independents, and assisting in the presentation of programs to several chain buyers

PROFESSIONAL ASSOCIATIONS:
Treasurer, Indonesian Advertising Association–1997
Vice-President, Executive Women Association–1995
Member, Indonesian Chamber of Commerce and Industry
Member of the National Women's Network Group

PERSONAL:
Married, two children. Excellent health. Interests include tennis, diving, renovating old homes.

履 歴 書　　平成 11 年 12 月 20 日現在

ふりがな	アダム　スミス
氏 名	Adam Smith

1964 年 12 月 24 日生（満 35 歳）　※ 男・女

ふりがな		☎ 03
現住所 〒		4567-1234
	東京都 渋谷区 広尾 1-2-3-205	

ふりがな		☎
連絡先 〒	（現住所以外に連絡を希望する場合のみ記入）	

年	月	学歴・職歴など（項目別にまとめて書く）
		学 歴
昭和56年	9	(USA) マサチューセッツ工科大学機械工学科 入学
昭和61年	6	マサチューセッツ工科大学機械工学科 卒業
平成 3年	10	東京日本語学院 入学
平成 4年	10	東京日本語学院 修了
		職 歴
昭和59年	6	アルバック（ボストン）インターンシップ
昭和59年	9	アルバック（ボストン）インターンシップ 修了
昭和61年	9	ニッサンアメリカ 入社
平成 3年	9	一身上の都合により退社
平成 5年	4	NTT東日本㈱東京本社 入社
		現在に至る
		以上

記入上の注意　①鉛筆以外の黒または青の筆記具で記入。　②数字はアラビア数字で、文字はくずさず正確に書く。
③※印のところは、該当するものを○で囲む。

No. _____

自己紹介書

平成11 年 12 月 20 日現在

ふりがな 氏 名	アダム スミス Adam Smith	現住所 〒 東京都渋谷区広尾1-2-3-205	☎ 03 4567-1234

年	月	免許・資格・専門教育
成 5年	12	普通自動車第一種免許取得
平成6年	4	日本語検定一級 取得

その他特記すべき事項　プレジデント リスト（MIT, 1986年）

得意な学科	スポーツ
機械工学, 経営学	野球
趣　味	健康状態
旅行	良好

志望の動機

今までの経験, 知識を発揮できると思ったから。

本人希望記入欄（特に給料・職種・勤務時間・勤務地その他について希望があれば記入）	通勤時間 約　　　時間　　　分
	扶養家族数（配偶者を除く） 0 人
	配偶者 ※ 有 （無） ／ 配偶者の扶養義務 ※ 有 （無）

保 護 者（本人が未成年者の場合のみ記入）
ふりがな

氏　名	住所 〒	☎

採用者側の記入欄（志望者は記入しないこと）

HIROSHI TANAKA
1-4-12 Minami-Aoyama, Minato-ku, Tokyo 123-0032
Phone/Fax: +81 3 3678 1245
E-mail: htanaka@gol.com

SUMMARY OF QUALIFICATIONS
—Eight years experience in high-technology industry.
—Experience working with US-based companies.
—Strong bilingual skills. Read, write, and speak both Japanese and English fluently.

PROFESSIONAL EXPERIENCE
3/96–Present **Kobayashi Data Systems, Tokyo, Japan**
A trading company of computer related products with annual revenue of US$30M.

Sales Engineer
—Responsible for sales, including promotion, direct and indirect sales as well as correspondence with U.S. software manufacturer.
—Conducted market research to measure product demand.
—Achieved double sales against planned annual budget (1998).

4/91–2/96 **ETC Information Systems, Tokyo, Japan**
Software development company with annual revenue of US$15M.

Technical Support
—Provided technical support of graphic library software imported from the U.S. to the sales group.
—Provided installations and documentation assistance as required.

EDUCATION
Jun '90–Jan '91 Language Institute for English
Rutherford, New Jersey
English language course

1990 Graduated from Waseda University (Tokyo, Japan)
Bachelor in Architecture, Department of Science and Engineering

SPECIAL SKILLS
—Fluent in several PC-based applications including: MS Word, Excel, PowerPoint, and various digital-imaging applications. Very familiar with several Internet products.
—English proficiency test TOEIC 750 points (1991).

PERSONAL INFORMATION
Date of Birth: February 3, 1966
Marital status: Married

JUAN C. DELA CRUZ
110 Acacia St., Rolling Hills,
Pasig City
(632) 722-2466

Education:

1998–2000   Rotterdam School of Management
Erasmus Graduate School of Business
Candidate, Master of Business Administration in General Management

1987–1992   University of the Philippines
Bachelor of Science in Chemical Engineering

Professional Experience:

Summer 1999   LAMBERTS INTERNATIONAL, INC. *Amsterdam, Netherlands*
Information Systems Solutions Provider
Business Consultant
—Planned and implemented strategic marketing plan for product-launch of software products.
—Helped develop positioning strategy and managed client network.
—Developed communication materials.

1992–1998   PROCTER & GAMBLE PHILIPPINES INC, *Philippines*
Manager, Detergents Process Manufacturing
—Managed detergent-making operations for USD 90 million detergent-bar business.
—Program leader back-up and member of site-safety in all operations.
—Involved in setting-up P&G's newest site for next generation work systems.
—Trained and qualified P&G's orientation and specialization training modules.

Honors and Awards:

1992   Won University of the Philippines Engineering Research & Development Foundation, Inc. Student Project Award in Chemical Engineering for: Production of Iron-Dextran and High Fructose Syrup for Molasses.

1987–1992   Awarded Scholarship for Chemical Engineering by Government's Department of Science and Technology (five time winner).

Skills:

Languages: English, Tagalog, and German

Extracurricular Activities:

1991–1992   University of the Philippines Tennis Varsity Team
1990–1991   University of the Philippines College of Engineering Soccer Team

Interests:

Tennis, basketball, soccer, scuba diving

Personal:

Date of Birth: July 22, 1969
Age: 30
Nationality: Filipino

Name: ALEXEI IVANOV
Age: 36
Marital status: Married. One daughter
Telephone: 7 812 326 97 28

EDUCATION AND QUALIFICATIONS:
State Engineering Academy, St. Petersburg
Master of Engineering 1994

Additional courses and seminars:

1998   Beverage Leadership Program ("Financial Management", "Projects Leader-ship", "Crisis Management", etc.), Pepsi Cola General Bottlers Training Centre

1996   Banking and Accounting program, Commercial Business College Toronto, On-tario. "Finance Basics", "Sales Management", "Presentation Skills", Pepsi-Cola International Management Institute

Languages: Fluent English

EMPLOYMENT HISTORY:
11/96–Present   Pepsi Cola General Bottlers, St. Petersburg
Sales & Marketing Director for Northwest Russia

Responsibilities:
—Control over P&L results including sales volume, pricing, margins, etc.
—Supervise sales and distribution activity, trade channel development, and routing efficiency
—Control over all marketing initiatives and programs in the region
—Development and launch of new products, brand positioning, and segmentation
—Media planning and ordering
—Purchasing of marketing materials, execute marketing budget for the region
—Organization of effective marketing on-premise program
—Preparation of business plan for new projects (new distribution centre openings)
—Sales forecasts and expense planning
—Manage staff 50 people

4/96–11/96   TMG International, Toronto, Canada
In-store Promotions Coordinator

Responsibilities:
—Organized promotional activities in specialized stores to promote new Motorola products

2/95–4/96   Pepsi Cola International, St. Petersburg
Business Development Manager

Responsibilities:
—Started up the business in northwest Russia
—Formulated sales and marketing strategy to successfully reach targets
—Coordinated marketing policy and organized several projects
—Achieved annual sales and expense goals through penetration of key accounts

—Developed and implemented a business plan for sales representatives
—Prepared CAPEX for Pepsi Project in Estonia and executed investments and product distribution activities

7/94–2/95   **Pepsi Cola International, St. Petersburg**
District Sales Manager

Responsibilities:
—Structured routes within the territory
—Managed 5 sales people
  Developed merchandising standards in the district

1/94–7/94   **Pepsi Cola International, St. Petersburg**
Customer Representative

Responsibilities:
—Searched for new customers
—Developed merchandising standards

9/93–1/94   **PLT Toyota, St. Petersburg, Russia**
Show Room Administrator

8/86-9/93   **Baltic Shipping Company, St. Petersburg**
Engineer

Name: JOHN TAN WAH CHONG
Address: Blk 115 Tampines Avenue 4 #15-09
Tampines
Singapore 520115
Telephone: 278 8655
Date of Birth: 20 February 1970
Nationality: Singaporean
Marital Status: Single
Languages: English and Mandarin
Computer Skills: Microsoft Office, Word, Excel, & PowerPoint

Education: Master of Business Administration (1996–97)
University of New South Wales, Australia

Bachelor of Business Administration (1990–93)
National University of Singapore
Gold Medallist

Awards: Certificate of Achievement
Microsoft Excel for Windows

Military
Service: Lieutenant
Singapore Armed Forces
Awarded Sword of Honor 1990

Extracurricular Activities:
- President, Student Association 1997
- Committee Member of AEISEC 1992
- Participated in community social services—current

Personal
Interest: Play piano and guitar
Photography
Rugby
Reading

Professional Work Experience:

Sept 1997 to date: Procter & Gamble Senior Brand Manager
After completing my M.B.A., recruited by Procter and Gamble to return to Singapore as Senior Brand Manager in charge of the Baby Napkin brand.

- Carried out test-marketing in Singapore and Malaysia
- Produced an advertising launch
- Designed a marketing plan which received higher trade acceptance in Malaysia and Singapore than in Hong Kong or Thailand
- Gained market share to 8% in 6 months despite a 35% price increase
- Did not cannibalize other in-house brands
- Charged with developing a brand franchise for products under charge

June 1993–Aug 1996   **Colgate Palmolive**

Management Trainee (June 1993–June 1994)
- Joined the company as a Management trainee

Assistant Brand Manager (July 1994–August 1995)
- Promoted to Assistant Brand Manager in a record time of 13 months due to strong performance in the launch of Baby Napkin products.
- Performed sales training with outstanding feedback from the Sales Manager and sales team and was asked to join the Sales team. Orchestrated the "X" Baby Napkin Brand Trade launch for 1000 trade customers within 10 days in both Singapore and Malaysia.

Brand Manager (Sept 1995 to August 1996)
- Was sent to Hong Kong as Brand Manager, overseeing the China market.
- Revitalized "Y" brand, an aging shampoo brand, with new copies, packaging, and fresh marketing concepts. Grew the business by 47% in six months.
- Portfolio included "Z" brand, another declining brand for the previous two years. Revived it with totally new advertising strategy and store promotion. Broke all sales records and scored an 83% purchase-intent when launched.

Decided to leave Colgate Palmolive to pursue an MBA in Australia.

NAME: MICHELLE ANNE BROWN
DATE OF BIRTH: 05.02.1969 (31)
MARITAL STATUS: Married (no children)
ADDRESS: 29 St Moritz   Postal: P O Box 32598
12 Horizon Road   Birchleigh
Birchleigh   1961
Gauteng
TELEPHONE: (011) 454 1584 (Bus)
(011) 641 9875 (Res)
(083) 845 3256 (Cell)
E-MAIL: mbrown@global.co.za
NATIONALITY: British
South African Permanent Residence
LANGUAGES: English (home), Afrikaans (good), French (fair)

EDUCATION
QUALIFICATIONS:

1985–1987   **St Mary's School for Girls, Johannesburg**
Matriculation Exemption

1988–1990   **University of the Witwatersrand**
Bachelor of Commerce
1991   Post Graduate Diploma in Accountancy

1992   **Public Accountants and Auditors Board**
Chartered Accountant (South Africa)

1997   **University of Cape Town Graduate School of Business**
Management Development Programme

EMPLOYMENT HISTORY
01/92–09/95   **Deloitte and Touche, Johannesburg**
01/92–12/94   Articled Clerk
01/94–09/95   Audit Senior

06/1995–Date   **Leisure Resorts (Pty) Limited**
06/95–03/98   Financial Accountant
04/98–date   Financial Manager

PERSONAL ATTRIBUTES
A solid financial executive who is able to see the bigger picture. Hands-on experience with good attention to detail. Committed and hardworking, someone who gets the job done. Energetic and enthusiastic, reliable and patient. A very organized individual who is able to manage multiple issues at the same time. A team player. Good IT skills.

CAREER HISTORY
01/1992–   **Deloitte and Touche, Johannesburg**
09/1995   *Articled Clerk and Audit Senior*

Key Performance Areas:
—Company audits
—Tax returns for individuals and companies including Receiver of Revenue queries

—Share valuations
—Going concern valuations and proposals to turnaround ailing companies
—Dividend certificates in terms of South African exchange control regulations
—Senior work in liquidation and insolvencies
—As an Audit Senior in charge of a number of large statutory audits
—Clients included both listed and private companies in the Hotel and Leisure, Fast Moving Consumer Goods, and Pharmaceutical sectors

Reason for Leaving: To pursue a career in commerce

06/1995–date   Leisure Resorts (Pty) Limited
Leisure Resorts (Pty) Limited is the holding company for five hotel and leisure resorts located throughout South Africa

Financial Accountant
• Involved in all financial issues for the company, specifically:
   —internal auditing systems
   —standard costing records and the revaluation of standard cost constituents
   —company secretarial and taxation matters
   —preparing monthly accounts
   —ad hoc feasibility studies
• Achievements:
   —Review and implementation of changes in the company's accounting and costing systems and internal control procedures
• Report to: Financial Manager
• Staff Responsibility: Two Financial Clerks
• Financial Accountability: No financial or budget responsibility

Financial Manager
• Involved in all financial issues for the company and specifically:
   —financial year end reports
   —tax planning
   —monthly operations meetings at each of the resorts
   —evaluating feasibility for new projects and if approved, monitoring the cost, cash flow, tax, legal, and funding efficiency
   —computer systems development
• Achievements:
   —Identified tax structuring to save company R50 million in taxes
   —Successful implementation on time and without problems of new general ledger accounting package
• Report to: Financial Director
• Staff Responsibility: Financial Accountant
                                Management Accountant
• Financial Accountability: Indirectly R550 million turnover

Motivation to   Current Financial Director is in his late 30's and a shareholder in the business.
Leave: Therefore, further progression within the organization is effectively blocked.

Name: ESPERANZA GÓMEZ
D.N.I. or Passport Number: 15236791
Address: Calle Columela 5, 3ª Plta., 28001 Madrid
Date of birth: 24.10.72
Telephone (mobile): 91 880 43 66
E-mail: espe@wow.es
Driver's license: M-123356-R

ACADEMIC DATA

- Degree in Telecommunications Engineering (January, 2001—University of Cataluña)
- Master in Business Administration, Instituto de Empresa (October 97–June 98)
- Languages: English written, read, and spoken at high level
  —First Certificate in English, University of Cambridge (December, 1991)
  —Certificate in Advanced English, Univ. of Cambridge (December, 1996)
  —French basic level

Computer:
- Operative Systems: MS-DOS, Windows 3.x, Windows95, OS/2, UNIX.
- Programming languages: Pascal, Fortran, C, MATLAB, Visual Basic.
- User computing: MSOffice (Access, Excel, Word, PowerPoint), H. Graphics.

PROFESSIONAL EXPERIENCE

April, 2000 to present: **AT&T Unisource**
Assistant Operations Technician: (Internship)
- Operation and maintenance of AT&T Unisource's communications node in Madrid
- Direct interface with multinational customer for incidence solving
- Network project implementation support in Spain

July 1998 to March 1999: **MCI-Worldcom**
Operations Trainee: (Internship)
- Assisted the operations department in the setup of new programs to service industry clients (part-time).

OTHER

- Hobbies: skating, tennis, and swimming
- Teach math and physics classes part-time
- I am dynamic, responsible, interested in meeting people and solving problems on the job.

ANDERS ERICSSON
Folkungagatan 33
134 21 Gothenburg
4610 3524 31
aericsson@hotmail.com
Born 1965   2 March, Denmark
Civil status 1993   Married. Daughter born June 1994; son born July 1995

Education	1984	Student, mathematics physics, Denmark
	1988	B.Sc. in Economics and Business Administration Copenhagen Business School, Denmark
	1993	M.Sc. in Economics and Business Administration, Copenhagen Business School, Denmark Concentration: "Marketing and Strategic Planning"

Experience   1990   Marketing Coordinator, Monitor Consulting, Denmark
—Development and implementation of marketing database system.
—Responsible for national and international campaigns.
—Responsible for preparing and updating marketing-, customer-, and competitor-analysis.
—Participated in marketing, planning, and budget control.
—Coordinated and published company newsletter.
—On occasion, worked in a sales capacity.

1998   Marketing Coordinator, Catalyst Programs, Denmark
—Responsible for all marketing activities, e.g., brochures, presentation material, design and implementation of a sales- and marketing-database, conduct market, consumer, and competitor analysis.
—Responsible for preparation of sales- and marketing-budgets, and marketing plans.
—Presentation and sale of software-/debt collection concept.

Languages   Danish (Mother tongue), Swedish (Very Good), English (Fluent) German (Good), French (Some).

Computer Skills   PC including Windows applications.

Other   Studied acting at Sören Weis, Copenhagen 1987
Camp leader, Surf-Camp of Denmark, St. Tropez, France 1990–92
Importer of silk from China, 1995–1998

PAT JOHNSON
35 South Commons Lane
Apartment # B 4
Cambridge, MA 02163
Telephone & Fax (617) 555-1234
E-mail: pjjohnson@hgs.edu

Objective: To seek a challenging assignment working in the Marketing, Operations, or Engineering functions in a multinational corporation.

Education: **HARVARD UNIVERSITY—HARVARD BUSINESS SCHOOL** Boston, MA
Master of Business Administration   May 2000

University of Virginia   Charlottesville, VA
Bachelor of Science in Mechanical Engineering   May 1997
GPA: 3.0/4.0

Experience: **EASTMAN CHEMICAL COMPANY**   Raleigh, NC
Project Engineer   June 1997–August 1998
- Worked on strategic packaging projects from development through rollout phase.
- Recommended improvements to management that increased production efficiency and decreased operating costs.
- Identified and analyzed new and emerging engineering technologies.

GENESIS CORPORATION   Richmond, VA
Operations Intern   June–September 1996
- Conducted work process flow analysis to identify steps that could be modified, shortened, or eliminated.
- Assisted in developing strategy to minimize material wastes in department.
- Evaluated material management and manpower planning.

Honors:
- Awarded GENESIS, NCSEE, and IBM Scholarships.
- Named Outstanding Sophomore Engineering Student.
- Dean's List.

**Extracurricular
Activities:**
- Member of Harvard MBA Student Speakers Bureau.
- Orientation team leader for new MBA students.
- Habitat for Humanity Boston.
- Member of Pi Tau Sigma and Tau Beta Pi—Engineering Honor Societies.
- President of Professional Engineers Society.
- Elected student representative from School of Engineering in Student Senate.

- Intramural Football, Track, and Lacrosse.
- Vice-President of Dorm Council during sophomore and junior years.

Volunteer Activities:

- Served as mentor and basketball coach for Charlottesville Boys Club.
- Big Brothers and Big Sisters of America Student Board Member.
- Volunteer for American Red Cross.

Technical Skills: Proficient with Microsoft Excel, Word, PowerPoint, Access, Corel Draw, DOS, Lotus 1-2-3.

Languages: English (native); Fluent in Spanish.

Other Information:

- Traveled extensively in the U.S. to 40 states and internationally to 25 countries in Europe, Asia, and Central and South America.
- Spent Junior year of high school as an exchange student in Madrid, Spain.
- Willing to relocate or travel domestically or internationally.

References: Furnished upon request.

APRIL B. DAVENPORT
1234 North Hampton Drive
Atlanta, Georgia 30329
Telephone (404) 123-0094
E-mail: adavenport@aol.com

PROFESSIONAL EXPERIENCE

Results oriented team player with extensive business experience, proven leadership skills, and a strong customer service focus. Organizational skills and project management experience in a variety of different areas are also key strengths, along with multifunctional team experience which resulted in revenue increases for the company.

The Anaconda Company   Atlanta, GA and London, England   1997 to present
Customer Marketing Manager
- Selected by President of the Company for 6-month assignment to London to spearhead Customer Account Team (CAT) project in Europe.
- Responsible for northwest European Division and international accounts.
- Established and headed commercial group for making strategic commercial decisions in the local market place resulting in increased presence in major retailer outlets.
- Developed future commercial strategy for distributors together with advisory group.
- Training and coaching of sales management in region and division locations.

Brand Manager   Atlanta, GA   1995 to 1997
Anaconda USA
- Project manager for new product roll-out in North America, resulting in 60% market penetration in first year.
- Developed Latin America into the largest export market and worked with local representatives in establishing new distributors in Mexico and Central America.
- Developed an information matrix of marketing and advertising procedures and requirements for all USA operations.

Sara Lee Corporation   San Francisco, CA   1993 to 1995
Assistant Brand Manager
- Developed rollout plan of new product launches in western US.
- Coordinated new hosiery package conversion rollout.
- Led task force in development and implementation of extension of new product line.
- Researched and assembled annual review of all customer sales volume reports and developed improved report distribution mechanism which resulted in significant cost savings.

EDUCATION:
Thunderbird, The American Graduate School of International Management
Master of International Management
(Focus: Marketing and Financial Reports Analysis)   Glendale, AZ   1993

Honors and Awards:
- Teaching Assistantship—Marketing Department
- Awarded Cecilia M. Blankenship award as top Grade Point average in Marketing Dept.
- Founder of Thunderbird Humanitarian Organization—Raised $50,000 for charity groups
- Member of International Marketing Club. Elected Treasurer.

The University of Michigan   **Ann Arbor, MI**   **1991**
Bachelor of Science in Marketing
Honors and Awards:
- Dean's List—Junior and Senior years
- Awarded Ann Arbor Rotary Club Scholarship
- Member of Gold Key National Honor Society
- Member of Theta Kappa Psi—National Marketing Honorary Fraternity
- Elected President of 120 member social sorority; responsible for overall operations of house, finances, etc.

Specialized Training: Certified instructor in Dimensions of Professional Selling (DPS)—1994
Certified trainer in Strategic Selling Techniques (SST)—1995
Interview and Selection Methodology Training—1996

Technical Skills: Experienced user of Microsoft PowerPoint, Access, Word, Excel.
Cobol language, extensive Internet experience (Netscape, Internet Explorer).

Languages: English—fluent/native. Conversant in French and German.

Volunteer and Other Activities:
- Mentor to local junior high school student
- Member of Fulton County Red Cross Auxiliary
- Active Member of Atlanta Women's Soccer League—Team Captain 1997

Other Information: Willing to travel and/or relocate domestically or internationally.

References: Available upon request.

AIESEC—Growing Tomorrow's Global Leaders

From its establishment in Europe more than 50 years ago, AIESEC, formerly the International Association of Students in Economics and Business Management, has grown to become the world's largest student-managed nonprofit exchange organization. Its unique combination of exchange and leadership programs reaches more than 50,000 students each year. The organization is comprised of students and recent graduates of institutions of higher education from around the world who are interested in economics and management. With chapters present on over 800 university campuses in more than 87 countries, AIESEC has taken a leading role in assisting students prepare for life after university.

AIESEC is the leading global network of young people for "developing socially responsible, entrepreneurial, culturally sensitive, active learners who are proactive agents of change." AIESEC offers almost 5,000 students (or trainees) the opportunity to work abroad every year. The principal aim of the exchange program is to develop key leadership characteristics, called "Global Results," in the individuals that they can then apply to the benefit of society. The program is based on the belief that the best way to develop future leadership is to provide young people with an opportunity to experience a diversity of cultures, community issues, and management styles.

Through AIESEC's exchange programs, students are given the opportunity to:

- ► Develop entrepreneurial attitudes and skills.
- ► Appreciate diversity and understand other cultures.
- ► Develop skills and attitudes regarding how they can work to make business socially responsible.
- ► Learn how to manage and deal with information in the evolving information society.

Traineeships predominantly take place in companies, but can also be in partnership with institutions and organizations. Special emphasis is placed on cultural experience and community involvement.

SOME CULTURAL ADVICE FROM AIESEC EXCHANGE PROGRAM PARTICIPANTS

Denmark

"Danish people are very direct, and can often shock you with what they say. It is, however, usually not meant to shock, but only the way they are!"

Finland

"If a Finn is being very sarcastic to you, it means that he/she likes you; that the ice is broken. It is their sense of humor. This applies to most Nordic countries."

"If you want to get to know Finns better, invite them to enjoy the sauna with you. Many business deals are made in the sauna. That's where the Finns 'de-freeze'."

France

"France is the country of laissez-faire and savoir-vivre. The process is sometimes valued more than the result. French people like to experience a bit of chaos and see what happens. In the end, it is more important to enjoy life than to organize everything in detail."

Germany

"Germany is the country of the *Meistermachers*. Everything needs to be perfect in Germany. A German is generally never satisfied with the status quo; he always strives for better. Punctuality, cleanness, and discipline are very important values to a German."

Malaysia

"In Malaysia, food is considered to be extremely important. If you meet someone, you always ask first: "Have you already eaten?" If the answer is 'No,' immediate action is undertaken and you proceed directly to one of the hundreds of food stores."

Philippines

"It is best to use euphemisms when speaking to a Filipino, especially when you are about to say something negative. Filipinos get insulted very easily, although they extend a greater amount of understanding to foreigners who say things too frankly."

Poland

"When doing business with traditional Polish managers, you might be invited out for the evening and invited to drink vodka. You can refuse, but it is better to try just a few shots as vodka is the best icebreaker."

FIND OUT MORE AIESEC

Find out more about AIESEC, its exchange programs, and the local committee nearest you by visiting its web site, www.aiesec.org. AIESEC's global headquarters is situated in the Netherlands:

AIESEC International
Teilingerstraat 126, 3032-AW
Rotterdam, The Netherlands
Phone: +31 10 443 4383
Fax: +31 10 265 1386
E-mail: info@ai.aiesec.org

The Global Experts in
Executive Search and Recruitment ____

AMROP INTERNATIONAL

Founded in 1977, Amrop International is a group of locally owned and managed executive search firms operating in more than 40 countries. Clients who seek the best talent in the local markets feel they receive superior insight from the owner-managers they deal with in Amrop. When a client's management needs require assistance in other countries, its Amrop partner is able through Amrop International to introduce the client to similarly qualified individuals. Find out more about Amrop International at www.amrop.com.

AON CONSULTING

Aon Consulting is one of the world's leading designers of processes and technologies that enhance human and organizational effectiveness, and provides a complete range of human resources consulting services. A fully integrated human resources consulting company, Aon Consulting specializes in linking human resources strategies with business initiatives for improved performance. Aon is headquartered in Chicago, Illinois (USA), and serves clients through an extensive network of more than 60 offices worldwide. Learn more at: www.aon.com.

LATIN AMERICA SEARCH ASSOCIATES (LASA)

Latin America Search Associates (LASA) specializes in the recruitment of bilingual executives with international experience for companies with Latin American headquarters or subsidiaries within Latin America. Over the years, LASA has built up an extensive network of bilingual and trilingual executives with considerable Latin American experience. LASA has excellent research capabilities in every country and prides itself in undertaking a full search for every assignment without strictly relying on inventories of previously interviewed executives. Find out more about LASA at www.latamsearch.com.

MARIA PAULA SAMPAIO CONSULTORES/MARLAR INTERNATIONAL

Maria Paula Sampaio Consultores has been in the human resources market since 1981, conducting executive search by applying headhunting techniques to identify executives in their specific universe. The recruiting is undertaken by true hunting and not by advertising in newspapers. The firm is based in the city of São Paulo, the headquarters for its Brazil operations. Maria Paula Sampaio Consultores is affiliated worldwide with Marlar International. For more information about the organization, contact mpsampa@mandic.com.br.

MERCURI URVAL

Since its formation in Sweden in 1967, Mercuri Urval has been a pioneer in helping organizations improve their competitive edge and business results through their employees. With over 1,000 people working from 78 offices in 20 countries, Mercuri Urval is represented throughout Europe, the United States, and Australia. Its client portfolio encompasses a wide range of industry sectors. Focused on developing working partnerships with clients, Mercuri Urval actively promotes business success through the recruitment, selection, and development of people. Mercuri Urval believes that people are the only truly active resource that can be rapidly mobilized. As a result, Mercuri Urval's method for the assessment of people, their potential and aptitudes, is one of the keys to the firm's success. The Mercuri Urval method is practiced by all of its firms worldwide, and is a global guarantee of consistency and efficacy. Read more about Mercuri Urval at www.mercuri-urval.com.

NICHOLSON INTERNATIONAL

Nicholson International is a global human resources management consulting group that includes 31 offices in Western and Eastern Europe, Near/Middle East, Asia-Pacific region, United States, and Latin America. Specializing in the executive search and selection of middle to senior management, Nicholson International sources individuals within a variety of disciplines including general management, information technology and telecommunications (both technical and managerial), sales and marketing, finance, human resources, research and development, engineering, manufacturing, operations, logistics, legal, and consultancy. You can visit Nicholson International at www.nicholsonintl.com.

OAK ASSOCIATES

In the year 2000, Oak Associates celebrated its 20th year in business in Japan. It was one of the first international human resources companies in the Japanese market, as well as one of the first privately owned foreign-owned companies allowed by law. The company performs searches for start-up operations in the Japanese market, contingency recruiting for bilingual professionals for global enterprises of all origins, skill and development training, performance support services, orientations for foreigners new to Japan, and career consulting. Oak Associates has a client base of over 300 firms from all industries. Visit its home page at www.oakassociates.co.jp.

PRICEWATERHOUSECOOPERS (PWC)

PricewaterhouseCoopers (PWC) is the world's leading professional services organization. Its services are underpinned by its resources: globally it has the combined learning and experience of more than 150,000 professionals in 150 countries.

Over the years, PricewaterhouseCoopers has developed a reputable and highly successful executive recruitment practice. Its professional consultants have profound experience in conducting executive search and selection engagements in all areas of management in virtually every category of business and across a wide spectrum of management disciplines. In addition to executive recruitment, the firm also provides guidance and advice on recruitment and retention issues, remuneration and benefits, employment contracts and agreements, psychometric testing, outplacement, and human resources policies and procedures. For more information about PWC, visit www.pwc.com.

SIGNIUM INTERNATIONAL

Signium International is a global network of retained executive search firms. Formerly known as the Ward Howell International Group, the network rebranded as Signium in late 1998. The name Signium embodies the values of entrepreneurship, in-depth local expertise, and international collaboration, which have been hallmarks of the group for almost 50 years. The network's unique structure enables it to attract leading national firms and an outstanding list of international clients. The network offers comprehensive access in the global marketplace combined with personal service delivered by committed local partners. For more information about Signium, see www.signium.com.

WOODBURN MANN (PTY) LIMITED, WHITEHEAD MANN PLC GROUP

Woodburn Mann (Pty) Limited, based in Johannesburg, South Africa, is one of the leading executive search consultancies in Southern Africa and is a member of the United Kingdom–based Whitehead Mann PLC Group. Woodburn Mann has been operating in South Africa since 1982. The company's mission is discreet and confidential research-based executive search. Woodburn Mann has the largest team of graduate research consultants dedicated to executive search in the Southern African market. Woodburn Mann offers its clients management selection and supportive consulting in the fields of executive remuneration services, management asset valuation and assessment, counseling of senior executives, and psychometric testing. A hallmark of Woodburn Mann is that it is able to view an organization from a holistic point of view, using a well-qualified multidisciplinary team approach. Learn more about the organization by contacting mail@woodburn.co.za.

About the Contributors

Argentina: Dr. José M. Llaberia, PricewaterhouseCoopers
Dr. José M. Llaberia is a PricewaterhouseCoopers partner, responsible for the Global Human Resources Solutions division in Argentina. He has worked as an organization consultant for 30 years, managing different projects related to organizational structure, human resource processes, information systems, and process reengineering. Learn more about the group at www.pwcglobal.com.

Australia: Watermark Search/Signium International
The authors of the Australia chapter are Leanne Munro, research analyst at Watermark Search/Signium International, along with Joanna Gore, consultant, and Bob Lewy, director. For more information, contact the group at search@watermarksearch.com.au.

Austria: Bernadeet Hasslinger and Doris Furthmayr, Jenewein Management Consulting/Amrop International
Bernadeet Hasslinger is a management consultant who specializes in professional search and research for multinational companies in the areas of industry, services, and telecommunications. Doris Furthmayr is a management consultant who specializes in professional search and research for multinational companies in the areas of Fast Moving Consumer Goods (FMCG), trade, and services. Jenewein Management Consulting/Amrop International is one of Austria's most reputable personnel consultancies working in the fields of executive search and selection, management audits, and consultancy for international start-ups. Read more about the company at www.jenewein.at.

The Baltic States: Lithuania, Latvia, and Estonia: Audrone Tamulionyte and Dr. Woody Sears, Aon Consulting
Audrone Tamulionyte, a Lithuanian-American, is director of Aon's Central Eastern European office in Vilnius, Lithuania. Dr. Woody Sears is an organization development consultant and a former human resource manager for an international consulting firm. He and Ms. Tamulionyte are completing a book on manager development in Central and Eastern Europe, as yet untitled, but due for publication in fall 2000 by Gulf Publishing Company.

Belgium: Fanny Bodart, Nicholson International
Fanny Bodart is senior consultant with Nicholson International. She specializes in executive searches for positions in sales and marketing, human resources, communications, procurement, and the law. Nicholson International Belgium publishes its opportunities on www.jobs-career.be/nicholson.

Brazil: Maria Paula Sampaio, Maria Paula Sampaio Consultores/Marlar International
Maria Paula Sampaio Consultores has been in existence since 1981, conducting executive search by applying headhunting techniques to identify executives in their specific universe. The firm is based in the key city of São Paulo, the headquarters for its Brazil operations. Maria Paula Sampaio Consultores is affiliated worldwide with Marlar International. Learn more about the organization by contacting mpsampa@mandic.com.br.

Canada: Charles M. Lennox, PricewaterhouseCoopers

Charles M. Lennox is a vice president at PricewaterhouseCoopers Executive Search, where he is responsible for leading the Information Technology and Technology Industry Executive Search Practice in Canada. He has worked as a senior manager with one of Canada's largest multinational organizations and has extensive experience in management consulting, human resource development, executive recruitment, administration management, and information systems. For more information on PWC's operations see www.pwcglobal.com/executive/ca.

Chile: Veronica Morgan, MV Amrop International

Learn more about the organization by contacting: mvamrop@entelchile.net.

China: Fiona Yung, PricewaterhouseCoopers

Fiona Yung has been in the executive search and selection industry for more than 12 years. She was previously director of recruitment for Coopers & Lybrand in Hong Kong. Fiona completed her secondary education in the United Kingdom and her university degree in the United States. Learn more about the organization at www.pwcglobal.com.

China: Sheldon Zhou, Amrop International

Sheldon Zhou has a wide range of experience in business consulting, manufacturing management, and staff development as well as executive search. Before joining Amrop, he was General Manager of Moore Hong Leong Guangzhou. He has also worked with Avery Dennison China, first serving as Finance and HR Director, then as Business Director. Previously, he was with Arthur Anderson Shanghai where he was responsible for HR and internal accounting. In the early 1990s, Sheldon was a pioneer of executive search in China.

For more information, please contact Sheldon Zhou or Luo Ming at:

Phone: 86-21-63758994-96
Fax: 86-21-63758997
E-mail: amropsha@online.sh.cn or shanghai@amrop.com

Czech Republic: Kvetoslava Peerova, PricewaterhouseCoopers

Kvetoslava Peerova, Ph.D., is the director of executive recruitment services for PricewaterhouseCoopers in the Czech Republic. Her human resources background covers the full range of competencies in HR functions supported by extensive experience in the areas of executive recruitment, selection, and assessment. PricewaterhouseCoopers employs 500 employees in the Czech Republic. Learn more about the organization at www.pwcglobal.com/cz.

Denmark: John Macfarlane, Mercuri Urval

John Macfarlane has worked with Mercuri Urval Denmark for more than 20 years and holds the position of chief psychologist for the Mercuri Urval group. He has a master's degree in psychology and has been a human resources manager for Apple Computer.

Mercuri Urval Denmark consists of 135 employees located in five offices throughout the country. Read more about the organization at www.mercuri-urval.com.

Finland: Kirsi Paajanen, Mercuri Urval

Kirsi Paajanen has been a consultant/senior consultant with Mercuri Urval Finland since 1981. In addition to her work with Mercuri Urval in Helsinki, she has worked for the organization in Sweden and the United Kingdom. Mercuri Urval Finland (Oy MU Consultants Ab) employs 60 persons and has offices in Helsinki, Turku, Tampere, Lahti, and Oulu. Learn more about the organization at www.mercuri-urval.com.

France: Rose-Marie Ponsot, Mercuri Urval

Rose-Marie Ponsot has been a consultant with Mercuri Urval since 1988. She holds the titles of senior consultant and director. She assists many international firms with their recruitment needs both in and outside of France. Mercuri Urval France employs more than 100 people, including 65 consultants, who work in 11 offices: two in Paris and one each in Rueil-Malmaison, Lyon, Rennes, Brest, Nantes, Lille, Strasbourg, Metz, and Toulouse. Learn more about the organization at www.mercuri.urval.com.

Germany: Ann Frances Kelly, Signium International

Ann Frances Kelly is a senior associate with more than 12 year's experience in executive search. In addition to in-depth consulting on the domestic market, she has expertise in cross-border European assignments. Signium International Germany was founded in 1978 and includes a dedicated team of researchers and consultants offering a wealth of knowledge and experience in almost all industry sectors. Learn more about the organization at www.signium.de.

Hong Kong: Fiona Yung, PricewaterhouseCoopers

Fiona Yung has been in the executive search and selection industry for more than 12 years. She was previously director of recruitment for Coopers & Lybrand in Hong Kong. Fiona completed her secondary education in the United Kingdom and her university degree in the United States. PricewaterhouseCoopers Hong Kong has more than 110 partners and 2,300 staff. They have been successful in placing candidates for positions based not only in Hong Kong, but also in the People's Republic of China and elsewhere in the Asia region.

Hungary: Krisztina Csóka, PricewaterhouseCoopers

Krisztina Csóka is a PricewaterhouseCoopers manager responsible for the Executive Search and Selection Division in Hungary. She has extensive experience in search and selection assignments, conducting HR-related surveys, compensation issues, and HR-strategy consultancy. Learn more about the organization at www.pwcglobal.com/hu.

India: Atul Kumar, Amrop International

Atul Kumar has been a partner with Amrop International India for three years. He works primarily with the financial services, information technology, and automotive sectors. Prior to joining Amrop, Atul spent 12 years with Citibank and GE Capital and worked with an IT firm. Amrop International is a leading executive search firm in the Indian market. It was also the first global firm to set up shop in India; today it has two offices—in New Delhi and Mumbai. Learn more about the organization by contacting new.delhi@amrop.com.

Indonesia: PricewaterhouseCoopers

PricewaterhouseCoopers Indonesia's search and selection team has access to the expertise and collective experience of the extensive PWC network of partners and staff. They are professionals who can provide invaluable support throughout the recruitment process, from identifying and recommending search candidates to conducting in-depth interviews and assessing the right candidates for the right jobs. For more information, see PWC's web site at www.pwcglobal.com.

Italy: Annamaria Carrozza, Mercuri Urval

Annamaria Carrozza has 10 years' experience as a human resources consultant. She joined Mercuri Urval after extensive experience in managing various marketing and communication projects. Mercuri Urval Italy has approximately 60 employees in three offices. Learn more about the organization by contacting mail@mercuriurval.it.

Japan: Birgitta Lofving and Charlotte Kennedy-Takahashi, Oak Associates

Birgitta Lofving is a human resource consultant and career consultant with Oak Associates. She was previously a human resource professional with Volvo and ABB Kabeldon in

Sweden and Germany. Charlotte Kennedy-Takahashi, president and founder of Oak Associates, has been active in the human resource business in Japan for more than 20 years.

Republic of Korea: Kang-Shik Koh and Peter Manlik, Signium International

Mr. Kang-Shik Koh and Mr. Peter Manlik are executive search consultants with Signium International Korea, the company that has pioneered the Korean search industry since 1987. Working in long-term partnership with Fortune 500 multinationals and the top 100 Korean companies, the firm places approximately 300 highly qualified managers and specialists annually. Either contact the firm by e-mail at tbcs@headhunter.co.kr or visit its web site, www.headhunter.com.

Latin America: Victor P. Viglino, Latin America Search Associates (LASA)

Victor P. Viglino, the founder of Latin America Search Associates (LASA), has been an executive search consultant for more than 22 years in Mexico City, New York City, and Fort Lauderdale, Florida. Learn more about his organization at www.latamsearch.com.

Malaysia: May T. Lim, Signium International

May T. Lim is the managing director of Signium Malaysia. She has a B.A. in economics from Wellesley College and a M.Sc. in management from Massachusetts Institute of Technology. She has 20 years' experience working with financial institutions, regional multilateral development banks, and manufacturing companies in Asia and the United States. For further information on Signium Malaysia, write to the firm at contact@signium.com.my.

Mexico: José Hernandez

José Hernandez is a human resources professional with a private firm.

Netherlands: Cor Hoeboer, Mercuri Urval

Mercuri Urval Netherlands, with its main office in Amersfoort, employs 120 consultants in 11 offices throughout the Netherlands. Cor Hoeboer has been working as business unit manager for Mercuri Urval in the Netherlands since 1989. Learn more about the organization at www.mercuri-urval.com.

Norway: Sven Iversen, Amrop International

Sven Iversen has been a senior consultant with Amrop International for six years. He is a graduate of the Norwegian Naval Academy and has several years of active naval service. Prior to joining Amrop, he worked for several years in the computer industry, both in Norway and abroad. Learn more about the organization by contacting oslo@amrop.com.

Philippines: Ellen N. Escalona, Signium International ZMG

Ellen Escalona is a human resources consultant with Signium International ZMG. She supports the sales and marketing requirements of fast-moving consumer goods/manufacturing companies. With 17 years' experience in the executive search business, Signium International ZMG's success can be attributed to its five core values: professionalism, integrity, customer focus, teamwork, and trust/respect for colleagues. Learn more about the organization at www.signium.com.ph.

Poland: Dr. Rafal Dutkiewicz and Moritz Herfert, Signium International

Dr. Rafal Dutkiewicz, cofounder and partner of Signium International Poland, and Moritz Herfert, junior consultant, have written the Polish chapter. Signium International Poland is known for its expertise in search and selections in the areas of retail and distribution, FMCG (fast moving consumer goods), production, automotive industry, banking and insurance, and construction and building. Contact the authors at rafal@signium.pl or moritz@signium.pl.

Russia: Igor Chugay, Amrop International

Igor Chugay, a native of St. Petersburg, has worked with Amrop International Russia since 1997. His areas of responsibility include search strategy preparation and implementation, candidate interviewing, and preparing analytical reports on the Russian economy and politics. Igor Chugay specializes in searches for expatriate senior executives. He is fluent in English and Italian. Contact the firm at either moscow@amrop.com or st_petersburg@amrop.com.

Saudi Arabia: Nada M. Rizkallah, Amrop International

Amrop International—Rasd Limited is a pioneer and market leader in executive search services in the Middle East. The firm provides executive search services to world-class multinational companies and to top-ranking business institutions in Saudi Arabia, the Persian Gulf region, Egypt, Lebanon, and Jordan. It is the only international executive search firm that maintains permanent offices in Riyadh, Saudi Arabia, and in Beirut, Lebanon. Learn more about the organization at riyadh@amrop.com.

Singapore: Tan Soo Jin, Amrop International

Tan Soo Jin, partner, has been active in executive search since 1977 and helped to pioneer search work in Singapore and the ASEAN region. He has successfully conducted search assignments in Singapore, Malaysia, Indonesia, Thailand, and Hong Kong across a broad range of industries and functions. He has particular expertise in the banking, finance, and consumer products areas.

Tan Soo Jin was formerly a principal with Egon Zehnder and a senior consultant with Korn Ferry before establishing Amrop International in Singapore in 1984. Amrop International Singapore is the trading name of Gattie–Tan Soo Jin Management Consultants Pte Ltd. Learn more about the organization by contacting singapore@amrop.com.

South Africa: Woodburn Mann (Pty) Limited, Whitehead Mann PLC Group

Woodburn Mann (Pty) Limited, based in Johannesburg, South Africa, is one of the leading executive search consultancies in southern Africa. The ethos of Woodburn Mann is to work together as a team. The authors include: Dr. Trevor L. Woodburn, managing director; Peter M. MacIldowie, director; Aletta Saaiman, consultant; Cathy Dowsley, consultant; Jacky Cuffley, associate consultant; Carol Armstrong, associate consultant; Caroline Foote, senior research consultant; Charlotte Barton, research consultant; Lynn Whyte, research consultant; Shelley Jones, research consultant; and Orla Kellermann, research consultant. Learn more about the organization by contacting mail@woodburn.co.za.

Spain and Portugal: Alberto Fuentes and Helena Silva, Mercuri Urval

Alberto Fuentes has been a senior consultant for Mercuri Urval Spain for four years. He previously served in the U.S. Air Force in various management and training positions. Helena Silva has been with Mercuri Urval Portugal as a senior consultant for four years and previously held a variety of human resource positions with several organizations. Mercuri Urval Spain was established in 1982 and today has offices in Madrid and Barcelona. Mercuri Urval Portugal has operations in Lisbon and Porto. Learn more about both organizations by contacting madrid@mercuriurval.es (Spain) and lisboa@mercuriurval.pt (Portugal).

Sweden: Hans Rosengren, Mercuri Urval

Hans Rosengren has been a senior consultant with Mercuri Urval Sweden for 10 years. He has a B.A. in economics and extensive experience with management and personnel administration in the public sector. Since its formation in Sweden in 1967, Mercuri Urval has been a pioneer in helping organizations improve their competitive edge and business results through their employees. The Swedish organization consists of 115 employees in seven offices. Read more about Mercuri Urval at www.mercuri-urval.com.

Switzerland: Petra Augustin, Amrop International

Petra Augustin is a consultant and director of research for Amrop International Spectrasearch AG, Zurich. She has more than 10 years' experience in executive search in Germany and Switzerland. Her main focus is IT/telecommunications as well as international search assignments in various industry sectors. Amrop International Spectrasearch AG, established in Switzerland 18 years ago, has three offices in Zurich, Geneva, and Lugan. The firm is one of the largest independent executive search companies in Switzerland. Contact the organization at zurich@amrop.com.

Thailand: Prapapan Bualek, Amrop International

Prapapan (Pinmora) Bualek works with Amrop International Bangkok, one of the world's leading executive recruitment firms. As assistant research manager, Prapapan is familiar with Thailand's employment market and has extensive experience with senior-level search assignments.

She holds a B.A. (Business Administration) from Bolton Institute of Higher Education, Lancashire, England. After 12 years of study in England, she joined Thailand's world-renowned luxury hotel on the banks of the Chaophraya River, in the position of executive secretary to the property's illustrious general manager.

For further information, contact Amrop International Thailand at bangkok@amrop.com.

United Kingdom: Mercuri Urval

Mercuri Urval United Kingdom began its operations in 1973 and now employs 50 consultants who work out of five centers: Harrow, Bristol, Birmingham, Manchester, and Leeds. The Mercuri Urval method of search and selection is renowned throughout Europe. Learn more about the organization at www.mercuri-urval.com.

United States: J. Lee Perrett, The Coca-Cola Company

J. Lee Perrett is a talent acquisition consultant with The Coca-Cola Company currently based in the company's corporate headquarters in Atlanta, Georgia. During his 16 years with Coca-Cola, he has held a wide variety of human resources positions, beginning in 1984 as senior marketing recruiter in the USA division. He has also been HR manager in Coca-Cola Fountain, manager of corporate and international staffing, and manager of college recruiting.

Mr. Perrett lived and worked in Scandinavia for two and one-half years, where he directed all recruiting and staffing activities for the start-up operations for three Coca-Cola business units in Sweden, Norway, and Finland. His most recent assignment has been as a talent acquisition consultant for Coca-Cola's Latin America group covering Mexico, Central America, and South America.

Prior to joining The Coca-Cola Company, Mr. Perrett spent four years with the John H. Harland Company in Atlanta, where he was manager of employment. He holds two degrees from Auburn University and resides in Atlanta, Georgia.

Interviewing across Cultures: Pamela Leri, UNIFI/PricewaterhouseCoopers

Pamela Leri has been a consultant, writer, facilitator, and trainer in the global business arena for more than 18 years. Ms. Leri recently joined PricewaterhouseCoopers, where she is a senior consultant with the global diversity practice in PWC's newly-established UNIFI division. During her career, Ms. Leri has consulted with corporate, governmental, and educational organizations on issues involving globalization, organizational culture integration for joint ventures and mergers, development of intercultural and culture-specific business competencies, global diversity, and multicultural and virtual teamwork. Ms. Leri began her career in Japan where she spent seven years working in advertising and consulting. She has also spent extended periods in Southern Africa, Asia, Europe, Mexico, and Canada. Ms. Leri holds a Master of Fine Arts degree in Creative Writing from the University of Iowa's Writer's Workshop, where she was the recipient of the prestigious Iowa Arts Fellowship. Ms. Leri can be reached via e-mail at pamela.l.leri@us.pwcglobal.com.

About the Author

Mary Anne Thompson lectures extensively throughout Europe on a wide range of topics crucial to developing successful employment strategies. Her seminars help new and experienced professionals structure their credentials and market their skills in globally competitive formats. Her advice focuses on job searching techniques, interviewing tactics, and preparing resumes and CVs for the international market. Her career advice is featured in numerous publications including *Jobline*, Europe's largest online employment network.

In addition, Ms. Thompson provides market research, strategic planning, and intercultural business communication training for companies interested in global market expansion. On the corporate level, she lectures on topics ranging from "American Corporate and Social Culture" and "Communication Skills for the Global Market" to "Leadership Skills for the New Millennium."

An American, Ms. Thompson is also a lawyer with 14 years' experience working with the federal government and private industry in Washington, D.C. She served as an attorney and adviser to President Ronald Reagan in the White House and with Secretary of Transportation Elizabeth Dole. She resides in Stockholm, Sweden, and Mobile, Alabama (USA).